RELIGION IN
NEW NETHERLAND
1623–1664

A Da Capo Press Reprint Series

CIVIL LIBERTIES IN AMERICAN HISTORY

GENERAL EDITOR: LEONARD W. LEVY

Claremont Graduate School

RELIGION IN
NEW NETHERLAND
1623-1664

By Frederick J. Zwierlein

DA CAPO PRESS • NEW YORK • 1971

A Da Capo Press Reprint Edition

This Da Capo Press edition of
Religion in New Netherland, 1623–1664,
is an unabridged republication of the first
edition published in Rochester, New York,
in 1910.

Library of Congress Catalog Card Number 72-120851

SBN 306-71960-6

Published by Da Capo Press
A Division of Plenum Publishing Corporation
227 West 17th Street, New York, N. Y. 10011

RELIGION IN
NEW NETHERLAND
1623–1664

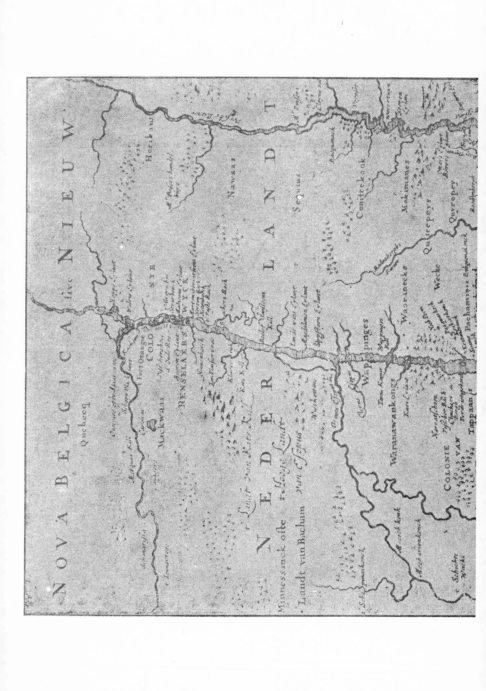

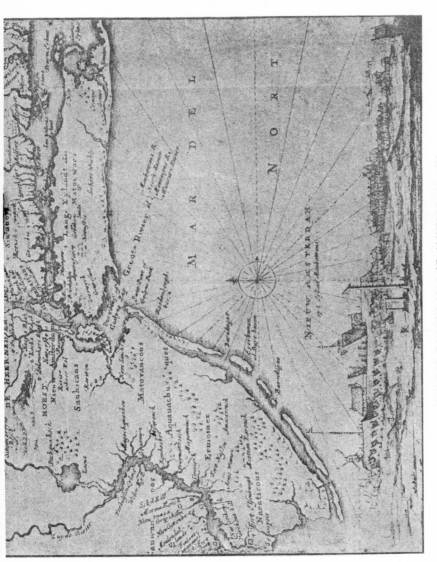

VAN DER DONCK'S MAP OF AMSTERDAM—1656

With view of New Amsterdam

RELIGION

IN

NEW NETHERLAND

———

A HISTORY

OF

THE DEVELOPMENT OF THE RELIGIOUS CONDITIONS
IN THE PROVINCE OF NEW NETHERLAND
1623-1664

———

A DISSERTATION PRESENTED TO THE UNIVERSITY OF LOUVAIN TO OBTAIN
THE DEGREE OF DOCTEUR ÈS SCIENCES MORALES ET HISTORIQUES

BY

FREDERICK J. ZWIERLEIN, L. D.
PROFESSOR OF CHURCH HISTORY AT ST. BERNARD'S SEMINARY
ROCHESTER, NEW YORK

———

1910
JOHN P. SMITH PRINTING COMPANY
ROCHESTER, N. Y.

OPUS QUOD INSCRIBITUR : *Religion in New Netherland, a history of the development of the religious conditions in the Province of New Netherland* (1623 - 1664) BY F. J. ZWIERLEIN, EX AUCTORITATE EMINENTISSIMI ET REVERENDISSIMI CARDINALIS ARCHIEPISCOPI MECHLINIENSIS ET LEGUM ACADEMICARUM PRÆSCRIPTO RECOGNITUM, QUUM FIDEI AUT BONIS MORIBUS CONTRARIUM NIHIL CONTINERE VISUM FUERIT, IMPRIMI POTEST.

P. LADEUZE,

RECT. UNIV.

Datum Lovanii, die 19 Aprilis, A. D. 1910

NIHIL OBSTAT

J. F. GOGGIN,

CENSOR LIBRORUM

IMPRIMATUR

† THOMAS,

EPISCOPUS ROFFENSIS

Datum Roffæ, die XI Maii, MCMX

PREFACE

Professor Cauchie of the University of Louvain, Belgium, first directed the author to limit his present work of historical research to the field of American Church History. Some results of this study are presented in this book to the University of Louvain as a dissertation to obtain the degree of Docteur ès Sciences Morales et Historiques.

The choice of subject was due to the fact, that the author's own State offered the best opportunity for the beginning of such a study, and also to the consideration, that the Belgians as well as the Hollanders of today still feel a great interest in the history of the former province of New Netherland.

It has been the author's constant aim to learn in the famous phrase of Ranke, "wie es eigentlich gewesen ist," by as close and extensive a study of documentary sources, as the time and the means at his disposal permitted. While there is room for improvement, there is hardly a statement in this book, which is not amply supported by the best of evidence.

The lack of such a systematic study of the religious development of the province of New Netherland with a mistaken conception of the nature of religious liberty in the Dutch Republic of the seventeenth century, has been the source of much error in many publications dealing with the beginnings of the State of New York. References to such histories, even when at varience with the main conclusions of this book, have been avoided as much as possible, as the author preferred to present the results of his work in a positive and not in a polemic light.

Special thanks are due to the officials in the Hall of Records of Kings County, and in the Hall of Records of New York, to the library staffs of Cornell University, of the Long Island Historical Society, to Mr. D. Versteeg of the Holland Society Library, and to many friends, who were always ready to give advice and assistance. In conclusion the author wishes to express his deep sense of indebtedness to Mr. Leo Kelly, who kindly corrected the proofsheets of this book.

St. Bernard's Seminary,
  Rochester, N. Y.,
    Easter, 1910

CONTENTS

INTRODUCTION

Three periods can be distinguished in the religious history of the Province of New Netherland. The first period embraces the years from the discovery of the country by Henry Hudson to the beginning of organized colonization under the authority of the West India Company. During this time (1609-1624), a few trading posts, but no religious institutions of any kind, were established by the Dutch. The second period begins with the practical establishment of the Dutch Reformed Church a few years after the arrival of the first colony and ends with the rise of organized dissent within the province in 1654. This marks the beginning of the third period, which is characterized by the promulgation and execution of oppressive colonial religious legislation down to the English conquest in 1664. These penal laws were a development of the clause in the charter of 1640 which allowed the public exercise of no other religion within the Province of New Netherland than the Reformed, and this provision of the charter was only an explicit expression of the spirit of intolerance which existed latent in the Dutch province from its very foundation. For "concerning the Quakers, Lutherans and other sectaries, their Honors (the Directors of the West India Company's Amsterdam Chamber) asserted that, from the beginning, they had established

(1)

the rule, that only the Reformed Religion should be exercised within your province."

The policy of religious repression pursued in the Province of New Netherland on the outbreak of organized dissent was not merely local in character. The colonial clergy, the natural custodians of the colony's orthodoxy, merited for their zeal in this regard the commendation of their ecclesiastical superiors in Holland, the Classis of Amsterdam, which insisted quite as vigorously with the Directors of the West India Company in the Amsterdam Chamber on the repression of dissent in the colony, as the colonial clergy did with the civil authorities in the Province of New Netherland. The Director General did not fail to adopt all measures he judged necessary to fulfill the oath which bound him to maintain the exclusive worship of the Reformed Religion, and the Directors in Holland did not at any time repudiate the policy of excluding all other worship, but they tried to persuade Stuyvesant to admit some connivance in regard to dissent, if this were possible, as they feared injury to the material interests of the Company, unless the policy of religious repression was tempered by some moderation. To insure this, all repressive ordinances were finally ordered to be submitted to the Directors before their promulgation in the province, but as late as the summer of 1663 one of the Directors plainly told the Quaker, John Bowne, that the religious liberty he demanded in New Netherland was not granted there.

Religious conditions, however, were not uniform throughout the entire province, but were differentiated largely by the character of the local immigration. The

Hudson River country, whether under the direct control of the Director General or of the patroon of Rensselaerswyck, was mostly settled by colonists of Dutch origin and of the Reformed persuasion. Here there was little chance for the organization of dissent and the attempts to organize a Netherland Lutheran Church were easily frustrated during the time of the Dutch rule. Greater difficulty was experienced on the mainland to the east and on the western end of Long Island, where the English from New England settled in large numbers under Dutch jurisdiction. This English immigration comprised two classes of colonists: Reformed, including Presbyterians and Congregationalists, and dissenters from the Reformed Religion. The Presbyterians were recognized as orthodox in "everything," and the Congregationalists as orthodox "in fundamentals." Both, therefore, received the full religious liberty extended to the Reformed believers in the province. The dissenters, however, were unorthodox in doctrine as well as polity, and did not enjoy this religious liberty, but liberty of conscience in the Holland sense of the word, which respected the personal belief of the individual, and its expression in the narrow circle of the family, but penalized the organization of dissenting worship in private and public conventicles. The magistrates of Gravesend appealed to their charter, which guaranteed them this liberty of conscience with "no molestation from any magistrate or Minister that may extend jurisdiction over them," against the marriage regulations of Stuyvesant; Captain Underhill represented the force used by the same Director General in saddling the ministration of Doughty upon the town of Flushing as a violation of its

charter, and finally the inhabitants of the same town at
the instigation of Tobias Feake appealed to the charter
in their protest against Stuyvesant's prohibition to give
entertainment to the Quakers, but not at any time nor
in any place did a body of English colonists[1] appeal to
their charter to justify the organization of "unorthodox" worship in public or in private conventicles.

The religious conditions obtaining in the South, or
Delaware, River country were closely dependent on the
political changes effected in the course of its history.
Occupied by a Dutch trading post and a few straggling
settlers, it could not resist the intrusion of the Lutheran
Swedes and the founding of New Sweden with the
establishment of the Lutheran State Church. The
admission of Dutch colonists from Utrecht with the
privilege of exercising the Reformed worship attests for
this region a greater degree of religious liberty than
existed in any part of the Province of New Netherland.
The conquest of New Sweden by the Dutch did not
terminate Lutheran worship on the South River, as the
outbreak of Indian hostilities necessitated the toleration of the Swedish worship with the ministration of
one of their ministers. The expenses of this invasion
put the Amsterdam Chamber of the West India Company deeply in debt to the City of Amsterdam, which
now in compensation for its loan acquired a tract of
land on the South River, where the exclusive exercise of
the Reformed worship was maintained, until the official
orthodoxy had to give way to obtain colonists to

[1] John Bowne appealed to the Flushing charter in his arguments
with the Directors at Amsterdam, but they refused to admit the
appeal, as the charter was granted before the arrival of Quakers in
the colony.

strengthen the territory against the encroachments of
the English settlers from Maryland. In 1662 the Mennonites received permission to settle in the territory
under the jurisdiction of the City of Amsterdam, and in
the same year Hinyossa, the vice-director, offered to sixteen or eighteen families, most of whom were Finns,
residing in the jurisdiction of the Company, the free
exercise of their religion with other inducements to
attract them to the City's colony.

There was, therefore, in all New Netherland, except
the South River territory, an absolute prohibition of
non-conforming religions outside of the family. No
individual but the Quaker, who was outlawed, was
molested for his personal belief, but no one was allowed
on the plea of conscience to refuse the rate established
by public authority for the support of a Reformed
church. The attempt made in the colony to exclude
the Jew failed, but various civic rights were only given
to the Jew after a great deal of agitation and on the
express command of the Directors in Amsterdam.
The motives advanced for this attempted exclusion of
the Jew and then of the restriction of his civic rights
were not only economic but also religious in character.

If we except the Quaker, no religious qualification
was required by the Dutch for citizenship in the
Province of New Netherland, but there was a manifest
tendency to restrict office-holding to members of the
Reformed Church, which was much accentuated on the
outbreak of organized dissent in the colony. The
Director General Stuyvesant was under oath to maintain exclusively the Reformed worship. There is no
evidence to show how his predecessors were bound in

this respect, but there is ample proof that the oath was administered to subordinates in the colonial government and to the officials of the patroon Kilian van Rensselaer. Officials of Rensselaerswyck swore to promote "the true and pure service of God in conformity with the Christian Reformed Religion." The "Nine Select Men", appointed by Stuyvesant in 1647 to represent the people, were also "to promote the honor of God and the welfare of our dear Fatherland to the best advantage of the Company and the prosperity of our good citizens, and to the preservation of the pure Reformed Religion." On the creation of a municipal court at New Amsterdam in 1653, the Burgomasters and Schepens were bound "under oath to help maintain the true Reformed Religion and to suffer no other." The vice-directors, appointed on the conquest of New Sweden for that region, were sworn "to promote the Reformed Religion," but Lutheran Swedes were also retained for inferior offices. Then on the erection of a small court of justice at Wiltwyck in 1661, the commissaries had also to swear that they would "maintain and exercise the Reformed Church service and no other." The judges were, therefore, to be "professors of the Reformed Religion." Even the court-clerk had to promise to promote "the glory of God and the pure service of His Word." There could hardly be any question of a religious qualification of this kind for office-holding in the towns settled almost entirely by English dissenters, but even here the Director General and Council did not fail to insist on a religious qualification when an opportunity to do so was presented. "The English do not only enjoy the right of nominating their own magistrates, but some of them also usurp the election and appointment of such magistrates, as they please, without regard to their religion. Some, especially the people of Gravesend, elect libertines and Anabaptists, which is decidedly against the laws of the Netherlands." In Jamaica, after the ravages of the Quakers, Stuyvesant purified the magistracy of the town by the appointment of Everett, Denton and Messenger, who could be trusted "to promote the Protestant cause," by repressing the exercise of any but the Reformed Religion in private as well as in public conventicles. Where the Reformed Church and the civil authority were so closely united as in Hempstead, appointment of any but church members to office was practically impossible. This was also true of the projected settlement of New Haven colonists on Achter Kol, where the magistrates were to be bound to "maintain the true and Protestant religion, soo as the same accordinge to the word of God is declared and in this province professed." Here the right of suffrage was to be restricted to church members.

This brief review of the religious factors in the development of New Netherland establishes the existence of a consistent religious policy, which was fostered, as far as possible, in the colony by the provincial government and clergy, and in the fatherland by the Directors of the West India Chamber and by the Classis of the Reformed Dutch Church at Amsterdam. The following chapters illustrate this conclusion in detail.

CHAPTER I

THE DUTCH BACKGROUND OF THE RELIGIOUS HISTORY OF NEW NETHERLAND [1]

A correct view of the religious conditions of the mother country is essential to an understanding of the religious development of its colonies. This is especially true, when the colonial church is identical with the church of the mother country, as was the case in the Province of New Netherland, where the Dutch Reformed Church was established a few years after the foundation of the colony.

[1] This introductory chapter differs greatly from the conventional sketches given in the books current in America, which seem to take little account of the results of serious historical study in the field of Dutch religious history The well documented studies of A. C. De Schrevel, Remi Drieux, évêque de Bruges et les troubles des Pays-Bas in the Revue d'Histoire Ecclésiastique, ii 828-839; iii. 36-65, 349-369, 644-688; iv. 645-678; of Eugène Hubert, Les Pays-Bas Espagnols et La République des Provinces Unis Depuis La Paix de Munster Jusqu'au Traicté D'Utrecht, 1648-1713, La Question Religeuse et Les Relations Diplomatiques (1907); of Knuttel, W. P. C. De toestand der Nederl. Katholieken ten tijde der Republiek, 2 vols. (1892-4), are invaluable for an understanding of the Dutch religious history of this period. It has not been thought necessary to reprint excerpts from the documentary evidence, which are the authorities for this general introductory study, as these are easy of access to the reader in the works cited. The articles on the Netherland history of this period in the Cambridge Modern History and, above all, Blok's History of the People of the Netherlands, 4 vols. (1907), are helpful guides. A good bibliography of the subject is given in all these works.

The religious history of the Dutch Republic in this period is closely interwoven with the history of its struggle against the Spanish power. Dissatisfaction with the Spanish administration in the Netherlands had become so general towards the end of the sixteenth century, that all provinces united to obtain from their hereditary sovereign the withdrawal of the Spanish soldiery and the recognition of their ancient charters and liberties. This national movement developed in spite of internal religious differences. In fact, a provisional settlement of the religious issue was effected in 1576 by the treaty of union known as the Pacification of Ghent. The fifteen Catholic provinces came to an agreement with the two Calvinist provinces and deferred the definitive regulation of the religious question in those places, where Calvinism had been established to the exclusion of the Catholic worship, until the convocation of the States General after the successful expulsion of the Spanish soldiers and their adherents. These regions comprised the two provinces of Holland and Zealand with Bommel and allied territories. Meanwhile, access to the Catholic and Calvinist provinces was to be free to the subjects and inhabitants of either side, provided nothing prejudicial to Catholic faith and worship was attempted outside of Holland and Zealand and their allied territories. Every infraction of this provision either by deed or word was punishable as a disturbance of the public peace. However, conditions were made quite tolerable for the Calvinists in the Catholic provinces, as all placards formerly published against heresy and all criminal ordinances of the Duke of Alva were suspended, except in a breach of the public peace as indicated, until further orders from the States General. Thus the exclusive exercise of the Catholic worship was maintained in the fifteen Catholic provinces, while the Reformed Establishment was provisionally tolerated only in the two Calvinist provinces. The provisional character of this settlement created some uneasiness in Calvinist circles, especially among the ministers of Leyden, but William of Orange reassured them by the statement that a long time would elapse before the convocation of the States General, upon whom the regulation of religion in these provinces would devolve. On the other hand, the Catholic party apologized for the toleration of the conditions obtaining in Holland and Zealand on the ground that the final settlement of religion in those rebellious provinces would result in the restoration of the Catholic Church by the future States General with its overwhelming majority of fifteen Catholic provinces.

The Prince of Orange now plotted to complicate the negotiations between the States General and the newly arrived Governor General, Don John of Austria. He worked for a more aggressive declaration of the country's determination to obtain redress for its grievances. Although his efforts were successful in this regard, through the formulation of the Union of Brussels, the Catholic party succeeded, in spite of his influence, in incorporating in the document of union a pledge to maintain the Catholic Religion. Nevertheless, the Calvinist provinces also signed, but with the reservation that the articles of the Pacification of Ghent should not in any way suffer derogation in virtue of this act. This was done in the expectation that Don John would refuse to yield to the demands of the States, and in the hope that the delay would bring about an infection of the Catholic provinces with Protestantism, which would furnish a pretext for the demand of the general toleration of Calvinism in all the Netherlands. The Calvinists were destined to be disappointed. When Don John was fully persuaded that the Pacification of Ghent contained nothing contrary to the Catholic Religion and the authority of the King, he came to an agreement with the States General, which was confirmed in the Perpetual Edict of February 17, 1577. While the eleventh article recorded the pledge given by the States General at Luxemburg to maintain in everything and everywhere the Catholic Religion, the sixteenth article was careful to note that all the provisions of the Edict were subject to the articles of the Pacification of Ghent, which remained in full force. Before the ratification of this treaty, the States General had sent an embassy to the Prince of Orange to inform him of its contents and to explain that the pledge of the States General to maintain the Catholic Religion in everything and everywhere had been taken at Luxemburg before the States of Holland and Zealand had joined the assembly of the States General at Brussels and consequently was binding only on the fifteen Catholic provinces.[1] The Prince and the States of Holland and Zealand made some complaints, but offered to sign the treaty, if the States General promised first to have recourse to arms

---

[1] This shows how erroneous is Blok's deduction: "The Catholic Religion was to be maintained everywhere (thus also in Holland and Zealand). This last stipulation was flagrantly at odds with the Pacification, etc." Blok. A History of the People of the Netherlands, iii. p. 114.

in case the Spaniards were not withdrawn, and then not to recognize any Governor General until the grievances of the country were redressed. Don John showed his good faith by hastening the departure of the Spanish soldiery through a loan of 27,000 florins to the States General. The withdrawal of the Spaniards again proved false the suspicions of the Calvinist party. Morillon wrote towards the end of April that the Consistorians of Holland and Zealand would never have expressed their readiness to submit to the decision of the States in regard to religion, if they could have conceived possible the departure of the foreign soldiery. Then he accused these Calvinists of trying to make their people, who were enraged at their submission to the fifteen Catholic provinces, believe that the Spaniards would soon return.

Meanwhile, Don John of Austria had come to the realization that the only obstacle to a complete pacification of the Netherlands at this time was the Prince of Orange with his adherents. The Governor did not hesitate to negotiate alone and in union with the States General, but all advances were met with new demands by the Prince, whose whole policy was now directed to undermine the authority of Don John and to create a rupture of the friendly relations of the States General with him. This open hostility of William of Orange convinced Don John of Austria that his life, or at least his liberty, was in danger and led him to seize the citadel of Namur to safeguard both. This fatal step wrought the triumph of William's policy. An Orange party began to dominate Brussels; the States General had to yield to pressure, and William was requested

to come to the city to give advice in the crisis. He
soon dominated the negotiations and frustrated the
attempts at a reconciliation with Don John. The
arrival of the Archduke Matthias complicated the
situation. He had been invited by some of the nobles,
under the leadership of the Duke of Arschot, to replace
Don John and to prevent the elevation of the Prince
of Orange to this position, but the Archduke soon
fell under the influence of William of Orange, who was
created his lieutenant general at the reques⁺ of
Queen Elizabeth of England. The Prince's power
had already been increased by his nomination as
Governor of Brabant, which had been obtained
from the States of that province by the exertion of
violent popular pressure under the influence of his
partisans. About the same time, the Duke of Arschot
had been elected Governor of Flanders, but in the
course of the session of the States of Flanders at Ghent
the Prince and his adherents fomented a revolt, which
resulted in the imprisonment of the Duke and some
other Catholic leaders. A reign of terror under Calvinist tyranny ensued in Ghent, during which churches and
monasteries were pillaged, monks and friars burnt alive,
and the Blood Councillor Hessels and the ex-Procurator
Visch hanged without any previous trial.[1] Similar
flagrant violations of the Pacification of Ghent also
took place elsewhere. Bruges, Antwerp and Brussels
were made the scenes of incredible excesses by fanatic
Calvinists. Retaliation on the part of Catholics ensued,

[1] The Rev. George Edmundson, M. A., writes: "William disclaimed any share in this act of violence, but it is difficult
altogether to exculpate him." The Cambridge Modern History,
vol. iii. chap, vi, The Revolt of the Netherlands, p. 248.

and in Artois and Hainaut the Protestant minority was
subject to persecution. The Prince of Orange now
thought the country ripe for a departure from the Pacification of Ghent. The way had already been prepared
on December 10, 1577, by a second Union of Brussels,
which tried to impose on Catholics and Protestants an
oath not to molest each other in the exercise of their
religion. This was a violation of the Pacification of
Ghent, as it extended the exercise of Calvinist worship
to the fifteen Catholic provinces. Finally, in the month
of June, 1578, William of Orange submitted to the
States General a project entitled the Peace of Religion,
which proclaimed full liberty of conscience and the
tranquil possession of property, ecclesiastical as well as
secular, until the assembly of a National Council.
The Catholic Religion was to be restored again in Holland and Zealand and other places, where its public
exercise had been interdicted. Wherever a hundred
fathers of families, Catholic or Protestant, should make
the demand, the free exercise of their worship was to be
conceded. In other places where the public exercise of
one or the other worship could not be granted on account of the small number of its adherents, a private
oratory was to be allowed within the home. Both
Catholics and Calvinists were to be careful to avoid
anything that might give offense to either party.
Finally, all public offices, universities, colleges, schools,
hospitals, hospices and public charities were declared
open to all. The project was referred by the States
General to the provincial States, where the scheme met
with decided opposition. Some cities accepted it under
pressure from the Prince of Orange, but they made no

attempt to execute its provisions. Meanwhile, the continuation of Calvinistic excesses made the Catholic party realize the necessity of united action. The Union of Arras was formed on January 6, 1579, to maintain the Pacification of Ghent, the Catholic faith, the obedience to the king and the privileges of the nation. Although the Union of Arras professed to be based on the Pacification of Ghent, the clause suspending the placards against heresy was suppressed. The formation of this Catholic league hastened the establishment of a Protestant league, already in process of formation, towards the end of the same month, the Union of Utrecht, also for the avowed purpose of strengthening the previous general union of the Pacification of Ghent. Nevertheless, according to this agreement, Holland and Zealand were free to act as they pleased in regard to religion, while the other provinces united in this league were to regulate themselves in accordance with the provisions of the Peace of Religion. While there was no straight line of cleavage produced between the North and South by the formation of these hostile leagues, the beginning was made that developed into the formation of two separate commonwealths. The southern cities of Ghent, Antwerp, Bruges, Ypres, Lierre and the Franc du Bruges gave their hearty support to the Union of Utrecht, but finally had to yield to the authority of the Duke of Parma, whom the Catholic Malcontents had recognized by the treaty of May 19. The conquests of Parma always entailed the restoration of the Catholic faith and of the placards against heresy, but capital punishment was no longer inflicted for heresy after 1597. Dissenters had the choice between reconciliation with the Catholic Church and exile, and those who preferred the latter were given time to liquidate their estates.

William of Orange now aimed at the consolidation of the northern union under a foreign sovereign. Finally, after much opposition, on September 19, 1580, the treaty was signed with the Duke of Anjou, who accepted the sovereignty of the Netherlanders. In virtue of this agreement, the Peace of Religion was to be observed in all the provinces with the exception of Holland and Zealand, where the Reformed Church was to be maintained as heretofore to the exclusion of the public worship of the Catholic religion. Nevertheless, even before the arrival of the Duke of Anjou, the first general placard against Catholics was promulgated on December 20, 1581. Catholics were forbidden to assemble either in churches or private houses for the purpose of assisting at mass or of hearing a sermon, if these assemblies were judged to be of the nature to create disorders, to facilitate secret machinations with the enemy, or to occasion harm to the public interests. For the infraction of this measure a fine of one hundred florins was to be inflicted on the master of the house and also on the priest officiating at the assembly. Furthermore, all means of Catholic propaganda were to be suppressed. The ecclesiastical dress was interdicted on the streets; no school could be opened without authorization from the local magistracy; the publication, sale and distribution of books, pamphlets, songs and other literature calculated to excite "the ignorant and weak" was prohibited under a fine of one hundred florins for the first offense and double the sum for the second offense.

Nevertheless, *all intention to burden or to make inqui-sition into any man's conscience was disclaimed by the legislators.*

The French protectorate proved a failure in spite of all the efforts of William of Orange after his recovery from the wound inflicted in the attempted assassination on March 18, 1582. The Duke of Anjou had arrived in the beginning of the year, after the States General had previously abjured their allegiance to Philip II. The failure of Anjou in his attempt to obtain independence by the seizure of several cities made a continuance of his sovereignty practically impossible. However, the Prince of Orange persisted in negotiating for a recon-ciliation until the day of the Duke's death, June 10, 1584, as he then saw no hope of help from the English Queen nor from the Lutheran Germans, who would have oppressed the Calvinists on the acquisition of power. Meanwhile, the States of Holland, Zealand and Utrecht were planning to confer sovereign authority over themselves on the Prince of Orange, who, according to one of the articles of the pact projected on this occasion, was to maintain exclusively the "true Re-formed Religion," but without molestation of anyone on account of his belief. Before these plans matured, William of Orange was murdered by Balthassar Gerard, to whom the publication of the King's ban had suggested the deed. This action entailed an increase of severity in the measures for the repression of the Catholics, amongst whom some had manifested satisfaction in the death of the main author of the revolt that had cost them the free exercise of their religion. The placard of November 21, 1584, decreed banishment for all organizers of Catholic worship within the United Provinces. The severity of this legislation was accentuated by the fact that Calvinism at this time was received universally only in the one Province of Zealand, while in all other provinces the Catholics were much more numerous than the Calvinists, especially in Utrecht and the regions to the east, but not to the same extent in Holland and Friesland.

After fruitless negotiations with the French King, the States sought protection from the Queen of England, with whom an agreement was finally concluded, according to which the surrender of the towns of Flushing, Brill and Rammekens was stipulated as pledges for the repayment of the expenses incurred by the Queen. The governorship was settled on Leicester, whose administration also proved a failure on account of the opposition excited by his measures against free trade with the enemy and his ambitious designs for the increase of his own authority at the expense of the States General with the help of the democratic opposition to the ruling oligarchies. His espousal of strict Calvinism gave him the support of the "precisians," who were working not only for the suppression of the Catholic Religion but also of all forms of Protestantism at variance with Calvinism, and even of the more liberal Calvinism then more in favor amongst the ruling classes. The failure of Leicester's design to seize several cities after his second arrival in the Netherlands hastened his final departure. Before this the "precisians" had taken the opportunity offered by the Governor's favor to convene a National Synod, which attempted a permanent organization of the Dutch Reformed Church on

the strict principles of the Calvinist zealots. The
Church Order then adopted was provisionally approved
by the States but *with the reservation of the right to exercise supervision over church and school.*

After the departure of Leicester, the executive
power of the Council of State, on account of the objectionable presence of the three Englishmen amongst its
members, was gradually absorbed by the States General,
in which the influence of Holland predominated. The
consolidation of these provinces into the federal state of
the Dutch Republic was largely due to the ability of
Holland's great statesman, the Advocate John van
Oldenbarnevelt, supported by the able soldier, Maurice
of Nassau, who had been appointed Captain General
and Admiral of the Union by the States General. The
union of all the Stadtholderates in the person of Maurice,
with the exception of Friesland, where his cousin William Lewis of Nassau held that position, was a great
step towards the unification of the country. There
was hardly any need of Holland to instruct this
ardent Calvinist as its Stadtholder to maintain the
Reformed Religion. As early as June 23, 1587, he
had published an ordinance prohibiting pilgrimages
and "other superstitions, "under a fine of twenty-four
Carolus florins for each offense. This oppressive placard
was renewed in 1588, 1590, 1591, and in more
vigorous terms in 1647, no doubt on account of its
frequent infraction. The offensive campaigns of Maurice
cleared the federated provinces of Spanish garrisons
and resulted in the formation of the new province
of Stadt en Landen by the union of the city of
Groningen with the Ommelands under the Stadtholder

William Lewis in 1594. Drenthe was also placed under this Stadtholder, but, unlike the newly created province, it had no individual seat in the States General. William Lewis organized the Reformed Church in both these provinces, where he hardly tolerated a vestige of Catholicism.[1]

The alliances concluded by the States General with Henry IV of France and with Elizabeth of England against Philip II effected little for the advancement of Dutch interests. Shortly before his death, Philip again tried conciliation by erecting the provinces into a separate, but only nominally independent realm under the Archdukes Albert and Isabella, his daughter, who were united in marriage. The establishment of the new government at Brussels failed to conciliate the revolted provinces. Under the new sovereigns, war was then vigorously pursued, with occasional brilliant victories on both sides, but finally this continuous warfare produced a state of mutual exhaustion. In spite of the opposition of Maurice and his strict Calvinist adherents,

[1] A very severe placard was issued by the provincial States of Groningen against Catholics and Anabaptists. A fine of ten Dalers was inflicted on the persons giving their houses for a reunion of Catholics or Anabaptists. The same fine was placed on the preacher for the first offense; in the case of a repeated offense the latter was subject to fifteen days' detention on bread and water, and for the third offense to banishment. Persons assisting at the services were also fined ten Dalers. Marriages contracted before a Catholic priest were punished as concubinage. Cf. Brandt, Hist. d. Reformatie, ii. 14-15.
In Drenthe, William Lewis of Nassau, on May 10, 1598, ordered the parish clergy to cease all divine service, to surrender the property of the churches and to leave their parsonages within three weeks. A new ordinance of March 19, 1599, forbade ecclesiastics to pass a single night in the province without special authorization. This severe legislation occasioned considerable emigration, and in a little time there was not an important Catholic population in any place but Koevorden. (Cf. Maguin, Overzicht der kerkelijke geschiedenis van Drenthe, cited in Knuttel, i. 40; Hubert, p. 86.)

the peace negotiations which ensued led to the conclusion of the truce for twelve years on April 9, 1609. The plenipotentiaries of Albert and Isabella, although supported by President Jeannin, the saver of the Huguenots of Dijon after the night of St. Bartholomew, could obtain no concession in favor of Catholic worship except the promise that the States and Prince Maurice would respect the exclusive exercise of the Catholic Religion in the Brabant territory occupied by the troops of the Republic. Soon frequent complaints were made of the violation of this promise by the Hollanders. During the negotiations for the truce, the States General had shown themselves absolutely opposed to the free exercise of "papist" worship within their territories, and even denied the King of Spain the right to raise the question, as all decision in this matter entailed the exercise of sovereignty, and consequently could only depend on the sovereign States themselves. Meanwhile, the Calvinist ministers were representing the demand of the King of Spain for freedom of Catholic worship as the initial step to the reconquest of the rebellious provinces. Under these conditions, the king, on the ratification of the truce, could only express the hope that the States would treat kindly the Catholics who went among them during the time of its duration. Jeannin, prior to his departure, insisted again on the concession of religious freedom to Catholics, but the States could only be induced to promise in a general way that they would act with moderation. As soon as the news of the murder of Henry IV (May 14, 1610), whom Prince Maurice was preparing to assist in the reduction of the Duchy of Cleves, arrived in the United

Provinces, there a was violent outbreak of hostility against "papists," manifested in the publication of a mass of insulting pamphlets. Also on this occasion, some Catholics were impolitic enough to add fuel to the flame. The States General were repeatedly urged to adopt stringent measures against papal superstition by the synods and classes of the Reformed Church and finally in response to this pressure an edict was published by this assembly in 1612 which prohibited instruction in foreign Catholic or Jesuit schools,[1] meetings to celebrate Catholic worship and the ministry of priests from the southern provinces, whence many had crossed the border since the establishment of the truce.[2] The Reformed were still in great fear of the Catholics, who even then formed two-thirds of the population, "la plus saine et la plus riche partie," as Oldenbarnevelt wrote to Carleton. The rule of the intolerant Protestant minority continued to be oppressive. In 1617, Rovenius, the Vicar Apostolic, made known to the Holy See the miserable condition of the faithful in his charge. In many places, Catholics who neglected to have their children baptized in Calvinist churches incurred large fines and Catholics whose marriages were not contracted before a minister of the Reformed persuasion were punished as if they were living in concubinage.[3] In Amsterdam,

[1] The States of Holland had placed a fine of 300 florins, March 12, 1591, on attendance at the Universities of Louvain, Dôle and Douay, where instruction was contrary "to the true religion" and hostile to the fatherland. Wiltens-Scheltus, Kerkelyck Placaatboek, i. 524.
[2] The States of Holland, Sept. 13, 1601, ordered the detention of foreign monks, seized within the province, in prison on bread and water for six months. Hubert, Les Pays-Bas Espagnols et La République des Provinces-Unies etc., p. 76.
[3] The States of Holland, July 1, 1594, issued an edict, placing a fine of 100 pounds upon persons recurring to the ministry of a priest

the Jews had their synagogues, the Mahometans their
meetings and all kinds of sects their conventicles; the
Catholics alone were excluded from all participation in
the toleration of Holland.   There were many Catholics
in Friesland,[1] but they could worship with safety only in
the castles of the nobles, of whom many still gave a
tepid allegiance to the old faith.   In Geldern[2] and Zealand, Catholics possessed little liberty and had to
assemble secretly for worship, while in Stadt en Landen
the adherents of the old faith suffered more active persecution.   However, the condition of the Catholics was
more tolerable in some of the cities.   Through the connivance of the magistracy, which in several places was
open to a bribe, the Catholics obtained a great deal of
liberty in the exercise of their faith in Harlem, Gouda,
Leyden, Alckmaar and Hoorn.[3]

for the baptism of their children and for the celebration of marriage.
A fine of 50 pounds was also placed on the witnesses and a fine of 400
pounds on the persons instigating the act.   The same penalties were
decreed for attendance at papist conventicles.   Wiltens-Scheltus,
Kerkelyck Placaatboek, i. 526.

[1] Persecution of Catholics was most violent in this province.
Thousands of Catholics found safety in flight, and only a small number of priests remained in the province in deep concealment.

[2] Here Catholics were numerous.   The policy of the government
was directed to paralyse their strength.   In 1624 the States deprived the clergy of the disposition of their revenues and declared
null and void the sale, mortgaging, donation, exchange or any alienation of property on the part of "pretended" ecclesiastics or of papists
in religious societies, sodalities and fraternities, etc.   It was pleaded
that many feared to adopt Calvinism and many returned to the old
faith lest they might be disinherited.   In 1640 the "klopjes"
were declared incapable of receiving an inheritance.   Finally
measures were directed to the prevention of assemblies, that the
Catholics attempted to facilitate by the removal of the walls
between neighboring houses.   For details cf. works of Knuttel and
Hubert, with documents cited.

[3] This was true to a certain extent at The Hague, where the
legations of the Kings of France and Portugal and of the Republic
of Venice had their chapels, which remained open also to the inhabitants of the city in spite of the frequent protests of the States of Holland at the instigation of The Hague consistory.

Meanwhile, the Reformed Church of the United Provinces was divided by the bitter controversies which raged between the "precisians" and the "libertines." In 1610 the liberal party, then also called Arminians from its chief exponent, assembled at Gouda and expressed in a "Remonstrance" their dissent from the teaching of strict Calvinism on the subject of predestination, election and grace, and appealed to the decision of a National Synod, convened under the control of the civil power, as the States had "the supreme direction and the highest jurisdiction over ecclesiastical and lay affairs under God and in accordance with His Word in these territories." The precisians, or Gomarists, as they were also called from their leader, replied with a Counter-Remonstrance, which upheld the strict Calvinist tenets in uncompromising rigor and denounced their opponents as guilty of Socinian, Pelagian and papistical heresies. The large majority of the Protestant population rallied to the support of the Counter-Remonstrants, while the burgher oligarchies favored their opponents, who commanded a majority in the States of Holland, Utrecht and Overyssel. A conference between the two parties arranged by the authority of the States of Holland and West Friesland failed to effect a reconciliation, and the attempt on the part of the States to establish *commissarissen politicq*, who were regularly to appear in the church assemblies and control the examination of candidates and the calls of the ministers, was bitterly resented by the stronger party, who feared favor for Remonstrant preachers. Finally, the Counter-Remonstrants, in 1613, confident of an overwhelming majority, also demanded the convocation of a

National Church Synod, but Oldenbarnevelt feared lest
the triumph of this party should lead to the domination
of the Church over the State, and through his influence
the proposals were rejected. To secure peace, the
States of Holland, in January, 1614, prohibited the discussion of disputed questions by the preachers in the
pulpits and enjoined moderation in such abstruse
matters. Violent opposition to this measure arose in
several important towns, also in Amsterdam, but
Oldenbarnevelt was determined to overcome all
opposition. When Maurice, who had begun to dis-
trust the Advocate, gave his support to the
Counter-Remonstrants and encouraged their opposition to the authority of the States, Oldenbarnevelt succeeded in inducing the States of Holland,
in December, 1616, to raise a force of four thousand
men to be at the disposal of the magistrates for the
enforcement of order. Although the two Stadtholders
commanded the votes of four out of seven provinces
in the States General, this assembly decreed the convocation of the National Synod by only a narrow
majority. The States of Holland, in spite of a powerful minority supported by Calvinist opinion throughout the province, refused to concur in the resolution
of the States General. The seizure of a church at
The Hague for the Counter-Remonstrants under the
direction of Maurice led to the adoption of the
"Scherpe Resolutie," proposed by the Advocate to
the States of Holland, which refused to approve
any convocation of a synod, national or provincial,
infringing the sovereign rights and supremacy of
the States in religious affairs. The city magistrates
were directed to uphold the peace and to levy new

forces for this purpose, if necessary; all officials, municipal and provincial, all soldiers in the pay of the province, were required to take an oath of obedience to the States of Holland on pain of dismissal. Levies of troops were raised in Leyden, Harlem, Rotterdam, Gouda and other towns. In the meantime, Oldenbarnevelt had gone to Utrecht, where the States under his influence refused to stop the levy on receiving the warning of the States General in regard to the dangerous character of such measures. Finally, Maurice, on the commission of the States General, entered the town at the head of his troops, and, on July 31, 1618, the troops of the States in obedience to his commands laid down their arms. The Prince as Stadtholder immediately created a new Municipal Council of Counter-Remonstrants and a majority of the same party in the Provincial States. On August 20, the States General issued a placard for the dismissal of troops of Holland within twenty-four hours, and on the 29th the Advocate and his chief adherents were placed under arrest, which terminated in their judicial murder. After these arrests, Maurice with a strong retinue made a tour of the towns of Holland and purged the Municipal Councils and the Provincial States of their Remonstrant majorities. His work was approved by the States General, which assembled in November, and with the destruction of all opposition the seven provinces unanimously approved the convocation of the National Synod.

The National Synod, assembled at Dortdrecht began its first session on November 13, 1618. The assembly consisted of more than one hundred members, amongst whom there were about thirty foreign divines

and eighteen political commissioners representing the
States. The Remonstrant minority was immediately
put on trial for its teaching by the remainder of the
Synod, from which they were finally ordered to with-
draw after violent altercation. They then assembled
in Rotterdam, where they denounced the tyranny of the
dominant party, who condemned the Remonstrants as
schismatics and heretics, and declared them unfit to
hold any position in the churches, schools and universities of the country. The former liberal movement in
favor of a revision of the Creeds of the Dutch Reformed
Church was definitely checked by the Synod's approval
of the Netherland Confession and the Heidelberg Catechism without any change, as the orthodox Calvinist
faith was thought to be briefly but completely set forth
in these. Now the States General imposed the "Act of
Cessation," on pain of banishment, which deprived the
Remonstrants of the right to preach and reduced them
to the condition of private individuals. Only one of the
Remonstrant members of the Synod signed; the remaining fourteen were forced to go into exile. In July, 1619,
the States General prohibited the assemblies of the
Remonstrants, but the ordinance was not enforced in
the larger towns, as Amsterdam, Rotterdam and Gouda,
although this connivance greatly annoyed the Calvinist
zealots. In all about two hundred Remonstrant
preachers were deposed and of these seventy signed the
Act of Cessation, about forty finally accepted the
articles of Dortdrecht, with restoration to the ministry
as a reward, and about eighty went into exile. These
last attacked the dominant party, "the little ministers
of the new Holland inquisition," with a mass of pam-

phlets and lampoons, emanating mainly from the press in Antwerp, the headquarters of the Remonstrants. The work of purification also extended byond the ministry. Church Councillors, schoolmasters, etc., who were suspected of the heresy were likewise removed from their offices. Some municipal governments were also changed, although a Remonstrant magistrate here and there retained his position, when his removal was more dangerous than his retention.[1] Under these circumstances the Arminian spirit persisted in spite of the oppressive measures.

The termination of the twelve years' truce brought an increase of severity in the treatment of the Catholics. Before this the Synod of Dortdrecht had petitioned the States General to see to the observance of the laws, to suppress definitively the exercise of Catholic worhip and to expel the Jesuits and foreign priests from the country. In response to a second request of this nature, the States General, on February 26, 1622, issued a placard which prohibited Jesuits, religious of either sex and foreign priests from residing permanently or tempora-

[1] With the victory of the strict Calvinists the tendency to restrict official positions throughout the provinces to the members of that party became still more pronounced. At the time of the formulation of the Union of Utrecht, it had been proposed to incorporate a clause excluding from such positions all persons who were not members of the Reformed Church. This measure was not adopted, but various limitations in regard to office-holding in the provinces dated from that time. In 1616 certain elective capacities were denied to Catholics. In the Provinces of Overyssel and Gelderland, no restriction was adopted until after the termination of the truce. Thirty years later similar laws were adopted in Holland, where many non-reformed had seats in the municipal colleges. Although some cities, like Gouda, gave the preference to members of the "true Christian Religion," until then no one in the majority of cities was legally disqualified for the exercise of political rights or for nomination to office upon theological or religious grounds. Cf. Blok, A History of the People of the Netherlands, iii. 486.

rily in the lands of the Republic, under the penalty of
being arrested and imprisoned as enemies of the State.
A second offense on their part entailed punishment for
disturbance of the public peace. Their hosts in the
land were subject to a fine of one hundred pounds
Flemish for the first offense, double the sum for the
second offense, and to the penalty of corporal punishment and banishment for the third offense. The
priests who previously had been authorized to reside
in the Republic were bound to report their names and
places of residence to the local magistrate, if they
wished to continue the enjoyment of this privilege.
All correspondence with foreign ecclesiastics was prohibited to the subjects of the Republic, and letters of this
kind were to be surrendered to the magistrate on their
receipt under a fine of fifty pounds for every infraction
of the law. Catholic ceremonies were interdicted not
only in the churches but also in private houses. The
master of the house was subject to a fine of two hundred
florins, each person present to a fine of twenty-five
florins, and the officiatingpriest to the penalty of banishment. The priests who preached disobedience to *these
laws* were to be prosecuted for sedition and subjected
to corporal punishment, "even unto death," according
to the gravity of the offense. Attendance at foreign
Jesuit schools was again forbidden, and parents were
ordered to recall their children from such places under
a fine of one hundred florins for each month of delay.
The congregations of devout women, "klopjes," were to
be dissolved at once. Protestant orphans were not to
be confided to the care of Catholic guardians, but to the
care of the magistrate, if they had no near relations of

the Reformed persuasion. Collections for all sorts of Catholic purposes were absolutely interdicted. Finally, the judges were commanded to execute the provisions of this ordinance without any relaxation, and they were threatened with the loss of their positions and with arbitrary punishment if they accepted a bribe from the delinquents. Those who denounced such practices were promised a reward of three hundred florins. Still there must have been a great deal of connivance, as this placard was renewed in 1624, 1629 and 1641, and as the synods multiply in course of time their complaints of the boldness and superstition of the papists, "Pauselijke stoutigheden ente superstitien." Nevertheless, the States General did not recede from its intransigent attitude towards Catholic worship, although the edicts against the Remonstrants and other Protestant dissenters, such as Mennonites and Lutherans, gradually lapsed into desuetude under the moderate policy dictated by the successor of Maurice, his brother Frederick Henry, and supported by the municipal governments, who feared the domination of the Dutch Reformed Church in the event of further repression. In 1630 the States General refused to listen to the petition of the French ambassador for the concession of religious liberty to the inhabitants of the conquered city of Bois-le-Duc. On March 13, 1644, the Count d'Avaux, previous to his departure for Münster, where he was to take part in the negotiations for a general peace, requested in the name of the Queen Regent of France a relaxation of the repressive ordinances against Catholics from the States General. This assembly protested against this presumptuous and unreasonable intervention of a stranger in the internal affairs of the Republic. A resolution was then passed by the States General to complete the penal legislation against Catholics on the plea that impunity to propagators of "Catholic superstitions" and the introduction of the papist hierarchy entailed undeniable dangers for public safety. The French plenipotentiary, Count d'Estrades, was not more successful in his attempt to have an article incorporated in the capitulation of the city of Hulst, granting the public exercise of the Catholic worship. When Frederick Henry transmitted the petition to the States General, the assembly expressed their great astonishment at this pernicious proposition. In the following year, when the French and Dutch planned a joint attack on Antwerp, Cardinal Mazarin was able to obtain only the grudging consent of his Dutch allies to the concession of four churches for Catholic worship on the conquest of this city. The joint expedition never took place.

The conclusion of the general peace of Münster in 1648 brought to the Republic a recognition of its sovereignty by Spain. The Catholics, sorely harassed in the past by the oppressive measures of the States General, which had often been anticipated and even reinforced by the penal legislation of the provincial States and of the town councils, hoped for some relaxation of the persecution with the cessation of hostilities, but the Calvinist clergy was loud in its protestations against any concession to "Roman idolatry," which would surely bring upon the Republic the anger of God. In spite of the opposition of the States of Holland, some relaxation was ordered by the States General within the territory proper of the Republic, but severe measures of repression were adopted for the territory recently annexed in the south, where, notwithstanding all the efforts of the Spanish plenipotentiaries, the supremacy of the States was asserted in spiritual as well as temporal matters. The death of the Prince of Orange with the birth of an heir eight days later gave an opportunity to the States of Holland to use its influence for an increase of the powers of the States by the reassumption of many rights that had been acquired under stress of previous political necessities by the Princes of Orange. The Great Assembly of the United Provinces, opened January 18, 1651, to discuss the situation, reindorsed the decrees of the National Synod of Dortdrecht, which were to be maintained in each province "with the power of the land." The five delegates from the provincial Synods were not satisfied with this. They demanded drastic measures against "popish idolatry, superstition and hierarchy," against the "innumerable Jesuits, priests, curates and monks," overrunning the land "in thousands like locusts"; they insisted on the enforcement of the placards against other dissenters, against the public worship of the Jews, and against all attacks on the Reformed teaching, with the suppression of all crying public sins, lest it appear that the authorities have received the "sword" in vain. Holland protested against the adoption of the measures of the Spanish Inquisition after the sacrifice of so much blood for liberty of conscience, but Zealand, with Friesland, Groningen and Overyssel, was willing to satisfy the demands of the Synods, while Gelderland and Utrecht hesitated. Finally, Holland was able to have its reso-

lution adopted by the assembly, which decreed the maintenance of the ordinances of the National Synod of
Dortdrecht, the enforcement of the placards against
the Catholics and the retention of other sects "in all
good order and quiet." The execution of this decree
fell far short of the desires of the Calvinist ministers,
who continually assailed the civil authorities with
their remonstrances, and Catholics and sometimes
adherents of other persuasions had continually to fear
the penalties that might be inflicted according to law
by the magistrates under pressure of the ministers.
Government circles were not so inimical to the consider-
ations which De la Court advanced. He believed that
self-interest should prevent the dominant Calvinists
from the attempt to suppress people of other persuasions, who were in the majority even in Holland, as persecution might provoke their emigration, to the great loss
of the country. He tells us that most of the "old inhabitants," peasants, moneyed men, and nobles in that
province were still Catholics, while there were also
many Protestants, but mostly Mennonites or Rijns-
burgers. In spite of all past vexatious measures,
Catholics still formed a large majority of the population
in the Provinces of Utrecht, Gelderland and Overyssel,
although many of the Reformed were to be found in
some districts, as the Veluwe, since John of Nassau
was able to throw his influence into the balance. De la
Torre's report of 1656 gives a very small number of
Catholics for the three northern provinces, and Blok in
his history estimates the number of Catholics above the
Meuse at about half a million. This geographical distribution of the confessions represents the condition of

religion in the Dutch Republic at the very moment
when the colony of New Netherland passed into the
hands of the English, on the eve of the second English
war, in 1664.

CHAPTER II

GENERAL RELATIONS OF CHURCH AND STATE
IN NEW NETHERLAND

THE successful organization of the Dutch East India Company in 1602 rendered feasible the formation of a West India Company to realize more effectually the humiliation of the power of Spain. Very early William Ussellinx, an ardent Calvinist and an enemy to "all heretics and erring spirits," advocated the organization of such a commercial company to prey on the Spanish possessions, from which their enemy drew the "sinews of war," and to plant there the saving faith and the gospel of Jesus Christ, whereby the heathen might be rescued from the darkness of idolatry and be preserved from papistry.[1] Although the plan became popular, it was opposed by the East India Company, which feared for its monopoly, and by Oldenbarnevelt, who was anxious to avoid new complications with Spain. The successful negotiation of a truce in 1609 made any further effort on the part of Ussellinx fruitless. Nevertheless, in the very same year, the discoveries of Henry Hudson on the North American coast, while employed by the Dutch East India Company in the search of a

---

[1] Cf. O'Callaghan, Hist. of New Netherland, i. 31; prospectus for W. I. Co., Arg. Gust. p. 51, Jameson, William Usselinx,A. H. A. Papers, ii. 39.

passage to the East Indies, opened a period of Dutch
discovery and fur-trade, which was increased considerably after the incorporation of the United New Netherland Company in 1614, with exclusive trading privileges
for three years. After the fall of Oldenbarnevelt,
Ussellinx was conscious of a better chance to realize his
projects, especially as there was no doubt of the renewal
of hostilities on the expiration of the twelve years' truce.
He was, however, disappointed by the refusal of the
States General to adopt many of his ideas in the charter
of the new company. Ussellinx had planned a charter for the formation of a Protestant (Calvinist) colonial
empire under a well-ordered administration, subject to
regular supervision by the state, to control the merchants "who have gain for their north star and greed for
a compass, and who would believe the ship was keeping
to its right course, if it were almost wrecked by profit."[1]
The States General obtained considerable influence in
the new association through its deputies on the governing board, the College of the XIX, and through the
requirement of its approval for warlike operations.
For the West India Company was modeled after the
East India Company, mainly for spoils and privateer-
ing, according to the more warlike plans of the
maritime cities of Holland.

While no mention of religion was made in the charter of the West India Company, or in the subsequent
agreement between the managers and the principal
adventurers, religious motives were not absent in the
adoption of the charter. Abraham Sixt, ambassador

[1] Blok, A Hist. of the People of the Netherlands, iv. 3-5;
Jameson, William Usselinx, A. H. A. Papers, ii. 66-67.

of the Elector Palatine Frederick, is said to have urged
this scheme to promote the Protestant cause in the
Bohemian war. During the discussion of the drafts
of the charter of the West India Company, Ferdinand
had become Emperor, the Elector Palatine, the nephew
of Prince Maurice and Count Frederick, had been
chosen King of Bohemia, and the combination had
been formed for the overthrow of the latter. The
cause of Protestantism in Bohemia and especially of
the German Calvinists appealed to the sympathies of
the party now ruling in the United Provinces, but in the
end the controlling factor in shaping the new organization was the proximate expiration of the truce with
Spain and the renewal of hostilities.[1]

The interests of the new company naturally centered
in the Spanish seas about Brazil and the West Indies,
while the Province of New Netherland received scant
attention,   although   organized   colonization   began
there almost as soon as the time for the subscriptions to
the company terminated in 1623. When the question
of religion presented itself in regard to the colony,
the   West   India   Company,   the   proprietor   of the
province, assumed the same authority which the civil
power exercised in religious matters within the United
Provinces. In addition, the right of patronage was
claimed by the company over the colonial church.
Usselinx had proposed in his plan the establishment of
a council or college of theologians, who were to supply
the company with godly ministers and teachers to
instruct not only the colonists and their children, but

---

[1] Jameson, William Usselinx, A. H. A. Papers ii. 66-67.

also the Indians, in religion and learning.[1] Although no such provision was made in the charter finally adopted for the company, the deputies on foreign affairs of the Classis of Amsterdam soon acquired such a position in the ecclesiastical affairs of the Province of New Netherland. The stockholders of the company had been organized into five chambers representing various sections of the United Provinces, to whom was given a proportional representation in a general executive board, the College of the XIX. In the general distribution of the various enterprises amongst the individual chambers of the company, the most important chamber, located at Amsterdam, received the immediate management of New Netherland from the College of the XIX,[2] which practically lost all its power over the province when it refused to contribute to the expenses of the colony after the company's bankruptcy in 1645 in consequence of the vast expenditures entailed in its ineffectual efforts to retain the Dutch conquests in Brazil.[3] Henceforth, the Amsterdam Chamber bore the expenses alone and assumed a still more independent administration of New Netherland.

The Directors of the Chamber in the establishment of churches and the appointment of preachers and other ministers of religion followed the rule adopted in

[1] Van Rees, ii. p. 117, makes this a subject of a memorial to the Synod of Dort. Cf. Jameson, William Usselinx, A. H. A. Papers, ii. 61-62.
[2] Cf. charter in O'Callaghan, Hist. of New Netherland, i. 399; Osgood, The Am. Colonies in the 17th Century, ii. 96. Van Rensselaer-Bowier MSS. (1908), gives a revised version of the charter.
[3] Directors to Stuyvesant, Jan. 27, 1649. Col. Docs. N. Y., xiv. 104.

1624 by the Synod of North Holland, which gave to the
Classis the charge of all the ecclesiastical interests in the
colonies under the care of the Chamber located within
the limits of its jurisdiction.[1] This practical solution
of the question of the supervision of the colonial
churches was immediately protested by deputies from
Utrecht, Overyssel and especially of Gelderland, who
held that the matter equally concerned all the churches
of the land, and demanded that at least deputies from
their respective synods might be admitted to a general
assembly of delegates from the churches and classes,
which had charge of colonial churches.[2] Such a general
assembly, which had first been suggested by the Synod
of North Holland at the expense of the commercial company with jurisdiction over these colonies,[3] never was
realized, and the individual classes continued to take
charge of the colonial churches of the respective chambers within their jurisdiction. According to this rule,
ministers were first sent to the colonies by the Classes of
Hoorn and Enkhuysen, but, with the concentration of
business at Amsterdam, this classis acquired almost
exclusive control of the colonial churches, although it
was not authorized to do this any more than other
classes, where there were chambers of the companies.[4]
As early as 1628 Michaelius, the first minister of New
Netherland, recognized the consistory of Amsterdam as
the superior ecclesiastical authority of the colony.[5]

[1] Synod of North Holland, Aug. 6, etc., 1624.   Eccl. Recs.
N. Y., i. 38-39.
[2] Synod of North Holland, 1625, Aug. 12, etc.   Ibid. 39.
[3] Synod of North Holland, Aug. 6, 1624.   Ibid 38-39.
[4] Synod of North Holland, Aug. 1, 1639.   Ibid. 126.
[5] Michaelius to Smoutius. Ibid. 54.

This course of action continued to be followed, but in 1639 a decided attempt began to be made on the part of the protesting synods for the formation of an ecclesiastical body that would have represented the entire Dutch Church in the supervision of colonial churches. In case of a refusal or a longer delay, these synods threatened to appeal for a remedy to the States General, whom their deputies were instructed to interest in this matter.[1] The majority of the classes in the Synod of North Holland declared the change unadvisable, but agreed by way of compromise to send the ecclesiastical acta of the colonial churches to the corresponding synods,[2] but this did not satisfy them. Deputies from the Synods of Gelderland, South Holland, Utrecht, and Overyssel submitted a remonstrance to the States General, who were requested in the grant of new charters to give charge of everything necessary for the welfare of the East and West India churches to a board of deputies from the synods of all the United Provinces. On the advice of the States General, the Synod of South Holland agreed to a conference with the Synod of North Holland in the presence of the correspondents from the other synods. The old rule was maintained, but the classes in charge of colonial churches were to submit a full annual report of the condition of these churches to their synods, of which a summary was to be incorporated in the synodal acts, and communicated to all the synods of the United Provinces. The correspondents were to take with them, at their own expense,

---

[1] Synod of North Holland, 1639, Aug. 1, etc., Eccl. Recs. N. Y., i. 123-126; 1640, Aug. 21, etc., Ibid. 132-134; Oct. 30, Ibid. 135.

[2] Synod of North Holland, 1641, Aug. 13, etc., Art 29, Ibid. 138-139.

copies of the minutes of these classes and of any documents bearing on these matters. If any difficulties
arose in regard to doctrine or church polity in the colonial churches, which could not be readily solved by the
particular classis or synod, the advice of the synods of
the land was to sought, unless there could be no delay,
and then the facts of the case were to be communicated
to them. The last article in this plan shows that the
protesting synods wished to make it possible for persons
under their jurisdiction to serve the colonial church.
Those who manifested such a desire were to be held in
good commendation by the classes in charge of such
churches, provided they had the necessary qualifications.[1] Although the Synod of South Holland provisionally accepted these propositions, it gained the
approval of other synods very slowly.[2] By 1648 it was
accepted by all the synods, except Utrecht, which
finally also agreed to the plan two years later.[3] Thus
the Classis of Amsterdam remained undisturbed in the
direction and supervision of the colonial church of New
Netherland. Ministers, Comforters of the Sick, and
Schoolmasters had to qualify themselves for work in
New Netherland before the Classis, who then presented
them to the Directors of the Amsterdam Chamber, and
on their appointment gave them the necessary call, for
which a special formula had been adopted in 1636.[4] The

[1] Synod of North Holland, Aug. 12, etc.   Eccl. Recs. N. Y.
i. 158-161.
[2] Synod of North Holland, 1643, Ibid. 173-4, etc.;
1644, Aug. 11, etc., Art. 28. Ibid. 183-4; 1645, Aug. 8, etc., Art
20. Ibid. 190.
[3] Synod of North Holland, 1648, Aug. 11, etc., Ibid.232; 1650,
Aug. 6, etc., Ibid. 277-8.
[4] Cf. Ibid. 92-99.

correspondence of these ministers in the colony of New Netherland manifests in detail the influence of the Classis of Amsterdam on the religious conditions which developed in the colony and forms one of the main sources of information for the history of this period.

Although the States General frequently intervened in the civil administration of the Province of New Netherland,[1] there is hardly any trace of its intervention in ecclesiastical matters. The condition of religion in the colony, revealed in the Remonstrance of the people of New Netherland to the States General in 1649, seemed to call for redress in spite of the opposition of the Company. In the following year, the States General resolved that "New Netherland, being at present provided with only one clergyman, orders shall be given forthwith for the immediate calling and support of at least three preachers, one to attend to divine service at Rensselaer's colony, the second in and about the city of New Amsterdam, and the third in the distant places; and the commonalty shall also be obliged to have the youth instructed by good schoolmasters,"[2] but the Directors of the Amsterdam Chamber claimed that " the colony of Rensselaerswyck must provide its own clergyman, while New Amsterdam is provided and there is none yet required in the outlying places."[3] There was again fear of the intervention of the States General in the separatist movement of the Lutherans from the Reformed Church of New Amsterdam, although the States General had approved the exclusive establish-

[1] Cf. Osgood, The Am. Colonies in the 17th Century, ii. 97-98.
[2] Provisional Order for the Government, Preservation and Peopling of New Netherland. Col. Docs. N. Y., i. 389.
[3] Observations of Chamber of Amsterdam. Ibid. 392.

ment of the Dutch Reformed Church in the charter of
Privileges and Exemptions of 1640. At this time, the
Classis of Amsterdam feared that an appeal on the part
of the Lutherans for freedom of public worship might be
allowed by the States General, but their fear was ground-
less, and nothing was done to revoke the exclusive
establishment of the Reformed Church of New Netherland.

Within the Province of New Netherland, the government was vested in the Director General, assisted by an
advisory council, upon whom all other officials of the
company in the colony were dependent for their
authority.[1] The Director, as supreme magistrate,
retained the direct control of the colonial church even
after the establishment of inferior local courts in villages and in the city of New Amsterdam. The local
courts had no jurisdiction over criminals and delinquents guilty of blasphemy, violation of God's Holy
Name and religion. Such cases were reserved to the
judgment of the Provincial Court.[2] All measures relative to the erection of churches and schools and the
support of these institutions had to be confirmed,
approved and commanded by the Director General and
Council, except when there was question of churches
established within patroonships, such as Rensselaerswyck on the North River and New Amstel on the South
River.[3] Comforters of the Sick, ministers and schoolmasters were usually appointed by the Directors of the
Amsterdam Chamber, commissioned by the Classis of

[1] Cf. Osgood, The Am. Colonies in the 17th Century, ii. 100, sqq
[2] This is the reason why the town minutes of this period contain
little information on the religious life of the people.
[3] Cf. Col. Docs. N. Y., xiii. 198.

Amsterdam, but inducted by some colonial official in the name of the Director General. When an appointment was made directly by the Director General to the ministry of a Dutch Reformed Church, as in the case of Polhemus, this was subject to the approval of the civil and ecclesiastical authorities in the fatherland. Such approval was not sought for the English orthodox ministers, who came into New Netherland with their congregations, but the exercise of their ministry needed the approval of the provincial government. This is the reason of the censure incurred by the Reverend Mr. Fordham, who gave up the exercise of the ministry in Hempstead without the wish and the knowledge of the provincial government. Stuyvesant, therefore, refused to admit him "in such mennor of comminge again."[1] Later the Director General and Council appealed directly to the Chamber of Amsterdam and the Classis of Amsterdam for orthodox English ministers. The fulfilment of these requests would have brought the appointment of English ministers into full conformity with the appointment of the Dutch ministers.

Appointments to minor offices within the churches illustrate still more the close dependence of the church on the chief magistrate. When Megapolensis needed a new chorister in his church at New Amsterdam, he requested the appointment from the provincial council.[2] When the term of office for a church warden had expired, the local magistrates presented a double num-

[1] Stuyvesant to the magistrates of Hempstead, July 14, 1657; Doc. Hist. N. Y., iii. 118-119; Col. Docs. N. Y., xiv. 396.
[2] O'Callaghan, Cal. Hist. MSS. (Dutch), i. 146.

ber of persons for the office, from which the Director General and Council selected a new church warden.[1]

The school, which was also a religious institution, was likewise under the direct control of the colonial government. The presumption of Jacob van Corlaer to teach in a school without the order of the Director General and Council brought a very clear assertion of the powers of the government, which then refused to grant the requisite permission even in spite of the humble supplication of the Burghers and inhabitants and the intercession of the Burgomasters and some Schepens. Stuyvesant declared that "school teaching and the induction of a schoolmaster depends absolutely on the right of patronage."[2] This principle found a good illustration in the petition of the magistrates of Boswyck, who requested the approval of their contract with Boudewyn Maenhout as reader and schoolmaster. The Director General and Council fulfilled the request on the condition that the schoolmaster be first examined by the reverend clergy of New Amsterdam and declared fit for the performance of his duties.[3] This regulation was probably due to the place of religion in the Dutch colonial school, where the principles and fundamentals of the Christian religion were also to be inculcated. One of the last ordinances of the Dutch provincial government ordered the two schoolmasters of New Amsterdam, Pietersen of the principal school and Van Hoboocken of the branch school in the Bouwery, to bring their children to the church on Wednesday to be

---

[1] Cf. Recs. New Amsterdam, vii. 142, 144, 175, 237, passim.
[2] Ibid ii. 348; Col. Docs. N.Y., xiv. 412, 413-14.
[3] Council minute, Dec. 28, 1662, Ibid 519.

examined after the sermon in the presence of the reverend ministers and elders in the catechism taught during the week.[1]

The right of patronage, while it conceded the privilege of church control in the appointment of the ministers, entailed the obligation of furnishing a revenue sufficient for their support. The budget of the Company for New Netherland contained the monthly item of one hundred and twenty florins for the support of a clergyman, and of thirty florins for the support of a schoolmaster, who was at the same time precentor and sexton.[2] On the formation of patroonships, the patroon and the colonists were bound to seek ways and means to support their ministers of religion. This was the case in Rensselaerswyck and New Amstel. The colonists in the jurisdiction of the Company desired the formation of a glebe, as appears in the Remonstrance of 1649, but no glebe was formed until the arrival of Polhemus, in 1654, on the petition of the court of Midwout. Here the attempt was made to find all support of the ministry amongst the people. Later the Company offered to contribute six hundred guilders for the support of a minister on the condition that the inhabitants raise an equal sum.[3] These arrangements only affected the Dutch Church; the English had to support their ministers without any aid from the government of New Netherland.

Governmental control extended not only to the regulation of the affairs of church and school, but also

[1] Laws and Ordinances of New Netherland, p. 461.
[2] Col. Docs. N. Y., i. 155.
[3] Doc. Hist. N. Y., iii. 434.

to the observance of general public morals. This was
especially true of the directorship of Peter Stuyvesant.
He published with much greater frequency than
his predecessors days of public prayer and thanksgiving, which he ordered to be celebrated with
sermons and prayers in the English as well as the
Dutch churches of the province. This was done
sometimes to placate divine wrath, outraged by the sins
of the people, sometimes to avert the impending evil
of an Indian war or of a pestilential disease, sometimes
to preserve the purity of the Calvinist faith endan-
gered by the growth of dissent; in a word, to implore
temporal and spiritual blessings for Church and State.[1]
Wherever he noticed grave abuses in the religious and
moral life of the people, he attempted to remedy the
evil. Although there was an ordinance not to tap beer
during divine service, as early as 1641, the conflict
between the former minister of New Amsterdam, the
Reverend Everardus Bogardus, and the former Director General William Kieft, had trained the people to
the violation of the Sabbath. Shortly after his arrival,
Stuyvesant saw that "the disregard, nay contempt, of
God's holy laws and ordinances, which command us to
keep holy in His Honor His day of rest, the Sabbath,
and forbid all bodily injury and murder," was due to
the prevalence of drunkenness amongst the inhabitants.
He, therefore, prohibited all brewers, tapsters and inn-
keepers, on the Lord's day of rest, to "entertain people,
tap or draw any wine, beer or strong waters of any kind
and under any pretext before two o'clock in case there
is no preaching, or else before four, except to a traveler

[1] Passim in Col. Docs. N. Y., i, ii, iii, xii, xiii, xiv.

or those who are daily customers, fetching their drinks to their homes." There was a double punishment attached to the violation of this ordinance. One affected the person found drinking liquor, who was subject to a fine of six guilders, and the other affected the brewer, tapster or innkeeper, who was to be deprived of his occupation for the violation of the law. Furthermore, no liquor was to be sold on any day after the ringing of the bell in the evening, which took place at about nine o'clock.[1]

In the following year, the Director General discovered that his orders "against unreasonable and intemperate drinking" were not observed, "to the great scandal and reproach of this community and neighboring strangers, who visit this place, also to the vilification and contempt of God's Holy Word and our ordinance, based thereon." He complained that "this way of earning a living and the easily made profits therefrom please many and divert them from their first calling, trade and occupation, so that they become tapsters and that one full fourth of the City of New Amsterdam has been turned into taverns for the sale of brandy, tobacco and beer."[2] After he had arranged "for the further obervance of the Sabbath with the knowledge of the servant of God's Word" by a sermon, in the afternoon as well as in the forenoon, with the usual Christian prayers and thanksgiving, he requested and charged all officials, subjects and vassals to assist at these services, during which "all tapping, fishing, hunting and other usual occupations, handi-

[1] Recs. of New Amsterdam, i. 1-2, May 31, 1647.
[2] Ordinance, March 10, 1648. Ibid., 7-8.

crafts and business, be it in houses, cellars, shops, ships, yachts, or on the streets and market places," were forbidden, "under the penalty of forfeiting all such wares, goods and merchandise and of redeeming them with the payment of twenty-five florins, to be applied until further orders for the support of the poor and the churches, besides a fine of one pound Flemish, payable by purchaser as well as seller, employee as well as employer, half of it going to the officer, the other half at the discretion of the court." Any person violating the Sabbath by excessive drinking, "to his disgrace and the offense of others," was subject to arrest by the Fiscal or any superior or inferior officer, and to arbitrary punishment by the court.[1] Regulations were also made to restrict the number of taverns, and to punish the sale of liquor to the Indians.

The ordinances for the observance of Sunday were not intended to be enforced only at New Amsterdam. As soon as the whole of the South River again came under the authority of the West India Company, in 1655, the vice-director, Jean Paul Jacquet, and his commissaries were instructed "to observe and have observed the placards and ordinances made and published heretofore against drinking on the Sabbath and the profanation of the same."[2]

The severity of the law was increased considerably in 1656. The Director General and Council forbade on the Lord's day of rest "the usual work of plowing, sowing,

[1] Ordinance, April 29, 1648.   Recs. New Amsterdam, i. 9.
[2] Provisional Instructions. Nov. 29, 1655.   Col. Docs. N. Y., xii. 115.

mowing, carpentering, woodsawing, forging, bleaching, hunting, shooting or anything else, which on the other days may be a lawful occupation, under the penalty of one pound Flemish, payable by each person so offending." Double this fine was established for "any idle and forbidden exercises and plays, excessive drinking bouts, frequentation of taverns or tipplinghouses, dancing, playing cards, ball or trick-track, tennis, cricket, or ninepins, pleasure-boating, driving about in carts or wagons, before, between or during divine service." Tavernkeepers and tapsters could not keep open their places or sell to anyone any brandy, wine, beer or other liquor, directly or indirectly, before or during the sermon, except under the penalty of six florins for each guest. Each person found drinking was also subject to a fine of three florins. The same penalty was inflicted for the sale of liquor after the mounting of the guard or the ringing of the bell at night on week-days as on Sundays. An exception was, however, made in this regard in the case of servants and boarders or on public occasions, with the consent and by the order of the magistrates.[1] A violation of the Sabbath ordinance entailed a severe sentence on April 11, 1658, when Andrew Vrydach, a mason, was sentenced to lose six months' wages and to stand guard for the same period for being intoxicated and fighting during divine service.[2] In 1661, various forms of servile labor were interdicted on the Sabbath under a penalty of one pound Flemish for the first offense,

---

[1] Ordinance, Oct. 26, 1656. Recs. of New Amsterdam, i. 24; ii. 204, sqq.
[2] Council minutes. July 11, 1658. O'Callaghan, Cal. Hist. MSS. (Dutch), i. p. 198.

double as much for the second offense, "and four times double as much" for the third offense. The same penalties were decreed for the sale of liquor on Sunday, and the drunkard found on this day was to be conveyed to the guardhouse, where he was to remain at the discretion of the commissaries and in addition was to be fined one pound Flemish for the benefit of the officer who arrested the prisoner.[1] In 1663, Stuyvesant complained not only that the Sunday laws were not observed, but that they were "by some misinterpreted and misconstrued, as if the previously enacted placards referred to and applied to the maintenance and sanctification of only half the Sabbath." The Director General and Council, therefore, commanded the observance not only of a part but of the whole Sabbath, and warned the people that, "pending the Sabbath, from the rising to the setting of the sun, no customary labor shall be performed, much less clubs kept." The Director General and Council also forbade "all unusual exercises, such as games, boat, cart or wagon racing, fishing, fowling, running, sailing, nutting or picking strawberries, trafficking with the Indians or any like things, and amongst other things all dissolute and licentious plays, riots, calling children out to the streets and highways." The penalty for the violation of this ordinance was the forfeiture of the upper garment (het Oppercleet) or six guilders, according to the decision of the court, for the first offense, double for the second, and exemplary punishment for the third offense.[2] The pla-

[1] Ordinance, Nov. 18, 1661.   Laws and Ordinances of New Netherland, 415-16.
[2] Ordinance, Sept. 10, 1663.   Recs. New Amsterdam, iv. 301-2.

card was sent to the Burgomasters and Schepens, but they did not publish it, because they "found themselves aggrieved in several particulars." Their successors, in the spring of 1664, judged the observance of the ordinance highly necessary, but they did "not dare to publish such a placard, as divers sections thereof are too severe and too much opposed to Dutch liberties."[1] The municipal court was constrained to come to some understanding with the Director General and Council, as various persons were brought before them on the usual court day for the violation of the Sabbath.[2]

The customs of the fatherland had been the occasion of friction before between the Director General and Council and the court of Burgomasters and Schepens. Some farm servants had intended to ride the goose[3] on the feast of Bacchus at Shrovetide, but Stuyvesant thought it "altogether unprofitable, unnecessary and censurable for subjects and neighbors to celebrate such pagan and popish feasts and to practice such evil customs in this country," while the Burgomasters and Schepens contended that such customs were "tolerated and looked at through the fingers in some places of the fatherland." Nevertheless, the Director General and Council sent the court messenger, Claes van Elsland, with a prohibition to the farm servants, who paid no respect whatever to the order of the Director General.

[1] Court minute, March 18, 1664. Recs. New Amsterdam, v. 38-39.
[2] Court minute, May 13, 1664. Ibid. 60.
[3] "There was a game called 'Pulling the Goose,' introduced at New Amsterdam in 1654. A goose with head and neck smeared with grease was suspended between two poles. Men rode at full gallop, and tried to grasp it as they passed." Tuckerman, Peter Stuyvesant, p. 152.

Some of the delinquents were then summoned before the Director General and Council to be tried and fined for contempt. Several behaved insolently towards the chief magistracy, and were committed by the Director General and Council to prison.[1] On the protest of the Burgomasters and Schepens, the Director General and Council informed them that the establishment of an inferior court of justice under the name Schout, Burgomasters, and Schepens or Commissaries in no way infringed or diminished "the power and authority of the Director General and Council to enact any ordinances or issue particular interdicts, especially those which tend to the glory of God, or the best interest of the inhabitants, or will prevent more sins, scandals, debaucheries and crimes, and properly correct, fine and punish obstinate transgressors."[2] When Cornelius van Tienhoven informed the Burgomasters and Schepens of the country-people's intention to ride the goose again in the following year, he was instructed, in response to his inquiry, "seasonably to declare the same to be illegal," as it had been forbidden by the Supreme Councillors.[3]

The prevalence of concubinage and irregularities in contracting matrimony, which occasioned the former, also called for Stuyvesant's intervention soon after his advent to the Province of New Netherland and repeatedly during the course of his administration. According to the laws of the Netherlands, and the

[1] Stuyvesant to Schout, Burgomasters and Schepens. Feb. 26, 1654. Recs. New Amsterdam, i. 172; Col. Docs. N.Y., xiv. 249.
[2] Stuyvesant to Schout, Burgomaster and Schepens. Feb. 26, 1654, Recs. New Amsterdam i. 173; Col. Docs. N. Y., xiv. 249.
[3] Court minute. Feb. 8, 1655. Recs. New Amsterdam. i. 286

adjoining provinces and countries, persons desiring to enter the state of matrimony had to give notice of their bans, which were to be published on three consecutive days of prayer or of court session in the jurisdiction, place or village where the two contracting parties were residents and had lived for the past year. If these parties were residents of different villages, places, or districts, the bans had to be published in both places and proof of no lawful hindrance had to be produced to the magistrates or beadles at the place, where, after the publication of the bans, they wished to be married.[1] In violation of this legislation, William Harck, the sheriff of Flushing, had solemnized a marriage between Thomas Nuton, a widower, and Joan, the daughter of Richard Smith, against her parents' consent and contrary to law. On April 3, 1648, the sheriff was fined six hundred Carolus guilders, dismissed from office, and the marriage was annulled; Thomas Nuton was sentenced to pay a fine of three hundred guilders and to have the marriage again solemnized after three proclamations.[2] Although the clergy of New Amsterdam were the commissaries of matrimonial cases, Stuyvesant himself sometimes intervened, as in the case of the maid Willemeyntje, who had been deceived by a promise of marriage by Ralph Clark.[3] In spite of the law, magistrates again published the bans of matrimony for persons who resided outside of their jurisdiction, and solemnized such marriages, but on January 19, 1654, an ordi-

[1] Stuyvesant and Council to magistrates of Gravesend. Feb. 10, 1654. Col. Docs. N. Y., xiv. 245-6.
[2] Council Minute. April 3, 1648. O'Callaghan, Cal. Hist. MSS. (Dutch), i. p. 116.
[3] Ibid. pp. 126-127, 130.

nance was issued that prohibited this practice and
bound the contracting parties to prove that their bans
had been published where they had resided for the
previous year.[1] This legislation had been occasioned
especially by the illegal proceedings of the Court of
Gravesend, which published the bans of matrimony
between Johan van Beeck and Maria Verleth, residents
of New Amsterdam, without the consent of Stuyvesant,
who had been made the guardian of the bridegroom by
the father in Holland. This breach of the correct
practice of the ecclesiastical and civil order of New
Amsterdam was thought to prepare "a way whereby
hereafter some sons and daughters, unwilling to obey
parents and guardians, will, contrary to their wishes,
secretly go and get married in such villages or elsewhere."[2]   The magistrates of Gravesend contended
that van Beeck was a freeman of their village and that
the intervention of the Director General in this matter
was a violation of their charter, but Stuyvesant retorted
that he was also a freeman of New Amsterdam and
of Amsterdam, that matrimony must be concluded
according to divine and human laws, with the consent
of parents, tutors or guardians, and that no infraction of
the privileges of their charter was intended.[3]   On February 10, 1654, the court messenger was sent to Gravesend to renew the marriage ordinance of the Province of
New Netherland, and to declare all marriages not concluded according to this statute, unlawful, "as contrary
to all civil and political laws and ordinances, in force

[1] O'Callaghan. Cal. Hist. MSS. (Dutch) i. p. 134.
[2] Court minute, Jan. 26, 1654. Recs. New Amsterdam, i. 155.
[3] Stuyvesant to magistrates of Gravesend, Jan. 20, 1654, Col.
Docs. N. Y., xiv. 243; Feb. 10, 1654, Ibid. 245-6.

here, in our fatherland and among all our Christian
neighbors."[1] On the same day, the Burgomasters and
Schepens of New Amsterdam, requested by Johan van
Beeck to proclaim properly the bans of his marriage
with Maria Verleth, remonstrated with the magistrates of Gravesend for their action in this case and
attempted to obtain a mutual promise to prevent such
irregularities in the future. Johan van Beeck continued to push his petition for a publication of the
bans of his contemplated marriage before the municipal court. The circumstances of the case were carefully weighed by the magistrates: the institution of
matrimony, the teaching of the Apostle of the Gentiles,
the proper ages of the contracting parties, the consent
of the parents of the girl, the distance of the fatherland and the difficulty of communication on account
of the war between Holland and England, and finally
the danger of disgrace for both families from further
delay. While the magistrates admitted the correctness
of the views of the Dutch theologians, that "we must
not tolerate or permit lesser sins, in order thereby to
avoid greater ones," they thought that "by a proper
solemnization of marriage the lesser and greater sins are
prevented." The Burgomasters and Schepens of New
Amsterdam, therefore, were of the opinion that the
proper ecclesiastical proclamations of the bans between Johan van Beeck and Maria Verleth ought to be
made at the earliest opportunity, to be followed after-
wards by their marriage.[2] Some days later a poster

[1] Col. Docs. N. Y. xiv. 245.
[2] Council minute, Feb. 19, 1654.   Recs. New Amsterdam, i.
165.

was put up by Johan van Beeck in various places of the
city that contained this resolution of the Burgomasters
and Schepens, the difficulties opposed by Director
Stuyvesant to his marriage at Gravesend and at New
Amsterdam, and his reasons for leaving the neighborhood to seek a safe retreat elsewhere.[1] Stuyvesant
immediately demanded a copy of the resolution of the
municipal court,which he reiterated again a week later,
and sent a letter to all governors, deputy governors,
magistrates and Christian neighbors, setting forth that
Johan van Beeck and Maria Verleth had run off to New
England to get married, and requesting them not to
solemnize the marriage, but to send back the runaways.[2] When Stuyvesant learned that Van Beeck had
been married by an unauthorized countryman,
named Goodman Crab, living at Greenwich, against the
laudable customs and laws of the United Netherlands,
contrary to the advice and command of his lawful
guardian, the Honorable Director General, and without a previous publication of the bans, he declared the
marriage unlawful, and condemned Johan van Beeck
and Maria Verleth to live separately under the penalty
of being punished according to law for living in concubinage.[3] Nevertheless, two years later Maria Verleth, the widow of Johan van Beeck, in the lawsuit for
a surrender of letters addressed to her husband, that
had arrived after his death, received a favorable decision from the Burgomasters and Schepens who based

---

[1] Council minute. Feb. 27, 1654. O'Callaghan, Cal. Hist. MSS.
(Dutch), i. 135-136; Stuyvesant to Burgomasters. etc., March 2,
1654, Recs. New Amsterdam, i. 174.
[2] O'Callaghan, Ibid.
[3] Council minute. Sept. 14, 1654.   Col. Docs. N. Y., xiv. 291.

their decision on the order of the court, of the 19th of February, 1654, according to which "respect must be paid to the proclamation of the church and consequently to the marriage tie of the said young people." They could not, therefore, pronounce the marriage illegal.[1]

New legislation seemed necessary to the Director-General and Council in 1658. Some persons did not proceed to the solemnization of their marriage, even after the bans had properly been proclaimed three times, but delayed the ceremony even for months to the detriment of good order and the customs of the fatherland. The Director, therefore, ordered the marriage to be celebrated within at least a month of the third proclamation, if there was no legal opposition; in the case of further delay, he commanded the reasons to be submitted under a penalty of ten florins for the first week after the expiration of the month and twenty florins for each successive week, until the parties reported the reason of their disobedience. Furthermore, no man and woman were allowed to keep house together like man and wife, before they were legally married, "under a fine of one hundred florins, or as much more or less as their position admitted." Such persons were to be fined anew every month, according to the orders and customs of the fatherland.[2] In 1660, Stuyvesant addressed a circular letter to the clergy from Fort Orange, in which he notified them, that they were not to publish any bans of

---

[1] Court minute. Feb. 7, 1656. Recs. New Amsterdam. i. 36.
[2] Ordinance. Jan. 15, 1658. Ibid. 37-38; ii. 304.

marriage, unless the parties had lived at least a year and a half to two years in their district.[1]

There was, therefore, no lack of paternal legislation to uplift the tone of public morality and religion in the Province of New Netherland, at least during the directorship of Peter Stuyvesant. However, most of the measures adopted for this purpose found little response in the life of the people. The Dutch inhabitants were largely indifferent to religion; the professed members of the Dutch Reformed Church never manifested great zeal in the practice of their faith; and all attempts at the organization of dissenting worship were strictly prohibited by law, and did in fact entail persecution.

[1] O'Callaghan. Cal. Hist. MSS. (Dutch), i. 215.

CHAPTER III

THE DUTCH REFORMED CHURCH

No provisions for religion are found in the Records of New Netherland until the arrival of the Director General Peter Minuit in 1626. For during the first two years of organized colonization under May and Verhulst, the small number of settlers, who were for the most part Protestant Walloons, exiles from the southern Provinces of the Spanish Netherlands, seem not to have had any kind of public worship. The public religious life of the Dutch colony, therefore, really began with the arrival of the two Comforters of the Sick, Sebastian Jansz Crol and Jan Huyck, in the company of the Director Peter Minuit.[1] This office in the Church of Holland had attached to it the particular duty of admonishing and comforting the sick according to an elaborate form, "The Consolation of the Sick" or "Instruction in the Faith and the Way of Salvation to Prepare Believers to DieWillingly,"[2] but in places destitute of an organized ministry the Comforters of the Sick conducted divine service, although they were warned under no pretext to arrogate to themselves whatever

---

[1] Doc. Hist. N. Y. iii, 28, citation from Wassenaer, Historie van Europa, xii, 38.
[2] Cf. Form in, Eccl. Recs. N. Y. i. 47; Manual of Reformed Church of America, Corwin, pp. 18-19.

properly belonged to the ministerial office. This divine service was very simple. It consisted of prayer. singing of psalms, the reading of some chapters of the bible and of some sermon of an orthodox Reformed minister.[1] This later became the model for the public worship allowed by the provincial authorities in the new settlements, English as well as Dutch, that could not be provided with an orthodox minister.[2] In all gatherings of the people, the Comforters of the Sick led in prayer according to the nature of the occasion. In the community, they were to be the watchful custodians of the faith and of the moral law, who were to instruct the ignorant, admonish sinners to repentance and amendment of life, and encourage the weak to perseverance in virtue. Accordingly on Sundays, Sebastian Jansz Crol and Jan Huyck read from the Scriptures and the commentaries to the commonalty that Minuit had concentrated on Manhattan Island. Meanwhile, François Molemacker was busily engaged in building a horsemill, over which was to be constructed a spacious room that would accommodate a large congregation. This structure was to be adorned with a tower, in which were to be hung the Spanish bells captured at Porto Rico by the Dutch fleet the preceeding year.[3]

[1] Cf. Instructions for the Comforters of the Sick, Adopted in Classis of Amsterdam, May 5, 1636, Eccl. Recs. N. Y. i, 96-97.
[2] The same policy was also adopted in Brazil by the College of the XIX. "The smaller places shall be served by precentors, Comforters of the Sick and schoolmasters, who shall offer up public prayers, read aloud from the Old and New Testament and from printed sermons; and tune the psalms." Proceedings of the College of the XIX. Ibid. 193.
[3] Narratives of New Netherland. Wassenaer's Historical Verhael. p. 83-4. Dyer points out the fact that, while the wooden structure erected solely for church purposes by Wouter Van Twiller

This provisional form of worship ceased with the arrival of the first Dutch minister, Jonas Michaelius, in the spring of 1628, whose services had been engaged for three years.[1] The population of New Amsterdam then numbered about two hundred and seventy souls, including men, women and children, but a portion of the Walloons were going back to the fatherland, either because the years of their service had expired or because they were of little use to the company.[2] Although the people were "for the most part rather rough and unrestrained," Michaelius found consolation in the love and respect which most of them manifested towards him. A consistory was at once organized, which comprised, besides the minister, two elders, Peter Minuit and Jan Huyghens, and the deacon Sebastian Crol. The latter, being also vice-director of the trading post of Fort Orange, was seldom in New Amsterdam. This led to the election of the two elders to assist the minister in all ecclesiastical matters that might occur. Both these elders, the Director of the Dutch colony, Peter Minuit, and his brother-in-law, Jan Huyghens, had formerly held ecclesiastical offices, the one as deacon and the other

became a landmark in drawing up deeds and mortgages, no reference of this kind occurs in regard to the horsemill until some time after the introduction of the English rule, in 1667. There were probably not two such primitive establishments for grinding the grain, as windmills were soon erected. Dyer believed that the lack of reference is probably due to its location on the waste lands north of the town, where in fact the horsemill of 1667 stood, viz., on Mill street, formerly Sleyck Strege. Cf. Dyer, A. M. Site of the first Synagogue of the congregation Shearith Israel of New York. Am. Jewish Hist. Soc. Pubs. No. 8. pp. 26-41.

[1] Michaelius to D. Johannes Foreest, August 8, 1628. Manhattan in 1628. Dingman Versteeg. 1904. p. 64.

[2] Michaelius to Smoutius August 11, 1628. Eccl. Recs. N. Y. i, 53-54. Col. Docs. N. Y. ii, 763 etc.

as elder in the Dutch and French churches respectively in Wesel. In the place of one of these elders, a new one was to be chosen every year from a double number lawfully proposed to the congregation. The occupation of all the members of the first consistory in public business with the exception of the minister made Michaelius fear the possibility of confusion and disorder in ecclesiastical and civil matters. To avoid this danger, he requested precise instructions for the governors of the Province and the Synodal acts for himself, so that the relations of Church and State might be well regulated.[1] It is generally asserted that there is no trace of any misunderstanding between Minuit and Michaelius, but the Van Rensselaer-Bowier Manuscripts disprove this. When the Director General and the secretary, Jan Van Remund, came into conflict with each other, the minister is declared to have been "very energetic here stirring up the fire between them; he ought to be a mediator in God's Church and community but he seems to me to be the contrary."[2] Kiliaen van Rensselaer in writing to Wouter van Twiller puts the blame on the colonial secretary, who had excited the minister against Minuit.[3]

The church organized at New Amsterdam comprised the Walloons and French, as well as the Dutch, although the Sunday service was performed only in the language of the latter, which all but a few individuals could understand. There was, therefore, no necessity for any special service in French, but Michaelius did

[1] Eccl. Recs. N. Y. i. 52-53.
[2] Van Rensselaer Bowier MSS. ed. by A. S. Van Laer, 1908. p. 169.
[3] Ibid. pp. 267-8.

administer the Lord's Supper to them in their native language. At this first administration of the Sacrament, there were fully fifty communicants, including the Walloons and the Dutch. Some of these made their first profession of faith, demanded prior to their admission to the Lord's Supper; others had certificates from their churches in the fatherland. Michaelius, however, could not insist upon the usual formalities in regard to all, as some had neglected to bring these testimonials with them under the impression that no church would be organized in the colony, and others had lost them in a general conflagration. He had, therefore, to be content with the testimony of their neighbors and with their conduct while in the colony. For the future, the Sacrament was to be administered every four months, until the advent of a larger number of people should make some other arrangement necessary.[1]

From the beginning, Jonas Michaelius was forced to share in the hardships of colonial life. He had been promised some acres of land instead of the free table, which was his due, but the conditions of the colony were such, that it was impossible to procure either labor or live-stock even for money. Neither butter nor milk was obtainable and the minister anticipated a hard winter with nothing but stale food imported from Holland, that was bad for his children as well as for himself. The loss of his wife by death made these hardships even more difficult to bear.[2]

The following year witnessed the explicit legal

[1] Michaelius to Smoutius, August 11, 1628, Eccl. Recs. N. Y. i, 53-54.
[2] Ibid. 63-64.

recognition of the Dutch Reformed Church in the Province of New Netherland. The slow progress made in the colonization of the country led the Company to grant to its members who should plant colonies there a charter of privileges and exemptions,[1] by which feudal rights were guaranteed to such patroons. At the same time, freedom of colonization with liberal privileges was also offered to private persons in the United Provinces, who should settle there either on their own account or in the service of their masters. According to the twenty-seventh article, *"the Patroons and colonists shall in particular, and in the speediest manner endeavor to find out ways and means, whereby they may support a Minister and schoolmaster, that thus the service of God and the zeal for religion may not grow cool and be neglected among them, and they shall from the first procure a Comforter of the Sick there."*[2] Thus the first charter granted for the colonization of New Netherland by the West India Company made the maintenance of the ministry of the Reformed Church obligatory on the part of the patroons and the colonists. The Dutch Reformed Church, therefore, obtained a legal recognition of its establishment in the Province as early as 1629. At the time of the negotiation of this charter, the West India Company was anxious to appear in the light of the champion of the Dutch national

[1] Col. Docs. N. Y. ii. 551-7. Laws and Ordinances of New Netherland. 9.

[2] The provision of the charter was not a piece of legislation adopted in particular for New Netherland, but is also found in the draft of the conditions for colonies in general by the College of the XIX, June 12, 1627 and November 22, 1628. Cf. Extract from Dutch Archives. U. S. Commission on Boundary between Venezuela and British Guiana. ii, pp. 52, 63.

cause and Faith, as the Directors feared the successfu conclusion of a truce with Spain to the great detriment of the interests of the Company, whose members, according to their remonstrance, had "most at heart the maintenance of the Reformed Religion and the liberties of our beloved Fatherland."[1]

Michaelius most probably left the colony shortly after the expiration of the three years for which his services had been engaged by the West India Company.[2] The Classis of Amsterdam then sent Everardus Bogardus to New Netherland,[3] where he arrived in the spring of 1633 with the new Director, Wouter Van Twiller.

The welfare of the Reformed Church was now advanced by the advent of the first schoolmaster, Adam Roelandsen, who was also sent out by the Classis of Amsterdam with the approbation and consent of the Directors of the Company. The duty of a Dutch schoolmaster in colonial days was not only to instruct in reading, writing and arithmetic, but also to implant the fundamental principles of the "true Christian Religion," to teach the children the customary prayers, and to train them to modesty and sobriety.[4] The building activity, with which Van Twiller inaugurated his directorship, included the erection of a church, later

[1] West India Co's Consideration on a truce with Spain. November 16, 1629. Col. Docs. N. Y. i, 40-2.
[2] Jonas Michaelius was again proposed after his return to Holland by the Classis of Amsterdam in 1637 for the New Netherland mission, but was rejected in 1638 by the Assembly of the XIX.Cf. Eccl. Recs. N. Y. i, 111, 114, 116.
[3] August 17, 1632, et. seq. Synod of North Holland at Alkmaar Art. 38. Ministerial changes. In the Classis of Amsterdam, Ibid. 82-3.
[4] Instruction and Credential Letter for Schoolmasters going to the East or West Indies or elsewhere. Ibid. 98-99.

68 RELIGION IN NEW NETHERLAND

characterized by De Vries as a "mean barn,"[1] with a dwelling house and stable adjoining for the use of the minister, the Reverend Bogardus.

In the summer of the following year, the friendly relations between the Church and the Provincial authorities were again disturbed.[2] Although the occasion of the quarrel is unknown, Bogardus was accused of having sent a letter to Wouter Van Twiller, which was not dictated "by the spirit of the Lord," but "by a feeling unbecoming heathens, let alone Christians, much less a preacher of the Gospel." He is said to have described the Director as "a child of the devil, an incarnate villain, whose buckgoats are better than he," and to have threatened him with "such a shake from the pulpit, on the following Sunday, as would make him shudder."[3] Somewhat later the peace of the Church of New Amsterdam was again disturbed by the trouble arising between the minister and the Schout Fiscal of the Province, Lubertus van Dincklagen, who in 1636 was sent to Holland by the Director and deprived of his wages for three years for his censure of the bad administration of the Province. He claimed he had been excommunicated by the machinations of the Reverend Everardus Bogardus and driven into the wilderness to escape the persecution instituted against him, where for days he

[1] Extracts from Voyages of David Pieterzen de Vries. N.Y. Hist. Soc. Col. 2d. Ser. iii, 101.
[2] Kiliaen van Rensselaer also puts the blame for this upon the secretary, Jan van Remund, who had stirred up the minister against Wouter Van Twiller. The Governor was accused of running "out on the street after the minister with a naked sword;" of being "proud and puffed up, always drunk as long as there is any wine... lazy and careless, hostile to the minister and no defender of religion, etc." Van Rensselaer Bowier MSS. pp. 267-8, 271.
[3] Summons of Bogardus before Council by Kieft. June 11, 1646. Col. Docs. N. Y. xiv, 69.

had been forced through the lack of necessary food to sustain himself on the grass of the field.[1] On his arrival at Amsterdam, he instituted proceedings against Wouter Van Twiller with the States General for the recovery of his salary and against Bogardus with the Classis for the removal of the excommunication.[2] He submitted a lengthy paper to the ministers of the Classis with an accusation against Everardus Bogardus, which "referred to his bad government of the Church, as well as his conduct and walk."[3] The States General finally "seriously" urged the College of the XIX to grant Lubbertus Van Dincklagen full redress, but the Classis postponed action until the return of the minister to Holland, which was expected to occur soon. William Kieft, meanwhile, superseded Wouter Van Twiller as Director. When Bogardus, in the summer of 1638, requested of the Council permission to depart for the Fatherland to defend himself against Lubbert Van Dincklagen, his request was refused, as the Council judged it "necessary to retain the minister here, so that the Church of God may increase more and more every day."[4] The consistory of New Amsterdam repeatedly sent testimonials to the Classis in favor of their minister, whose cause was also espoused by the new Director, William Kieft.[5] While the Classis promised to take to heart their case "in order to maintain the honor of their

[1] Acts of Classis of Amsterdam. March 19, 1640. Eccl. Recs. N. Y. i, 127.
[2] Acts of Deputies. May 7, 1640. Ibed. 129.
[3] Acts of Classis of Amsterdam. April 7, 1636. Ibid. i, 88.
[4] Council minute. July 8, 1638. Col. Docs. N. Y. xiv, 10.
[5] Acts of the Deputies. November 19, 1641, Eccl. Recs. N. Y. i, 142; April 7, 1642, Ibid. i, 149; April 22, 1642, Ibid. 151.

worthy pastor, the Reverend Everardus Bogardus,"
the ministers were determined to do justice towards
Lubbertus Van Dincklagen.[1] The case was still pending
in May, 1642, but the published documents of the Classis fail to disclose its issue.

A new impulse to colonization was given on July
19, 1640, by the publication of a new charter of Freedoms and Exemptions which was extended to all in
friendly relations with the Netherlands. The West
India Company took this occasion to establish still more
formally the Dutch Reformed Church. *"And no
other religion shall be publicly admitted in New Netherland, except the Reformed, as it is at present preached and
practiced by public authority in the United Netherlands;
and for this purpose the Company shall provide and maintain good and suitable preachers, schoolmasters and Comforters of the Sick."*[2] Although this clause was intended
to strengthen the position of the Dutch Reformed
Church in the Province of New Netherland, the privileges extended by the charter to foreigners became the
occasion of a large growth of dissent with the consequence of an attempt to infringe upon the exclusive
establishment of the Reformed Church, which led to
persecution.

Greater zeal for the Reformed Religion was also
manifested after the publication of the new charter of
Freedoms and Exemptions. The need of a new and
more substantial church had been felt for some time.
In 1640 the Director and Council appropriated a portion of the fines imposed by the court of justice to raise

[1] Acts of Deputies, May 5, 1642. Eccl. Recs. N. Y. i, 152.
[2] Col. Docs. N. Y. i, 123.

the funds necessary to defray the expense of the new building.[1] In spite of this, nothing was accomplished until two years later, when Captain De Vries urged Kieft to follow the example of the English, who always build a fine church immediately after the erection of their dwellings. The West India Company ought not to be less zealous, as it "was deemed to be a principal means of upholding the Reformed Religion against the tyranny of Spain." Kieft demanded that De Vries show his love for the Reformed Religion by the donation of one hundred guilders, which the latter promised to do, if the Director himself would generously subscribe for this purpose in behalf of the Company. They were in hopes that the remainder could be raised by the community.[2] A favorable opportunity for this presented itself in the wedding of the daughter of the Reverend Bogardus. The Director "set to work after the fourth or fifth drink; and he himself setting a liberal example, let the wedding guests sign whatever they were disposed to give towards the church. Each, then, with a light head, subscribed away at a handsome rate, one competing with the other; and although some heartily repented it when their senses came back, they were obliged, nevertheless, to pay."[3] Accordingly a contract was let to John and Richard Ogden, of Stamford, to build a stone church at New Amsterdam,

[1] O'Callaghan. Hist. of New Netherland. i, 259.
[2] Extracts from the Voyages of David Pieterzen de Vries. N. Y. Hist. Society Coll. 2d. Ser. iii (1857), 101-2. From the "Korte Historiael Ende Journaels Aenteyckeninge," by David Pieterz. de Vries. Narratives of New Netherland. p. 212.
[3] Remonstrance of the People of New Netherland to the States General, Col. Docs. N. Y. i. Representation of New Netherland. Narratives of New Netherland. p. 326.

seventy-two feet long, fifty-two feet wide and sixteen
feet high, for the sum of two thousand five hundred
guilders.[1] On the advice of De Vries, a site was chosen
for the new church within the fort, that the faithful
while assembled in worship might be guarded against
a sudden attack of the Indians. The walls of the
building were soon raised and the roof covered with oak
shingles, but the immediate completion of the building
was retarded by the rise of factions within the Dutch
community and by the outbreak of Indian hostilities.
The inscription on the church even became a matter of
complaint to the commonalty against the government
of Kieft, who asserted therein that he had the community build the temple.

Anno 1642;
William Kieft, Directeur-Generael;
Heeft de Gemeente desen Tempel Doen Bouwen.

A grievance was also later found in the position of
the church in the fort, as "a fifth wheel to a coach,"
whereas the opponents of the governor would have preferred it in a more central location for the greater acco-
modation of the people at large. However, these
objections were only urged after the development of
unpleasant relations within the colony.[2]

The building activity of the church wardens at New
Amsterdam had been stimulated largely by the intelligence that the colonists of Rensselaerswyck contemplated the erection of a church. Although this colony had

---

[1] Cf. copy of the contract in O'Callaghan, Hist. of New Netherland, i, 262 note 1.
[2] Remonstrance of the People of New Netherland to the States
General, July 28, 1649, Col. Docs. N. Y. i, 271-318; or Representation of New Netherland. Narratives of New Netherland, p. 320.

been founded in virtue of the charter of Freedoms and Exemptions granted in 1629, the settlers had remained without the religious comforts which a church and resident clergyman might bring to them in the wilds of America. Nevertheless, the public exercise of religion was not neglected in the colony. The officials were bound under oath to promote "the true and pure service of God in conformity with the Christian Reformed Religion . . . taught and maintained in the churches and schools of the United Provinces."[1] Whenever a council meeting was held, a prayer had "to be offered up by the most suitable person,in order that the blessing of God" might rest upon the assembly and bestow upon its members "wisdom and understanding" in their deliberations.[2] On Sundays and holidays, the people of the colony came together to hear read some chapters of the Bible and the special lessons and exposition of God's Holy Word assigned for the day in the Book of Homilies,which a Reformed divine,Schultetus, had composed for family use.[3] It was usually the duty of the "officer and schout" of the colony to read and to offer up public prayers in these assemblies.[4] Thus the patroon hoped to have his colonists trained in the commandments, the psalms, in pious reading, in modesty, love and decency, until means could be found to send a

[1] Cf. Instructions for Adriaen van der Donck, May 14, 1641, Van Rensselaer-Bowier MSS. 703.
[2] Kiliaen van Rensselaer to Jacob Albertsz Planck, May 10, 1638. Ibid. 415.
[3] Instructions to Rutger Hendricks van Soest, schout, and to the Council, July 20, 1632. Ibid. pp. 208.
[4] Ibid. 251. Contract between Kiliaen van Rensselaer and Jacob Albertz Planck, March 4, 1634.

minister from Holland.[1] The schout, Jacob Planck,
wrote that three hundred florins a year might be raised
in the colony, but Kiliaen van Rensselaer knew full
well, that no minister could be found to go there for that
sum.[2] Meanwhile, in response to the request of the
patroon, Kieft allowed the minister at Manhattan occasionally to go to Rensselaerswyck to console and
admonish the colonists there and to celebrate the
Lord's Supper with them.[3]

Ten years after the foundation of the colony the
exemption of the settlers from the payment of taxes
ceased, and the patroon then expected to develop
resources for the support of an organized ministry from
the tithes to be paid by the inhabitants.[4] He anticipated within a short time sufficient revenue from this
source for the erection of a small church, for which he
himself sent the model, of a parsonage for the minister
and of a dwelling for the sexton.[5] However, the people
of the colony opposed the payment of the tithes, to the
great annoyance of Kiliaen van Rensselaer, who
thought it "childish to think of a minister going there
from here to be paid by the inhabitants individually.

[1] Letter. Kiliaen van Rensselaer to Jacob Albertz Placnk
October 3, 1636, Van Rensselaer-Bowier MSS. 328. Commission
to Arent van Curler, as secretary and bookkeeper, May 12, 1639.
Ibid. 434.
[2] Letter. Kiliaen van Rensselaer to Pieter van Munnickendam,
May 8, 1638. Ibid. 408.
[3] Letter. Kiliaen van Rensselaer to William Kieft, May 17,
1638. Ibid. 404. William Kieft to Kiliaen van Rensselaer August
14, 1638. Ibid. 423, Kiliaen van Rensselaer to Kieft May 12, 1639.
Ibid. 431.
[4] Commission to Pieter Cornelisz van Munnickendam as receiver
of tithes and supercargo of the vessel, May 12, 1639. Ibid. p 436.
[5] Cf. Instructions for Cornelis Teunisz van Breukelen as the representative of the patroon, August 4, 1639. Ibid. 459. Kiliaen van
Rensselaer to Arent van Curler, July 18, 1641. Ibid. 561.

He who is a servant of Jesus Christ, would then become a servant of the people, and when it came into the farmer's heads, they would give nothing at all."[1] The patroon insisted on his right to the tithes, as it was "the means appointed by the Lord God himself," as it was "in use throughout all Christendom," and especially as "the patroons by the Twenty-seventh article of the Freedoms" were bound "to endeavor to find means for the promotion of the service of God."[2]

The new charter again urged the duty of maintaining a minister in the patroonships, and in 1642 Kiliaen van Rensselaer requested the Classis of Amsterdam to assist him in obtaining the services of the Reverend John Megapolensis, Jr., of the Church of Schoorel in the Classis of Alkmaar.[3] The ministers were most willing to second the efforts of the patroon, and so John Megapolensis was duly called to "proclaim Christ to Christians and heathens in such distant lands," and furthermore commissioned "to preach God's word there; to administer the holy sacraments of baptism and the Lord's Supper; to set an example, in a Christian-like manner by public precept; to ordain elders and deacons; to keep and govern, by and with the advice and assistance of the same, God's congregation in good discipline and order, all according to God's Holy Word; and in conformity with the government, confession and catechism of the Netherland churches, and the Synodal acts of Dortdrecht."[4] The patroon made liberal pro-

---

[1] Kiliaen van Rensselaer to Arent van Curler, May 30, 1640, Rensselaer- Bowier MSS. 489.
[2] Instruction to Arent van Curler, June 16, 1640. Ibid. 494.
[3] Classis of Amsterdam, March 17, 1642. Eccl. Recs. N. Y. i, 145-6.
[4] Call of Rev. Megapolensis, March 22, 1642. Ibid. i. 146-8.

visions for the maintenance of the minister, whose services were engaged for six years.[1] When the ship was
about to sail, the Directors of the West India Company
unexpectedly claimed the exclusive right to approve
the appointment of the colonial clergy. There was no
time to argue the case without delaying the departure
of the vessel, and a compromise was allowed by the
patroon, who consented to the approval of the minister's commission by the Directors without any prejudice to his rights as patroon of the colony.[2]

Kiliaen van Rensselaer did not limit the authority
of Domine Megapolensis to ecclesiastical matters, but
also made the minister the arbiter of all disputes
arising between the chief official of the colony,
Arent van Curler, and the next officer in rank,
Adriaen van der Donck. He was instructed to "have
an eye to the rights and advantages of the patroon,
that the common welfare may not suffer from misunderstanding, contention and the like." The
Domine's decision was to stand unquestioned until
the patroon himself could look into the matter at issue.[3]
However, there is no evidence of friction between the
minister and the officials. In fact, Arent van Curler

O'Callaghan's Hist. of New Netherland. i, 449; Munsell's Annals
of Albany. i, 21, 92.
  [1] Contract in O'Callaghan, Hist. of New Netherland. i. 448-9.
He was given free passage and board on ship for himself, wife and
four children. If he should fall into the hands of the Dunkirkers,
the patroon promised to ransom him and during his detention to
give forty guilders monthly for his support. A parsonage was to be
erected in the colony and a salary of one thousand and ten
guilders yearly, with an increase of two hundred and fifty guilders
yearly for the three following years, was stipulated.
  [2] Ibid. 449, also in Van Rensselaer-Bowier MSS. p. 606-8.
Dates differ; here April 6, in O'Callaghan, March 6.
  [3] Memorandum from Kiliaen van Rensselaer for Johannes Megapolensis. June 3, 1642. Van Rensselaer-Bowier MSS. 618.

wrote the patroon that he never failed to ask the minister's opinion before he began any new enterprise and always thankfully received his counsel.[1]

Megapolensis did not find a church edifice ready for his use. On August 17, 1642, he had to preach his first sermon in the storehouse, where about one hundred persons had assembled.[2] The minister did not find the people all that he desired,[3] and Kiliaen van Rensselaer had to confess that matters were "in such a state, that hardly any semblance of godliness and righteousness" remained. Many, hardened in their sins, now absented themselves from divine service, "so as not to hear the Word of God."[4] The patroon, therefore, sent a draft of an ordinance, which made attendance at divine worship, at least once a week, obligatory upon all adults, unless they were excused by sickness or some other good reason. Severe fines were to be decreed for the violation of this ordinance, and the minister was directed occasionally to preach at Rensselaers-Steyn, even on some week-day, to give the people of that region more opportunity to fulfill this obligation.[5] The worst crimes enumerated by the patroon as prevalent in the colony were dishonesty, licentiousness and drunkenness.[6] Kiliaen van Rensselaer suspected "that Fort Orange is a wine cellar

[1] Van Curler to Kiliaen Van Rensselaer, June 16, 1643. O'Callaghan, Hist. of New Netherland, i, 457.
[2] Kiliaen van Rensselaer to Johannes Megapolensis. March 13, 1643. Van Rensselaer-Bowier MSS. 652. A church was finished only a year later.
[3] Ibid. 647.
[4] Redress of the abuses and faults in the colony of Rensselaerswyck, September 5, 1643. Ibid 686-7.
[5] Ibid. 694-5.
[6] Ibid. 687-88.

to debauch my people, exhausting them as long as they
can find something to pay, and after that charging it to
my account."[1]   He, therefore, also planned severe
legislation to limit the importation of liquor into the colony according to the needs of each family, but to the
exclusion of dissipation and drunkenness. Offenses
of this kind were also to be punished by heavy fines,
which were to be doubled, if the culprit proved to be an
officer, "as wine and spirits are the cause of God's
wrath, of the patroon's loss and of all evils."[2]

On the outbreak of the Indian war, the Dutch minister at Manhattan, Everardus Bogardus, "many times
in his sermons freely expressed himself against the horrible murders, covetousness, and other gross excesses."[3]
On several occasions, the Dutch in their revolting
cruelty even outraged the blunted moral sense of the
Indian savage. The ravages of the war, which reduced the Dutch settlers almost to the last extremity,
made the government unpopular, and Kieft attempted
to shift the responsibility for the war upon his advisors.
One of these, Maryn Adriaesen, became so incensed at
this treachery of the Director General, that he made a
murderous but unsuccessful attack upon Kieft.
The minister espoused the cause of the unfortunate
man from the pulpit "in the most brutal manner."
Later he again attacked Kieft.[4]   "What are the
great men of the country but receptacles of wrath,

[1] Kiliaen van Rensselaer to William Kieft, June 8, 1642.   Van
Rensselaer-Bowier MSS. 622.
[2] Redress of the abuses and faults in the colony of Rensselaerswyck. Ibid.
[3] Broad Advice. N. Y. Hist. Soc. Coll. 2d. Ser. iii, (1857),
261-2.
[4] Col. Docs. N. Y. xiv, 69-73.

fountains of woe and trouble? Nothing is thought of but to plunder other people's property—to dismiss—to banish—to transport to Holland." It was unfortunate for the welfare of the Dutch community that this minister's life was also a scandal on account of his intemperance, which took away a great deal of the force of this telling criticism of Kieft's government. The Director General represented the minister as "a seditious man, who sought nothing else than to excite the people and the servants of the company against him, who was their sovereign ruler." Kieft now absented himself entirely from church attendance "to avoid giving greater scandal," but a series of recriminations took place between the Director General and the Dutch minister, which was unworthy of their respective offices and did great harm to the moral and religious life of the commonalty. Kieft's example drew away from the church the officials and servants of the Company, "who all did not attend the administration of the Lord's Supper, or even the meetings to hear God's Word."[1] The officers and soldiers were permitted to perform all kinds of noisy plays about the church during the sermon and scoffed at the faithful who came to partake of the Lord's Supper. While the minister was engaged in preparing the faithful for this solemn religious act, orders were given to beat the drum and to discharge the cannon several times. Kieft finally began

---

[1] Cf. also letter of John Backerus to Classis of Amsterdam, August 15, 1648. "I had to observe with my own eyes that none of the officers here would come to church, when our brother Domine Everardus Bogardus preached. For there was such important questions and differences between our said brother on one side, and his Honor, General William Kieft, with certain officials, on the other, that there was a mutual aversion."—Eccl. Recs. i, 233.

to realize that he could not continue in this course and attempted to obtain a reconciliation without compromising his dignity, but the minister had been too deeply outraged, and he naturally allied himself to the party, working for the removal of the incompetent governor, whom he openly attacked, outside of the church in the gatherings of the people on the occasion of weddings and christenings, and in the church in the course of his sermons. The matter came to a crisis in the beginning of 1646, when Kieft called upon Bogardus to answer for his continual opposition to the government. "Inasmuch as your duty and oath imperiously demand the maintenance of the magistracy; and whereas your conduct stirs the people to mutiny and rebellion, when they are already too much divided, causes schism and abuses in the church and makes us a scorn and a laughing stock to our neighbors, all which cannot be tolerated in a country where justice is maintained, therefore, our sacred duty imperiously requires us to prosecute you in a court of justice, and we have accordingly ordered a copy of these our deliberations to be delivered to you to answer in fourteen days." Bogardus, who had hitherto neglected to recognize any letter of the Director, was constrained to answer this bill of indictment, but his first reply was considered futile and absurd, and his second answer slanderous. After some further correspondence, the minister refused to enter into "a deep discussion of this affair" and challenged the competency of the Director and his council. The Director refused to allow that the matter transcended his powers, but, to obviate all pretext of slander, he declared his willingness to submit the case to the judgment of "impartial judges of the Reformed Religion," such as the ministers Megapolensis and Doughty and two or three impartial members of the Province, unless meanwhile another Director should arrive, who might then decide the matter. Bogardus saw his opportunity and immediately appealed to the new Director and Council, but Kieft refused to entertain this appeal, as the time of the arrival of the new Director was uncertain, and it was high time "to put a stop to the scandal and disorder which have prevailed hitherto." Nevertheless, the prosecution was not pressed in the end, probably on account of the intervention of Domine Megapolensis, who at the request of the Director was allowed by Bogardus to preach in his pulpit,"in order that we may with more fervor pray God in the midst of the congregation that he would dispose you and our hearts to a Christian concord." The termination of Kieft's tenure of office prevented a new outbreak of hostile feeling from either party within the colony, as both postponed further action in the matter until their arrival in the Fatherland. In the following summer, both Kieft and Bogardus embarked for Holland "to terminate their disputes of long standing before the Directors,"[1] but shipwreck in the Bristol Channel, where both perished, relieved them from rendering their accounts.

Peter Stuyvesant, the new Director General, who was joined at Curaçoa by the minister John Backerus, found New Amsterdam in a low state. "Where the

[1] John Backerus to Classis of Amsterdam, June 29, 1648. Eccl. Recs. N. Y. i, 232.

shepherd errs, the sheep go astray."[1] The congregation numbered about one hundred and seventy members, most of whom were "very ignorant in regard to the true religion and very much given to drink." John Backerus, whose services had been engaged temporarily, believed that "the source of much evil and great offense would be removed," if the seventeen taphouses were closed, with the exception of three or four. The vice of intemperance had obtained such sway that the minister despaired of being able to accomplish anything with many of the older people, who were "so far depraved that they are now ashamed to learn anything good."[2] His hope was with the children, who might be influenced by the pious example of a new pastor and of a good schoolmaster. The abuses that had developed during the strife between Kieft and Bogardus had retarded the growth of religion and education. The church, although begun in 1642, still remained uncompleted, no schoolhouse had as yet been erected, and Kieft had been accused of misappropriating the funds collected for both these purposes. As the resources of the Directors were too limited to allow any vast expenditure, Stuyvesant now endeavored to obtain assistance from the people by the formation of a representative board of "Nine Select Men," who, as good and faithful representatives of the commonalty, were "to promote the honor of God and the welfare of our dear fatherland to the best advantage of the Company and the prosperity of our good citizens, to the preservation

[1] Directors to Stuyvesant, April 7, 1648. Col. Docs. N.Y. xiv, 84.
[2] Backerus to Classis of Amsterdam, September 2, 1648. Eccl Recs. N. Y. i, 236.

of the pure Reformed Religion, inculcated here and in the churches of the Netherlands."[1] Arrangements were made to procure means to complete the church and to provide a schoolhouse with a dwelling for the school-master. Meanwhile, on the request of Stuyvesant and the church of Manhattan, William Vestensz was sent as Comforter of the Sick and schoolmaster by the Classis of Amsterdam, with the approval of the Directors of the West India Company.[2]

A total destitution of the ministry now threatened the Province of New Netherland. John Backerus demanded to be released of his temporary charge by the appointment of another minister, who "must have full liberty in denouncing sin, for which he will find the way already prepared, and he must do his duty with the good example of a decent life himself."[3] The authorities in Amsterdam felt constrained to grant his request, but they were put to great trouble, as the six years' service of Domine Megapolensis expired at this time and he also was anxious to return home to rejoin his wife and children and to attend to the liquidation of an estate, in which he was greatly interested.[4] Nevertheless, Stuyvesant, with the full approval of the Directors in Amsterdam, hoped to engage the services of Megapolen-sis after his dismission from the church at Rensselaers-wyck. The Classis of Amsterdam was also anxious that Megapolensis should accept a call to the church of

[1] Council minute, November 14, 1647. O'Callaghan, Cal. Hist. MSS. (Dutch) i, p. 114; Hist. of New Netherland, ii, 37-38.
[2] Classis to Megapolensis, January 10, 1650. Eccl. Recs. N. Y. i, 266.
[3] Backerus to Classis of Amsterdam, September 2, 1648. Ibid. 236.
[4] Directors to Stuyvesant, January 27, 1649. Col. Docs. N. Y. xiv. 107.

New Amsterdam. Although the patroons of Rensselaerswyck would gladly have seen Megapolensis continue his residence in their colony, they were not willing
to hold him there against his will. However, they
requested him to make some arrangements before his
departure for the continuation "of some form of worship, such as the reading of some chapters of God's
Word, or some good homily."[1]   When Megapolensis
arrived at New Amsterdam, on his way to the fatherland, Backerus had already left the town for Europe.
His departure had been hastened by the measures
adopted by Stuyvesant to repress any protest of the
people against his autocratic government, which he
feared might also be made the subject of this minister's
discourse in the pulpit. At the same time, he protested
that he did not wish to gain control of "ecclesiastical
affairs which are left at the full disposal of said ministers
and consistory," wherein the Director General offered
all the aid and assistance that could lawfully be demanded from the chief magistrate of the country.   In
regard to other things, the minister was personally
instructed by the Director General "not to read himself
or have read by any of the church officers from the pulpit or elsewhere in the church at the request of any of
the inhabitants any writing, petition or proposal having
relation to the municipal or general government," until
such writing had been signed by the Director himself
or by the secretary on the order of the Director and
Council.[2]

[1] Acts of Deputies. Classis of Amsterdam, March 29, 1649.
Eccl. Recs. N. Y. i. 249.
    [2] Council Minute, May 8, 1649.   Col. Docs. N. Y. xiv. 114.

On the departure of Backerus, the Director General and Council determined to press Megapolensis to remain and to supply here the service of the Word and the administration of the Holy Sacraments for the honor of God, the advancement of his Church, and the salvation of men.[1] Megapolensis finally yielded to these persuasive arguments of the Director and Council. Unlike his predecessors, he was of one mind and spirit with the provincial government on the religious and political issues which presented themselves in the course of time. This was especially manifested six years later in the policy adopted for the repression of religious dissent.

The abuses that had developed in the course of Kieft's administration, and the ineffectual efforts to obtain redress of their grievances from Stuyvesant, led the people to appeal directly to the States General in 1649.[2] The failure of the company to endow the Church of New Amsterdam with property sufficient to give a fixed revenue for the support of religion was urged in these complaints as a grievance of the commonalty. The education of the youth had also suffered from neglect. Some material had been gathered for the erection of a school, but the first stone had not yet been laid, although a plate had long been passed around to raise funds. However, the proceeds of this collection were not in the hands of the provincial authorities, but in the hands of one of the remonstrants, Jacob Couvenhoven. No charitable institutions in the nature of an hospital, or of an orphan asylum, or of a home for the aged had been erected. The Directors claimed that their re-

---

[1] Council minute, August 2, 1649.   Col. Docs. N. Y. xiv. 116.
[2] Col. Docs. N. Y. i. 217-300, 335, 340.

86   RELIGION IN NEW NETHERLAND

sources at present were too limited to allow the erection of buildings, which were not very necessary. They believed that the poor could be well cared for with the proceeds of voluntary offerings and the fines, that were given to the Deaconry, as it was able to loan the company in New Amsterdam the sum of nine hundred to a thousand guilders.[1]

The Remonstrance finally led to the incorporation of the city of New Amsterdam with a municipal court of Burgomasters and Schepens. The minutes of this court open on February 6, 1653, with a prayer, in which they thank God for his past blessings, beseech Him for strength and light in the administration of justice, so that they might be able to exercise the power entrusted to them "to the general good of the community and *to the maintenance of the church.*"[2] Stuyvesant had attempted in vain to obtain some financial assistance for the maintenance of the civil, ecclesiastical and military servants of the company.[3] Finally, in the fall of this year, Stuyvesant granted the Burgomasters and Schepens the usual excise on wine and beer consumed in the city of New Amsterdam, which they were to farm out to the highest bidder, if in return they paid subsidies for the maintenance of the works of the city, and the salaries of its ecclesiastical and civil servants.[4] When a semi-annual payment became due, the ministers Megapolensis and Drisius applied to Stuyvesant,

[1] Representation of New Netherland (1650). Narratives of New Netherland, p. 327.   Van Tienhoven's Answer. Ibid. p. 361-3.
[2] Recs. New Amsterdam. i, 48-9.
[3] Directors to Stuyvesant, June 26, 1653. Col. Docs. N. Y. xiv. 206.
[4] Court minute, November 29, 1653.   Recs. New Amsterdam, i. 130.

who ordered the Burgomasters and Schepens, in accordance with their promise, to provide the salaries of the ministers of the Gospel,[1] but the Burgomaster and Schepens now offered only to pay out of the excise the salaries of one minister, one precentor, who was at the same time schoolmaster, and of one beadle.[2] When Stuyvesant saw that these men were not willing to fulfill their promise, he revoked the concession of the excise, which he farmed out immediately to the highest bidder, to pay the clergy and place them above want.[3]

The incorporation of the city of New Amsterdam did not change the position of the deaconry of the Dutch Reformed Church in regard to the poor. The deacons were instructed by the Director General and Council to exercise as heretofore the office of orphan-masters towards the widows and orphans, but they were commanded now to apply to the Burgomasters and Schepens, or in case of necessity to the Director and Council for the appointment of curators, who were to be responsible to the municipal court.[4] However, in the following year, at the instance of the Burgomasters and Schepens, Stuyvesant appointed regular orphan-masters, who were organized February, 1656, into a separate body, "whose duty it shall

[1] Director General and Council to Burgomasters and Schepens. June 1, 1654. Col. Docs. N. Y. xiv. 268-9. Recs. New Amsterdam. i. 206.

[2] Burgomasters and Schepens to Director and Council. August 21 and 31. Col. Docs. N. Y. xiv. 288-9. Recs. New Amsterdam, i. 232.

[3] Council minute, June 1, 8. Col. Docs. N. Y. xiv. 268-9;271-2. Recs. New Amsterdam, i. 206.

[4] Council minute, February 26, 1653. O'Callaghan, Cal. Hist. MSS. (Dutch) i, p. 131. Cf. Minutes of Orphan Masters of New Amsterdam. Preface by Berthold Fernow. pp. vi-viii.

solely be to attend to orphans and minor children within the jurisdiction of the city and to administer their property in and out of the city and oversee such administration by others." The deacons retained the care of the poor, but such great demands were made upon them by the poor of other towns, that the deacons, on June 11, 1661, requested the Director General and Council to have the adjacent villages make weekly collections for their own poor.[1] Such provisions were made by the ordinance of October. It speaks well for the good sense of the Dutch that goods and merchandise, belonging to the board of deacons and other charitable institutions, were exempt from the fee for weighing. The weigh-master was instructed to weigh these free and for God's sake.[2] This was the only exemption allowed from such taxes. The question of exemption from the Burgher excise and a tax on slaughtered cattle in regard to the clergy was discussed in 1656 by the court of New Amsterdam, which finally decided that no person was to be exempt from such taxes, as the Director General himself offered to pay.[3] Nevertheless, in 1661 Alexander Carolus Curtius, the rector of the Latin school, contended that professors, preachers and rectors were exempt from excise taxes in Holland, but the court decided that the rector was to pay the excise.[4]

After the departure of Megapolensis from Rensse-

---

[1] Council minute, June 11, 1661, O'Callaghan. Cal. Hist. 226. MSS. (Dutch) i. Ordinance, October 22, 1661. Ibid. 230.
[2] Laws and Ordinances of New Netherland, April 11, 1661. p. 393.
[3] Court minute, October 2, 1656, October 26, October 30. Recs. New Amsterdam, ii, 179, 204.
[4] Court minute. January 25, 1661. Recs. New Amsterdam, iii, 253.

laerswyck, this colony remained without a clergyman until the arrival of the Reverend William Grasmeer in 1650. He was a son-in-law of Megapolensis and formerly pastor at Grafdyck in the Classis of Alckmaar, where he had been found guilty of domestic quarrelling, abandonment of his wife, and drunkenness.[1] He was deposed from the ministry and his deposition was confirmed by the Synod of North Holland. As soon as the Classis of Amsterdam learned of his resolution to go to New Netherland, the deputies earnestly warned 'the colonial authorities not to allow him to exercise any duties of the ministerial office, until he had given satisfaction to the Classis of Alckmaar. Nevertheless, William Grasmeer was able to obtain a call to the pastorate of the church of Rensselaerswyck by means of two certificates, which he had obtained under false pretenses from the deacons and elders of Grafdyck and from the pastor of Alckmaar, the Rev. Knierus (John Knyf).[2] The Classis of Amsterdam with the approbation of the patroon informed the church of Rensselaerswyck that they could not allow William Grasmeer to remain in the ministry of the colony, "lest God's Holy Name be blasphemed, your colony demoralized, and the good order and discipline of the church be trampled under foot."[3] This decided opposition led Grasmeer to return to Holland and seek a reconciliation with his ecclesiastical superiors in the hope of then receiving an appointment

[1] Classis of Amsterdam to church of Rensselaerswyck, February 20, 1651. Eccl. Recs. N. Y. i. 290.
[2] Classis of Alckmaar, November 28, 1650. Ibid. 283. Classis of Amsterdam, January 2, 1651, Ibid. 286.
[3] Classis of Amsterdam to church of Rensselaerswyck. February 20, 1651. Ibid. 289.

as the second minister at New Amsterdam.[1]   Stuyve-
sant had recommended the case of this minister to the
Directors of the Amsterdam Chamber, but the Synod of
North Holland had first to approve the reconciliation of
Grasmeer,[2] which was done only in August, 1652, after
a repentant acknowledgment of his sins.[3]

Meanwhile, the services of two ministers had been
obtained for the colonial church, which apparently pre-
cluded the return of William Grasmeer to the colony.
Stuyvesant had urged the appointment of a minister with some ability to preach to the English, who
had settled in New Amsterdam, and were members of
the Reformed Church.   At this time, disturbances in
England led the Reverend Samuel Drisius to retreat to
Holland, where he declared his willingness to the Classis of Amsterdam to be employed in the ministry of
New Netherland.   Immediately the deputies of the
Classis recommended his appointment as assistant to
Domine Megapolensis in the church of New Amsterdam,
as he was able to preach in both languages, English and
Dutch, and if necessary even in French, and thus would
prove "a great instrument for the propagation of God's
Holy Word and glory."[4]   The Directors readily con-
ceded the request of the Classis.   A few months later
Gideon Schaats, schoolmaster at Beets, received a call to
the church of Rensselaerswyck, for which he was or-

---

[1] Acts of Classis of Amsterdam, February 12, 1652. Eccl. Recs.
N. Y. i. 301.

[2] Directors to Stuyvesant, April 4, 1652. Col. Docs. N. Y. xiv.
174.

[3] Synod of North Holland, August 12, et seq., 1652. Eccl. Recs.
N. Y. i. 312-13.

[4] Directors to Stuyvesant, April 4, 1652. Col. Docs. N. Y. xiv.
173. Eccl. Recs. N. Y. i. 303-6.

dained by the Classis of Amsterdam.[1] His contract
with John van Rensselaer bound him "to use all Christian zeal there to bring up both the heathen and their
children in the Christian religion; to teach all the catechism and instruct the people in the Holy Scriptures,
and to pay attention to the office of schoolmaster for old
and young; and further to do everything befitting a
public, honest and holy teacher for the advancement of
divine service and church exercise among young and
old."[2] Thus while Gideon Schaats exercised the ministerial office, he also held the office of a schoolmaster in
the colony of Rensselaerswyck. With the new minister
there also arrived a new Schout of the colony, Gerrit
Swart, who was instructed "above all things to take
care, that Divine Worship shall be maintained .. conformably to the Reformed Religion," as publicly
taught in the United Provinces, and "that the Lord's
Day, the Sabbath of the New Testament, be properly
respected both by the observance of hearing the Holy
Word, as well as the preventing of all unnecessary and
daily labor on said day."[3] Gideon Schaats found a congregation of about one hundred members in the colony,
but sometimes there was an attendance of three or four
hundred at the church, and the new minister estimated
that there might be a congregation of six hundred, but
for the taverns and villainous houses, that had many
visitors. "There are many hearers, but not much saving fruit." He could hardly rely on any support
from the people, who preferred "to gamble away or lose

[1] Classis of Amsterdam, Acts of Deputies, 1652, April 15,
May 6. Eccl. Recs. N. Y. i. 308-9.
[2] Contract in O'Callaghan, Hist. of New Netherland, ii. 567
[3] Ibid. 566-7.

in bets a ton of beer at twenty-three or twenty-four guilders, or some other liquor." The better class were too few to be able to make up any deficiency of his salary. There was not even a house for the new minister, as the house that had been occupied by the former preacher was allotted to the new schout-fiscal,[1] and the congregation refused to build a new parsonage. The patroon of the colony only allowed the minister two hundred guilders for rent, while the rent of a decent domicile cost at least four hundred guilders. This forced the Rev. Gideon Schaats to come to some arrangement with the deaons of the church, from whom he obtained the use of the poor-house for his dwelling place, as there were then very few poor people in the colony. Meanwhile, a small new church had been erected in the heart of Beverwyck, which was then a village of about one hundred and twenty houses. Most of the inhabitants were in the employ of the West India Company, and when the second contract with patroon of the colony expired in 1657, van Rensselaer refused to pay any longer for services, which were mainly to the advantage of the servants of the company.[2] He was then reappointed "at the request of the inhabitants of Fort Orange and Beverwyck," by Stuyvesant at a salary of one hundred florins a month, which the company expected to be raised for the greater part by the congregation.[3] The labors of Gideon

----

[1] Commission of Gerrit Swart. O'Callaghan, Hist. of New Netherland, ii. 564.
[2] Schaats to Domine Laurentius, June 27, 1657. Eccl. Recs. N. Y. i 385-6.
[3] Directors to Stuyvesant, May 20, 1658. Col. Docs. N. Y. xiv., 419.

Schaats bore fruit in spite of the discouraging outlook, for in 1660 he estimated the number of church members at about two hundred, although at that time he was fearful of the ravages which might be inflicted upon his congregation by the toleration of Lutheran worship in the colony.[1]

The Dutch settlements on Long Island were dependent for religious ministration on the church of New Amsterdam until 1654, when the Reverend John T. Polhemus arrived from Itamarca, in Brazil, whence the Dutch had been expelled by the Portuguese. In the beginning of this year, the West India Company had invited the Classis of Amsterdam to find a suitable person to take charge of public worship on Long Island, and had appropriated for his support six hundred guilders as an annual salary. No one was found to take the place.[2] Thus the advent of Polhemus to the Dutch colony was opportune, and he immediately received a call to minister to the inhabitants of Midwout and the adjoining towns, subject to the approval of the Classis of Amsterdam and the Directors of the Company. It was resolved to erect in Midwout[3] a building, about sixty or sixty-five feet in length, twenty-eight feet in width and twelve or fourteen feet high. A chamber in the rear was planned for the use of the preacher, while the front part was to be devoted to divine service. The building was intended

[1] Schaats to Classis of Amsterdam, September 22, 1660. Eccl. Recs. N. Y. i. 483.
[2] Acts of Deputies. Classis of Amsterdam. March 2, 1654. Ibid. 324.
[3] Council minute, December 17, 1654. Col. Docs. N. Y. xiv. 310.

to become a parsonage and barn, as soon as the inhabitants collected more funds and the material necessary for a church. The erection of this edifice was confided to a commission, composed of the Reverend Megapolensis, Jan Snediger and Jan Strycker. On the erection of a parsonage and the grant of a parcel of land, Midwout felt too poor to bear further expenses alone[1] and permission was granted to call upon the inhabitants of Breukelen and Amersfoort to cut and hew timber to be used in the construction of a building for the exercise of Divine Service.[2] Poverty also made the support of the minister impossible for one single town, and Stuyvesant, on the petition of the magistrates, directed a collection to be taken up in the villages of Breukelen, Midwout and Amersfoort for the support of the minister, but Breukelen and the adjacent places agreed to contribute according to their means, only on the condition that Domine Polhemus would officiate alternately at Midwout and Breukelen, which the Director General and Council readily allowed.[3] This arrangement met with serious objections from the people of Gravesend and Amersfoort, who were thus compelled every other Sunday to travel four hours each way, "all for one single sermon, which would be to some very troublesome and to others utterly impossible," while Midwout was only two hours walk from each town. A compromise was now effected according to which the Sunday sermon was to be delivered in the morning at Midwout, which was nearly equally distant from the

[1] Council minute, June 15, 1655. Col. Docs. N. Y. xiv. 337.
[2] Council minute, February 9, 1655. Ibid. 311-12.
[3] Letter to Director General and Council, February 25, 1656. Ibid. 338.

three other towns, but the usual afternoon service was to be changed to the evening and was to be held alternately in Breukelen and Amersfoort.[1]

The lot of Domine Polhemus was not more enviable than that of Domine Schaats. He received no compensation whatever for almost the first two years of his ministry from the Dutch settlers of Long Island. In his poverty, he was compelled to draw from the Company's warehouse the necessaries of life to the amount of nine hundred and forty-two florins. This debt was remitted on the petition of the minister by the Provincial authorities in return for the services rendered during this time.[2] Another just cause of complaint was given to Polhemus, when winter set in, with the parsonage in such an uninhabitable state, that he with his wife and children had to "live and sleep on the bare ground and in the cold."[3] Stuyvesant had sent one hundred hemlock planks for the ceiling and wainscoting of the house, but the Commissaries Jan Snediger and Jan Stryker disposed of them to other persons and for other usages, so that the parsonage remained unfinished in spite of the approach of winter. A restitution of the stolen property and the completion of the dwelling-house was peremptorily ordered by the Director General.[4] A new difficulty was presented by the question of the minister's salary. It was finally determined to raise the sum from the three towns of Midwout,

[1] Council minute, March 15, 1656. Stiles, Hist. of Brooklyn, i. 130.
[2] Council minute, January 29, 1658. Col. Docs. N. Y. xiv. 411-12.
[3] Letter to Stuyvesant, December 14, 1656. Ibid. 370-1.
[4] Order of Stuyvesant, December 21, 1656. Ibid. 376.

Amersfoort and Breukelen, of which the first town
was to be assessed four hundred florins and the
other two three hundred respectively. In the beginning of 1657, the court of Midwout, with the consent of
Stuyvesant, levied a tax of ten florins upon each lot or
parcel of land, of which there were about forty in the
town.[1] The same plan was also pursued in Amersfoort,
which, with the voluntary contributions promised by
Gravesend, thus hoped to realize the three hundred
guilders, for which it was assessed for the support of the
minister.[2] Breukelen alone was not content. This
community was too small and too impoverished to be
able to satisfy the demands made upon its resources for
a ministry, which had not been engaged by the town,
but had intruded itself against the wishes of the inhabitants. Besides the service of Domine Polhemus had
proved unsatisfactory, inasmuch as the minister gave
them only "a prayer instead of a sermon, that was finished before they could collect their thoughts, so that he
gives small edification to the congregation." The magistrates thought that it might be more profitable to the
people, if one of their own number were appointed "to
read a sermon from a book of homilies every Sunday."
They did not dispute the good will of Polhemus, but
they believed that his faculties had been weakened by
old age. Nevertheless, if he should persist to minister
as before to them, they would give some voluntary contribution, but the congregation refused to be bound to
any fixed sum in spite of the former promise of the

[1] Council minute, March 28, 1656. Col. Docs. N. Y. xiv. 345.
[2] Council minute, ¡January 15, 1657. Ibid. 378-9.

magistrates of the town, as "there are many who cannot make any contribution, and whom it would be more necessary to support."[1] Stuyvesant refused to entertain the reasons alleged in this remonstrance and threatened to use force, and the intimidated magistrates agreed for this year to raise the promised three hundred florins, through the levy of a tax provided they were excused from any further contributions, unless conditions in the meantime improved in New Netherland and the fatherland.[2]

In the fall of the following year, 1658, Polhemus and Jan Stryker began to erect the church proper on the order of Peter Stuyvesant.[3] Meanwhile, the magistrates of Midwout had obtained from the Director General and Council an endowment for the support of the church, school and minister through the formation of a glebe. Twenty-five morgens were to furnish revenue to maintain the church in good repair; another lot of twenty-five morgens was set aside for the support of a school and divine service, and two more lots, containing together fifty morgens, were attached to the parsonage for the direct support of the minister, on condition that the inhabitants of Midwout would make up any deficiency in his salary. This arrangement was to hold

[1] Petition of Brooklyn, January, 1657. Col. Docs. N. Y. xiv. 380-2.

[2] Letter to Director and Council, January, 1657, Ibid. 382-3. The schout of Breukelen, Peter Tonneman, brought suit against Lodewyck Jan Martin, Nicolaes, the Frenchman, Abram, the mulatto and Gerrit, the wheelwright, for refusing to pay the levy of six guilders, "making none but frivolous excuses, one for instance, that he was a Catholic, the other that he did not understand Dutch, etc." They were condemned to pay twelve guilders, as a warning example to others. Council minute, March 26, 1658. Ibid. 413-14.

[3] Council minute. January 4, 1663. Ibid. 520.

good, until the tithes became due, when further orders would be given.[1] Thus the company was almost entirely relieved of the support of religion in Midwout with the exception of occasional subsidies.[2]

The inhabitants of Breukelen were never quite reconciled to this arrangement of divine service on Long Island and in 1659, "on account of the fatigue of the journey from Breukelen to Midwout and the great age of Reverend J. Polhemus, to whom it proves burdensome," they requested a preacher for themselves for the promotion of religion and their own edification.[3] Accordingly the Classis of Amsterdam, on the recommendation of the West India Company, called the Reverend Henricus Selyns to the ministry of the Church of Breukelen, where upon his ordination he was commissioned "to preach the entire and saving Word of God; to administer the Sacraments according to the institution of Christ; to lead in public prayers of the congregation; and in union with the officers of the church, to preserve discipline and order; all in conformity with the Confession of Faith of the Netherland Church and the Heidelberg Catechism."[4] On the arrival of the Reverend Selyns, the peace negotiations with the Esopus Indians so preoccupied the Provincial government, that his installation at Breukelen was delayed several months, during which the Company gave him an allowance for his support. Meanwhile, the magistrates of Breukelen

---

[1] Council minute, January 29, 1658. Col. Docs. N. Y. xiv. 410.
[2] Four hundred fls. advanced by Company, Sept. 30, 1660. Council minute, Ibid 482-3. Acknowledgment of subsidy of four hundred, fifteen and ten fls. Council minute March 29, 1661. Ibid. 499.
[3] Council minute, Sept. 3, 1660. Eccl. Recs. N. Y. i. 479-80.
[4] Call, February 16, 1660. Ibid. 466.

discovered that they could only raise three hundred guilders yearly towards the salary of Selyns, who had been promised one thousand two hundred florins a year. The company then had to contribute the tithes of the village, and Stuyvesant himself offered to give to the new minister two hundred and fifty florins a year on the condition that the Domine preached on Sunday evening at his own Bouwery.[1] This offer was accepted and on September 3, 1660, Nicasius de Sille, the schout fiscal of New Netherland and Martin Krieger, a Burgomaster of New Amsterdam were sent to Breukelen to install Domine Selyns in his new charge, where he was cordially received by the magistrates and the consistory, and greeted by Domine Polhemus. Divine service was carried on in a barn, but the people expected to erect a church the next winter. On his arrival at Breukelen, Selyns found one elder, two deacons, twenty-four members, thirty-one householders and one hundred and thirty-four people. His congregation also comprised the Ferry, Wallabout and Gowanus, and his audience was often increased by visitors from Midwout, New Amersfoort and even from Gravesend. People from Manhattan came to the service on Sunday evening at the Bouwery, which was also a place of relaxation and pleasure; Stuyvesant had there forty negroes besides the household families, and Selyns contemplated the organization of a separate consistory at this place or at least the election of one deacon, if not of an elder, who might take charge of the alms, which were then provisionally received by the deacons from New Amster-

[1] Council minute, August 30, 1660. Col. Docs. N.Y. xiv. 479.

dam.[1] A year after the organization of a separate
church in Breukelen, a schoolmaster, who was also sexton, chorister and precentor, was hired in the person of
Carel De Beauvois.[2] On the departure of Domine
Selyns after the expiration of his time of service in the
summer of 1664, the schoolmaster was commissioned to
read prayers and a sermon from an approved author
every Sunday in the church for the improvement of
the congregation, until another minister could be
found.[3] Selyns reported that during his ministry the
church membership with God's help and grace had
increased fourfold.[4]

There was also another minister, who had come to
the Province of New Netherland at the same time as
Domine Selyns, but had been ordained to minister to
the inhabitants of Esopus. This was the Reverend
Hermanus Blom, who had before been in the country
while yet a proponent, and at the invitation of Stuyvesant had preached in several villages, to the great satisfaction of his hearers. After an opportunity was given
by the Director General to the inhabitants of Esopus to
hear Blom,[5] they petitioned the provincial authorities
to give him to them as their minister, and resolved to
prepare a good Bouwery for his support, to which later
settlers would also have to contribute proportionately
to the obligations assumed by the present petition-

[1] Letter to Classis of Amsterdam, October 4, 1660. Eccl. Recs.
N. Y. i. 488.
[2] Contract, July 6, 1661. Stiles, Hist. of Brooklyn, i. 429.
[3] Stiles, Ibid. 145.
[4] Letter, June 9, 1664. Eccl. Recs. N. Y. i. 548.
[5] Stuyvesant to Lourissen at Esopus, August 11, 1659. Col. Docs:
N. Y. xiii· 102.

ers.[1] Stuyvesant recommended their case, and Blom, on his return to Holland, was ordained and commissioned to preach at Esopus with the full approval of the Company, which promised to pay six hundred guilders yearly, while the balance up to ten or twelve hundred guilders was to be raised by the community, but paid to the minister by Stuyvesant in his capacity of chief magistrate of the Province.[2] After some delay in his installation, which was also due to the Indian difficulties in the Esopus country, he finally was inducted in September of 1660. The anxiety of the new minister in regard to his support was put at rest by the promise of the inhabitants to raise seven hundred guilders as their share of his salary, if his farm should fail.[3] A primitive form of divine service had already been organized some years previous to the arrival of the new minister. The company had given the office of precentor to Andries van der Sluys, who led in prayer and read an approved homily at the Sunday meeting, catechised the children and taught them also the art of reading and writing.[4] On the arrival of Domine Blom, the church of Wiltwyck only counted sixteen members, but in the course of a few years the membership increased to sixty.[5] Stuyvesant did all in his power to foster the life of the church. On the erection of a small court of justice at Wiltwyck in 1661, the commissaries had also to prom-

[1] Petition, August 17, 1659. Col. Docs. N. Y. xiii. 103.
[2] Directors to Stuyvesant, December 22, 1659. Ibid. 129-30.
[3] Contract. March 4, 1661. Ibid. 194.
[4] Megapolensis and Drisius to Classis of Amsterdam, August 5, 1657. Eccl. Recs. N.Y. i. 397-8. Andries van der Sluys to Stuyvesant, September 28, 1658. Col. Docs. N. Y. xiii. 91.
[5] Letter of Blom, September 18, 1663. Doc. Hist. N.Y. iii. 582-3.

ise and swear in the presence of the Almighty and Everpresent God that they would "maintain and exercise the Reformed Church service and no other." The judges were, therefore, to be "professors of the Reformed Religion, as now preached in the United Netherland Churches in conformity with the Word of God and the order of the Synod of Dortdrecht." Even the court-clerk had to promise "to promote and help, as far as his position is concerned, the glory of God and the pure service of His Word."[1]

The church suffered a severe blow in 1663 from the hostilities of the Indians, who slew twenty-four persons, and carried off forty-five prisoners. The dead left behind them many intestate estates, which became the occasion of serious differences between the magistrates and the minister with his consistory, between whom relations had already become somewhat strained. The magistrates were accused of arrogating to themselves the disposition of what was collected in the community either for the church or for the poor, while Domine Blom and his consistory were accused of opposing the magistrates in the appointment of administrators and in the inventory of estates left without any heirs or testamentary disposition. The minister claimed that he had only opposed the payment of the surplus of such estates in a particular case after the settlement of all liabilities to the magistrates, until it had been ascertained whether the overseers of the poor had any claim to the money, as the church had the care of the poor, who were then a

[1] Council minute, Col. Docs. N. Y. xiii. 196, 398; Laws of New Netherland, 396.

heavy burden. Stuyvesant directed that the money should be placed in charge of the overseers of the poor, until there was proof who had a right to the money. The magistrates complained that this put the whole matter in the hands of Domine Blom and his consistory, Albert Heymansen, as no deacon had ever been appointed, who could read or write. They were still more dissatisfied by the fact that Stuyvesant had neglected to recognize their petition for the farming of the excise on beer and wine, as the expenses of the village were increasing and they were daily dunned for arrearage on the Domine's house.[1]

Even after the arrival of Selyns and Blom, Stuyvesant informed the Directors that there were still three or four villages in need of preachers, New Utrecht and Gravesend on Long Island, New Haarlem on Manhattan Island and Bergen, a newly planted village of about thirty families across the North River.[2] At Haarlem, a church, partly French and partly Dutch, had been formed, to which the Reverend Michael Siperius ministered for a short time in 1659 on his arrival from Curaçoa, where he had been located before.[3] Evil reports in regard to his life had reached the Classis of Amsterdam, which were not belied by this Dutch minister's conduct in New Netherland.[4] "He behaved most shamefully here, drinking, cheating and forging other people's writings, so that he was forbidden not

[1] Correspondence in Col. Docs. N. Y. xiii. 306-7; 311, 318.
[2] Letter, October 6, 1660. Ibid. 189.
[3] Beck to Stuyvesant, August, 1659. O'Callaghan. Cal. Hist. MSS. (Dutch), i. p. 331.
[4] Classis of Amsterdam to Drisius, December 5, 1661. Eccl. Recs. N. Y. i. 514.

only to preach but even to keep school." This soon led to his departure for Virginia,[1] and the church of Haarlem was not supplied with a new minister in spite of Stuyvesant's petition. The people of Bergen[2] declared their willingness to raise a goodly sum for the support of a minister in their village, but as in the case of other villages of New Netherland this petition was also in vain. There were no ministers in Holland with sufficient zeal to prompt them to abandon their native country to labor in the struggling colonies of New Netherland, and the Company felt its resources too limited after its bankruptcy to assume additional burdens for the rich endowment of colonial churches, that would attract to them the young ministers or candidates to the ministry, at the beginning of their career.[3] The only minister, who was ordained and sent to New Netherland on the eve of the English conquest, at the instance of the West India Company, was Samuel Megapolensis, the son of the old minister, who had recommended[4] him to the Classis of Amsterdam for this ministry, as he was qualified through several years' attendance at the Academy of Cambridge in New England to preach to the English, who were in great want of preachers, and consequently open to the inroads of schism and heresy.[5] In fact, Stuyvesant had asked the Directors to locate two English preachers in the English towns as early as 1659, but the Directors felt that it

[1] Drisius to Classis of Amsterdam, August 5, 1664. Eccl. Recs. N. Y. i. 555.
[2] Petition, November 1662. Col. Docs. N. Y. xiii 232-3.
[3] Cf. Classis of Amsterdam to Backerus, April 26, 1549. Eccl. Recs. N. Y. i, 250.
[4] Letter, September 25, 1658. Ibid. 436.
[5] Megapolensis and Drisius to Classis of Amsterdam, September 24, 1658. Ibid. 432-3.

would be dangerous to draw any preachers from England, while that country was so disturbed, "not only in her political, but also in her ecclesiastical government."[1] They wanted a minister "who would conform himself in government" with the churches of New Netherland, "free from Independent and other New England notions," as the Directors informed the Classis of Amsterdam.[2] Nevertheless, no one was sent until the appointment of Samuel Megapolensis, and when he arrived just previous to the departure of Domine Selyns, he was expected to take the place of this minister at the Bouwery and at Breukelen.[3] Thus the English villages were still left destitute, but they had already passed from the jurisdiction of the Company and soon all New Netherland was in the hands of the English. However, an article in the capitulation guaranteed the free exercise of the Reformed Religion.[4]

[1] Directors to Stuyvesant, December 22, 1659. Col. Docs. N.Y. xiv, 451.
[2] Acts of Classis of Amsterdam, January 5, 1660. March 1, 1660. Eccl. Recs. N. Y. i. 462, 470.
[3] Drisius to Classis of Amsterdam, August 5, 1664. Ibid. 554.
[4] Col. Docs. N. Y. ii. 250-53.

CHAPTER IV

Religion in New Sweden before and after the Dutch Conquest

The Swedish immigration to territory claimed by the Dutch became an important factor in the development of the religious history of the Province of New Netherland. The attention of the Crown of Sweden had been directed to American colonial enterprise by the original projector of the Dutch West India Company, the exiled Antwerp merchant, William Usselinx. After his departure from the Netherlands, he had been engaged by Gustavus Adolphus to assist in the establishment of a Swedish trading company to do business in Asia, Africa, America and Magellica, for which he received a commission from the King, December 21, 1624.[1] Although Usselinx had been a champion of orthodox Calvinism, who could not even regard the Remonstrants but as free-thinkers, heretics, apostates from the Reformed Religion, and enemies of the State, he did not apparently scruple to work for the extension of the Swedish power and consequently of the Lutheran faith, whose bishops and ministers he endeavored especially to interest in the project, "the good means, which God has

[1] Col. Docs. N. Y. xii. 1-2.

(106)

graciously granted and given to the Honor of his Name, and the growth of his Church." Through this company, he argued, the "glory of God would be much increased, His blessed Word and holy Gospel planted and spread among all kinds of people, and many thousand souls would be brought to the true knowledge and understanding of God, who until now have lived and still live in dreadful heathenish idolatry and great wickedness." Usselinx did not limit the inducements to motives of this highly spiritual order. The bishops and the inferior clergy with all other classes of society were to profit in the prosperity, which the establishment of the trading company would cause in the country; the preferment of the more learned of the clerical body "to dignities and positions" was thus to be promoted.[1] At the same time, Usselinx tried to move the Huguenots of France and also "all good Netherlanders, who for the sake of their faith and the freedom of the Netherlands have been exiled from Brabant, Flanders and the Walloon country and dispersed throughout Europe," to subscribe to his great commercial project.[2] In spite of all these efforts, the sum of only 110,000 Dalers was realized by subscription.[3] On June 14, 1626, Gustavus Adolphus, King of Sweden, signed the charter, which again insisted that the heathen and the savages were to "be made more civilized and taught morality and the Christian religion by mutual intercourse and trade."[4] Although

[1] Col. Docs. N. Y. xii. 5.
[2] Usselinx. Naerder Bericht, cf. Jameson. Am. Hist. Papers ii. 107-8
[3] Jameson. Ibid. 274.
[4] Col. Docs. N. Y. xii. 7.

Usselinx traveled extensively in the interests of the South Company of Sweden, little was accomplished to advance the realization of the colonial enterprise, which was still more impeded in 1629 by the demand made by the King upon the vessels of the Ship and the South Companies, then united into one.[1] Gustavus Adolphus had entered on his great war in Germany, that three years later led to his death on the field of battle.

Meanwhile, Usselinx had proposed an enlargement of the company, which was to become a great international Protestant association, but the amendment to the charter, drawn up to that effect on October 16, 1632, does not bear the signature of Gustavus Adolphus, whose death occurred three weeks later.   The Mercurius Germaniae of William Usselinx was intended to set forth the advantages of this commercial project to the Germans, whose religious zeal he attempted to enkindle by citing the example of the bishops and pastors in Sweden, where "a special prayer has been composed for this, and is read at public worship and hours of prayer."[2]   In the beginning of 1634, a charter was sanctioned, which in its amplified form also extended its privileges to the German Evangelical Nation. Usselinx now compiled the Argonautica Gustaviana to advocate this project, but the whole scheme collapsed, as far as Germany was concerned, with the defeat of Nördlingen.   He now went to France, but failed in his endeavor to obtain the support of Louis XIII, to whom he represented the South Company as a great

[1] Jameson. Am. Hist. Papers ii. 165.
[2] Ibid.

means to undermine the Spanish power. His attempt
to obtain a union of the West India Company and the
Swedish South Company, for which he received a commission from the Swedish Chancellor Oxenstierna, was
also barren of any result. Although the proposals
addressed to the States General in his memorial of April
21, 1636,were virtually rejected, some Dutch merchants
became interested in the project of a Swedish expedition to the coast of Guinea. As early as June 3, 1635,
the Swedish chancellor had received a letter from
Samuel Blommaert, a merchant of Amsterdam and a
partner in the Dutch West India Company, who requested some information in regard to the Guinea
trade.[1] The negotiations with these Dutch merchants
were not entrusted to William Usselinx, but to Peter
Spiring, another Dutchman in the service of Sweden,
who went to Holland in 1636 to obtain subsidies
for Sweden from the States General. He was also
instructed "to observe whether it might not be possible in this conjuncture to obtain some service in
affairs of commerce or manufactures."[2] In Holland,
Peter Minuit, the former Director General of the West
India Company's Province of New Netherland, was
recommended as the most competent person to give
advice on any enterprise of trade or colonization to
America.[3] Further negotiations led to the organiza-

[1] June 3, 1635. Odhner, The Founding of New Sweden. Hist.
Soc. Pa. Mag. Hist. and Biogr. iii. 273.
[2] Ibid. 274.
[3] Ibid. Brief van Samuel Blommaert aan Axel Oxenstierna.
December 26, 1635, in the collection published by G. W. Kernkamp in Bijdragen en Mededeelingen van Het Historisch Genootschap. Te Utrecht, 29 Deel, 1908, p. 90. Brief van Samuel Blommaert aan Axel Oxenstierna, November 26, 1636. Ibid. p. 104.

tion of a Swedish and Dutch combination, which,
however, had at its disposal very limited resources.
The whole capital invested did not exceed 24,000
florins,[1] of which one-half was subscribed in Holland by
Blommaert and Peter Minuit, and the other half in
Sweden by the three Oxenstiernas-Axel, the Chancel-
or, his brother Gabriel Gustafsen and the treasurer,
Gabriel Bengtson—the Admiral Clas Fleming and Spiring. This company had not been formed to realize the
projected expedition to Guinea, as this was considered
too expensive for its limited resources; it was now
resolved to trade and colonize on a part of the North
American coast, which had not yet been occupied by
either English or Dutch. Usselinx looked with an
unfavorable eye on this small enterprise, which realized
so little the gigantic schemes, that he had planned and
still advocated. He wrote to Beyer, the Queen's secretary: "There is in my opinion little to be obtained
thence but furs, skins and tobacco, which gave good
profit when it was worth as many gulden as it is now of
Lubeck shillings, besides the filthiness of it is to honorable people a great drawback, seeing how injurious it is
to the health."[2]

Two small vessels of the United South and Ship
Company, the Kalmar Nyckel and Gripen, were chartered and the whole expedition placed under the
charge of Peter Minuit, while Samuel Blommaert was
to remain in Holland as the commissary of the Dutch

[1] It finally took thirty-six thousand florins to fit out the expedition. Cf. Blommaert's letter to Axel Oxenstierna, January 6 1838,
G. W. Kernkamp in Bijdragen en Medeelingen van Het Historisch
Genootschap. Te Utrecht, 29 Deel, 1908, p. 146.
[2] Usselin to John Beyer, March 16, 1639. Ibid p. 147, note 1.

Swedish Company in Amsterdam. The Dutch partners of this corporation, who were also associates in the
West India Company, no doubt wished to avoid all col-
lision with the Company, and the letters of Blommaert
speak of this expedition as the "voyagen till Florida."[1]
This is also the title given to the instructions for Peter
Minuit, preserved in the Archives of the Kingdom of
Sweden at Stockholm. Sprinchorn concluded from the
fact that the document is without a signature, that
these instructions can only be regarded as an outline of
a plan for this expedition. According to this document, if Minuit was able to sail from Gottenburg
early in the year, he was to proceed directly to the "Ile
de Sable" and take possession of it on behalf of the
Crown of Sweden. Then he was to trade with the
Indians along the coast, while on his way to the South
River, where he was to take possession of a well-defined
tract of territory to be called by the name of Nya Sverige.[2] Only after the conclusion of commercial relations
with the Indians there, was the smaller vessel to be despatched to take possession of Florida and thus the
expedition also took upon itself the character of a hos-

[1] Blommaert, January 14, 1637, informed the Swedish Chancellor that Spiring and he had "goetgevonden een compagnie te for-
meren om te bevaeren en behandelen de custe van Florida te Terra
Nova." G. W. Kernkamp in Bijdragen en Mededeelingen van Het
Historisch Genootschap (te Utrecht), 29 Deel. 1908. p. 106. He
sent Minuit with "alle pampieren en becheiden, dienende tot een
voyage naer Florida en bygelegen landen." Letter, February 11,
1637. Ibid. 107. He wrote repeatedly to the Swedish Admiral
Fleming "wegen onse equipage naer Florida." Letter, June 6,
1637. He urged the expedition to sail "om vóor September de
kust van Florida aan te doen." Letter, September 9, 1637.
Ibid. 132.

[2] There is no evidence in Blommaert's letters to Oxenstierna,
that he knew of this intended settlement on the South River before
the actual occupation of this land by Minuit.

tile demonstration against Spain, whose adherents were to be "boldly attacked" wherever found, whereas the Dutch and English residing in New Sweden were to be treated as friends. The enmity towards Spain is still more patent in certain instructions, that amount practically to organized piracy against Spanish vessels in the waters of the West Indies.[1]

Minuit sailed from Gottenburg late in the fall. After stopping in the Dutch port of Medemblik, he directed his course to the South River, where he arrived early in 1638. The Director of New Sweden immediately purchased from the Indians a small piece of land at Paghahacking, upon which he later built a fort named Christina in honor of the young Queen of Sweden.[2] Although the Dutch at Fort Nassau further up the river and the provincial authorities protested against the advent of these colonists as an intrusion into territory within the Province of New Netherland, the Swedes, according to the orders of the Directors in Holland, were to be permitted on the conquest of New Sweden to hold the land upon which Fort Christina stood, with a certain amount of garden land for the cultivation of tobacco, "as they seem to have bought it with the knowledge and consent of the Company."[3] Yet the Chamber of the West India Company at Enck-

---

[1] Sprinchorn. The Hist. of the Colony of New Sweden. Penna. Mag. of Hist. and Biogr. viii. 254, note 1. Blommaert frequently included the capture of good Spanish prizes in West India waters in his projected instructions for Minuit and in his communications to the Swedish Chancellor. Cf. letters, ed. by Kernkamp in Bijdragen, etc. 29 Deel. pp. 122, 128-9, 133, 139.
[2] Details in Blommaert's letters: September 4, 1638, Ibid. pp. 157-8, November 13, 1638. Ibid. 161-167, January 28, 1640. Ibid. 170-189.
[3] Col. Docs. N. Y. xii. 90.

huysen seized a heavily laden Swedish ship arriving at
Medemblik in the fall of 1638 on the plea of illegal
trading within the Company's American territory.
The ship was released only at the command of the
States General in order to avoid any complication with
Sweden at the time.

The first period of the history of New Sweden
reflects the Dutch and Swedish elements in the constitution of the Company. However, the influence of
Sweden predominated from the very beginning. This
was largely due to the fact that its colonial expeditions
had to be organized in Sweden and carried out under
the Swedish flag on account of the fear of the Dutch
West India Company's power in Holland. The Directors in fact felt that Samuel Blommaert[1] and his associates, "although members of the same college," were
doing more harm than good. During the first years of
the colony's existence, there was a good percentage of
Dutch immigration into New Sweden. In fact, the

[1] Blommaert himself had scruples on account of his activity in
the Swedish project of colonization, as director of the West India
Company, even while he thought it was directed to the Florida
coast. He did not allow his subscription to be inscribed in his own
name but in that of Minuit. Letter, May 6, 1637, Bijdragen, etc.
p. 116-117; July 23, 1637, Ibid. 125. This may have led Blommaert to suggest the erection of a chamber of the West India Company in Gottenburg instead of an independent company, but this
was not done. Cf. Letter, August 22, 1637. Ibid. p. 130. When he
learned of the settlement on the Delaware, he communicated his
fears to the Swedish Chancellor, that he might have to suffer in consequence of a protest probably to be addressed to the States General
by the West India Company against this intrusion into its territory.
He then indicated the line of defense to be taken by the Swedish
Ambassador. The land between South River and Charles River
"is tot sonder possessie zewest," so that Minuit founded New
Sweden there. Cf. Letter, September 4, 1638, Ibid. 157; November
13, 1638, Ibid. p. 162. Aitzema. Staat en Oorlogh, p. 247. O'Callaghan, ii, 573.

first colonization under Minuit was almost entirely Dutch. Lieutenant Mans Kling, who was left in command of the twenty-three men in Fort Christina, when Minuit[1] sailed in the fall to the West Indies, is the only Swede expressly mentioned amongst the first colonists. This is probably the reason why no Swedish clergyman of the Lutheran faith accompanied the first expedition. The exclusive occupation of the colonists in the fur trade, which caused "about thirty thousand florins injury" to the Dutch West India Company in the first year, nearly proved the ruin of the colony. In the second spring, they found themselves under the necessity of choosing either to remain and perish, or to abandon New Sweden and seek relief with the Dutch. The authorities at Manhattan assured them a cordial welcome.

This happy solution of the Swedish question for New Netherland was prevented by the timely arrival of a new Director in the person of Peter Hollander with a goodly number of colonists and fresh provisions. The new members of the colony were mainly Swedes, in consequence of the action of the Swedish government, which had ordered the deportation of Swedish married soldiers with their families, who had evaded service or were guilty of some offense, under promise to permit them to return in two years. The spiritual wants of the Swedish population found their provision in the ministration of the Lutheran clergyman, Reorus Torkil-

---

[1] Minuit perished in a hurricane while visiting a Dutch captain in his ship Het Vliegende Hert. According to instructions, he was cruising for a rich Spanish prize. Blommaert to Oxenstierna November 13, 1638 and January 28, 1640, Bijdragen, pp. 161; 177-8.

lus, from Ostergötland, who labored in the colony until
his death in 1643. In the beginning of the same year,
which witnessed the organization of the first Swedish
Lutheran Church in America, Hendrik Hoogkamer and
associates from Utrecht[1] obtained a charter to establish
a settlement under the Crown of Sweden on the South
River, where they were authorized to take up as much
land on both sides of the river as they needed, but not
within "at least four or five German miles from Fort
Christina." The "unrestrained exercise of the so-
called Reformed Confession" was guaranteed to these
Dutch colonists, upon whom also devolved the support
of their ministers and schoolmasters with "a care of the
religion, instruction and conversion of the savages."[2]
A commission was also issued for Joost van Bogaerdt
as special commandant of the Dutch colony at an annual salary of two hundred Rix Dalers, "to be remitted
to his banker in Holland" by the Swedish resident at
The Hague. Bogaerdt arrived in New Sweden in the
fall of 1640 and settled three or four miles below
Christina. In the following year, a contingent of
"roaming Finns" and others, collected by Mans Kling
arrived in New Sweden, and increased the Lutheran
population of the colony.[3] The Swedes had purchased
additional land from the Indians and attested the sovereignty of their Queen in the purchased territory by the
erection of "the arms and crown of Sweedland." On the

---

[1] Cf. Blommaert to Axel Oxenstierna, January 28, 1640. Bijdragen, etc. pp. 173-4; Memorie van de Heer Hoochcamer on dem
Heer Resident Spierinck te Verthoonen. Ibid. pp. 189-192;
Gegenbedencken eingebrachtes Memorial, etc., Ibid. pp. 192-193.
[2] Hazard Annals, 51 seq. Odhner, 400-2.
[3] Odhner, C. T., Ibid. The Founding of New Sweden, Pennsylvania. Mag. of History and Biography, iii. 418.

arrival of Mans Kling, further purchases were made, so
that the Province extended "from the borders of the
Sea to Cape Henlopen in returning southwest towards
Godyn's Bay; thence towards the great South River, as
far as the Minquaaskil, where Fort Christina is constructed; and thence again towards South River, and
the whole to a place which the savages call Sankikah,"
now Trenton Falls.[1]

By this time the Dutch Swedish Combination, that
had been organized for the purpose of trade and colonization on the American coast, not yet occupied by
either the Dutch or the English, was transformed into a
national trading company of Sweden. The first step
towards the complete nationalization of the company
was the permission granted to the old Ship and South
Company of Sweden to embark its capital in this
association in return for a monopoly of the tobacco
trade in Sweden, Finland or Ingermanland.[2] When
the Dutch partners showed some opposition to the
plans of trade and colonization, pursued by the Swedes,
the government resolved to buy out the Holland partners, "since they are a hindrance." The Swedish resident at The Hague was instructed to pay 18,000 guldens
of the subsidies obtained from the States General to the
Dutch associates, on the condition that they abandon
all further claims.[3] This marks the second period of
the history of New Sweden.

A new company was now formed under the name of

---

[1] Col. Docs. N.Y. xii. 28 note.
[2] January 12, 1641. Ibid. 21-22.
[3] February 20, 1641. Kammararkivet. Odhner, o. c. Penna.
Mag. History and Biography iii, 400.

the West India, America, or New Sweden Company, which commissioned John Printz, a soldier of the Thirty Years' War, as the new Governor of the Crown's province in America. His instructions commanded him to "labor and watch that he render in all things to Almighty God the true worship which is his due, the glory, the praise, and the homage which belong to him, and to take good measures that the divine service is performed according to the true confession of Augsburg, the Council of Upsala, and the ceremonies of the Swedish church, having care that all men, and especially the youth, be well instructed in all parts of Christianity, and that a good ecclesiastical discipline be observed and maintained." In spite of this establishment of the Swedish Lutheran Church in the Province of New Sweden, the Dutch colonists, who had come there under the authority of the Crown of Sweden, were not to be disturbed in the rights, which had been guaranteed them in religious matters by their charter.[1] Printz was also instructed to treat the Indians "with much humanity and kindness" and try to convert them from their idolatry and "in other ways" to bring them to civilization and good government.[2] This zeal for religion led to the reinforcement of the ministry of the colony by the Reverend John Campanius Holm, who arrived, with the new Governor at Fort Christina on February 15, 1643.[3] While Printz strengthened his

[1] O'Callaghan, History of New Netherland. Cf. Hazard's Register of Penn. iv. 177, 178, 200, 219, 220, 221, 314, 373.
[2] Keen, New Sweden in Narrative and Critical History of America, ed. Justin Winsor. iv. 453. Acrelius, History of New Sweden, 35-39.
[3] Odhner, The Founding of New Sewden. Penna. Mag. History and Biography, iii. 409.

hold upon the South River by the erection of a strong
fort of heavy hemlock logs, called New Gottenburg, on
the Island Tinicum, about twelve miles below Philadelphia, and later of another fort on the east shore of
the bay near Salem Creek, sickness was weaken-
ing the population. During the summer, seventeen of
the male emigrants died, amongst whom was the first
pastor of the colony, the Reverend Reorus Torkillus.[1]
Thus the colonial ministry was again reduced to one
Swedish minister. About this time, the chancellor
Brahe wrote to Printz, hoping that he would "gain firm
foothold there and be able to lay so good a foundation
in tam vasta terra septentrionali, that with God's
gracious favor the whole North American Continent
may in time be brought to the knowledge of His Son
and become subject to the crown of Sweden." The
Chancellor further gives expression to his fear that the
Swedish colonists might be contaminated by the religious ideas and practices of the English and Dutch.
Therefore, says he, "adorn your little church and priest
after the Swedish fashion, with the usual habiliments
of the altar, in distinction from the Hollanders and
English, shunning all leaven of Calvinism," as "the outward ceremonial will not the less move them than others
to sentiments of piety and devotion."[2] The reply of the
Governor to this letter reveals the measures adopted by
the authorities for the public worship of God in the colony. "Divine service is performed here in the good old
Swedish tongue, our priest clothed in the vestments of the
Mass on high festivals, solemn prayer-days, Sundays, and

[1]Keen, 458. Narrative and Critical History of America. 12
[2]Keen, Ibid. 459.

Apostles' days, precisely as in old Sweden, and differing in every respect from that of the sects around us. Sermons are delivered Wednesdays and Fridays, and on all other days prayers are offered in the morning and afternoon; and since this cannot be done everywhere by our sole clergyman, I have appointed a lay-reader for each place, to say prayers daily, morning and evening, and dispose the people to godliness. All this has long been witnessed by the savages, some of whom we have had several days with us, attempting to convert them; but they have watched their chance, and invariably run off to rejoin their pagan brethren."[1] Campanius Holm in course of time succeeded in acquiring a knowledge of the Lenni-Lenape tongue, into which he translated Luther's catechism; the work was begun at Tinicum, but completed after his return to Sweden in 1648.[2] His efforts to convert the savages bore little fruit. He confessed that he only succeeded in convincing them of the relative superiority of the Christian religion.[3] The building activity, which followed the burning of New Gottenburg, also included the erection of a church on the Island of Tinicum, which was decorated according to the means at the disposal of the Governor "after the Swedish fashion." This church, with the burying ground adjoining, was consecrated by the Reverend Campanius Holm, September 4, 1646.[4] The arrival of two Lutheran clergymen, Lars Carlson Lock and Israel Fluvian-

[1] Keen. Narrative and Critical History of America, iv. 459.
[2] The catechism was printed at Stockholm in 1696. A copy is in the library of Am. Phil. Soc.
[3] Cf. Campanius Holm (grandson of minister). Description of New Sweden. Translation by Du Ponceau, Penn. Hist. Soc. Memoirs, iii. Separate edition, 1834.
[4] Keen, l. c. 461.

der, the son of Printz's sister, in the fall of the next year made it possible for the old minister to leave for the fatherland in the spring of 1648.[1] Israel Fluviander (Holgh?) either died or left New Sweden early in the year, as Lock was then the only clergyman residing in the Province.[2]

Printz himself was anxious to be relieved from the burden of his office. He wrote to this effect to Peter Brahe in 1650, promising his successor as good a position in the colony as he could find in Sweden. "I have taken possession of the best places, and still hold them. Notwithstanding repeated acts and protests of the Dutch, nothing whatever has been accomplished by them; and where on several occasions, they attempted to build within our boundaries, I at once threw down their work; so that, if the new governor brings enough people with him, they will very soon grow weary and disgusted, like the Puritans, who were most violent at first, but now leave us entirely in peace."[3] The necessity of strengthening the authority of Sweden on the South River by new settlements of Swedes, who were still few in number, became most patent in the following year, when Stuyvesant, instructed to maintain "the rights of the company," which was then contemplating a settlement of the boundary question between the two jurisdictions, invaded New Sweden with a force of one hundred and twenty men, who were joined at Fort Nassau by eleven sail. This post was dismantled and a new fort was erected on the west bank of the river,

[1] Sprinchorn, History of Colony of New Sweden, Penn. Mag. of History and Biography, viii. 22.
[2] Ibid. p. 245.
[3] Keen, Narrative and Critical History of America, iv. 466.

between Forts Christina and Elfsburg near the present
site of New Castle, which was called Fort Casimir,
where twenty-six families settled. As a result of Stuyvesant's activity, Printz had to abandon all but the three
principal posts: New Gottenburg and Christina on the
South River, and Nya Korsholm on the Schuylkill. At
this time, New Sweden counted a population of about
two hundred souls, who could attempt nothing against
the Dutch with the resources at their disposal.[1] The
precarious situation of the Province, where nothing had
been heard from Sweden for four or five years, finally
moved Governor Printz to leave the colony in the fall
of 1653 for Sweden. under promise to return in ten
months or send back a vessel and cargo.[2] Meanwhile,
a new expedition had been organized, and on February 2,
three hundred and fifty emigrants, including women
and children, sailed for the South River from Sweden,
where Printz arrived only in April. Two clergymen,
Petrus Hjort and Matthias Nertunius, accompanied
these new colonists.[3] A number of newly appointed
officials also embarked, amongst whom must be mentioned especially John Claesen Rising, Commissary and
Assistant Councillor to the Governor. He was commissioned as temporary governor, as soon as Printz's
departure from the Province became known in Sweden.
This was shortly after the departure of the expedition
from Gottenburg for America. When Rising arrived off
the Dutch Fort Casimir, and found it defended only by a
dozen soldiers under Gerrit Biker, he thought the time

[1] Keen, Narrative and Critical History of America, iv. 467-68.
[2] Ibid. 470.
[3] Sprinchorn, Carl. K. S., History of Colony of New Sweden,
Penn. Mag. of History and Biography, viii. 22.

had come "for action which it were culpable to neglect."
The Dutch submitted without any show of resistance.
The post was named anew Fort Trinity in honor of the
feastday on which it was captured.[1] The whole South
River was now in the power of the Swedes. When the
Directors of the Dutch West India Company in Amsterdam heard of the capitulation of Fort Casimir, they
ordered Stuyvesant to invade New Sweden as soon as
the ship De Waag, carrying thirty-six guns and two
hundred men, arrived at New Amsterdam.[2] Upon its
arrival, Stuyvesant had completed his preparations and
on August 26, 1655, he sailed with a force of three hundred and seventeen soldiers[3] for the South River, where
the Swedes, barely numbering five hundred souls, after
some resistance submitted to the Dutch.[4]

The condition of the Reformed Church on the South
River had never been satisfactory to the Dutch. The
religious issue, presenting itself on the conquest of New
Sweden, probably accounts for the presence of the
Dutch minister Megapolensis in the expedition, which,
according to Stuyvesant's proclamation,[5] was not only
to promote the welfare of the Province of New Netherland, and its good inhabitants, but also the Honor of
God's Holy Name and the propagation of His Holy

[1] Keen, Narrative and Critical History of America, iv 472-3.
[2] Col. Docs. N. Y. xii. 88-89.
[3] Cf. catalogue of Frederick Muller & Cie. Geographie-Voya-
ages, 1910. Deux lettres originales concernant la prise de forte-
resse Casimir au Zuydt Rivier (Deleware) par les Hollandais sur
les Suédois, en 1655, "Johannes Bogaert schrijver" á Bontemantel,
"den 28 augustij 1655 op de reede van de Menades" et "Int schip
de Waegh den 31 October, 1655,"4 pp. in fol. O'Callaghan gives the
number of soldiers at 600 to 700.
[4] Col. Docs. N. Y. xii. 98-106.
[5] Ibid. 92.

Gospel. These thoughts must have been prominent in the sermon preached to the Dutch troops on the Sunday after the occupation of Fort Casimir.[1] The separatist movement of the Lutherans in New Amsterdam had already entered an acute stage,[2] that boded little good for a religious settlement favorable to the Lutheran Swedes in the subjugated territory. There were then three Swedish Lutheran ministers on the South River: Lars Carlson Lock, Peter Hjort and Matthias Nertunius. It was the intention of the Dutch to expel all three, although they themselves had no preacher to place there, but while the negotiations for the surrender of New Sweden were pending, news of a serious outbreak of Indian hostility at New Amsterdam made it imperative for the Director General to conclude matters on the South River and return to Manhattan as soon as possible.[3]

These troubles made him consent to the seventh article of the capitulation, stipulating that "those who will then remain here and earn their living in the country, shall enjoy the freedom of the Augsburg Confession, and one person to instruct them therein."[4] When the West India Company received the account of these proceedings, the Directors did not hesitate to let Stuyvesant know that they would have preferred an unconditional surrender, as "what is written and surrendered in copy can be preserved for a long time and

---

[1] Col. Docs. N. Y. xii. 101.
[2] Cf. infra. chap. iv.
[3] Megapolensis and Drisius to Classis of Amsterdam. August 5, 1657. Eccl. Recs. N. Y. i. 395-6.
[4] Ibid. i. 395-6. Col. Docs. N. Y. i. 608.

sometimes appears at the most awkward moment."[1] However, the interests of the Reformed Church were also safeguarded by the oath, which the Director General imposed upon his vice-director on the South River, Jean Paul Jacquet. He had to promise and swear to maintain and advance as much as possible "the Reformed Religion, as the same is preached here and in the Fatherland conformably to God's word and the Synod of Dort."[2] The two ministers, Peter Hjort and Matthias Nertunius, who had been stationed at Fort Casimir and Fort Christina, were sent to New Amsterdam, and finally transported, with Governor Rising and others who refused to submit to Dutch authority, to Europe. Thus the Reverend Lars Carlson Lock was the only Lutheran clergyman, who remained to minister to the Swedes and Finns, of whom at least two hundred lived on the river above Fort Christina. The Dutch ministers of New Amsterdam do not give a very flattering report of this man. "This Lutheran Preacher is a man of impious and scandalous habits, a wild, drunken, unmannerly clown, more inclined to look into the wine can than into the Bible. He would prefer drinking brandy two hours to preaching one . . . Last spring this preacher was tippling with a smith and while yet over their brandy, they came to fisticuffs and beat each others heads black and blue; yea, the smith tore all

---

[1] Col. Docs. N. Y. xii. 119.
[2] Ibid. 117. This same oath (accidental changes of a word here and there) was taken by William Beeckman, appointed Commissary of the West India Company on the South River, July 30, 1658, by the Director General and Council.

clothing from the preacher's body, so that this godly minister escaped in primitive nakedness."[1]

The minutes of the administration of Jean Paul Jacquet, the vice-director on the South River, refer to this minister as the ecclesiastical deputy in matrimonial cases.[2] Under Jacquet's successor, William Beeckman, the Swedish minister came into a conflict with the authorities on account of his action in these matters, which was at variance with Dutch legislation on matrimony. Lock was fined fifty guilders early in 1660 for marrying a couple without the publication of the banns and against the will of the parents. One of the Swedish commissaries, Oele Stille, contended that the matter was not within the jurisdiction of the vice-director, who had nothing to do with the Swedish minister, but that the correction of such affairs belonged to the consistory of Sweden.[3] Trouble of a more serious nature arose for the Reverend Lars Carlson Lock, when he attempted a second marriage with a young girl of seventeen or eighteen years after he had obtained a divorce, subject to Stuyvesant's approbation, from his former wife, who had fled in a canoe with a depraved character named Jacob Jongh.[4] On April 14, 1662, he was informed by Beeckman that his marriage was illegal, as he had married himself, which was contrary to the law of matrimony; that he ought to have first asked and obtained a divorce from superior authority according to the laws of the fatherland. A heavy fine was imposed on him for taking an inventory of

[1] Megapolensis and Drisius to Classis of Amsterdam. August 5, 1657. Eccl. Recs. N. Y. i. 395-6.
[2] August 9, 1656. Col. Docs. N. Y. xii. 150-151.
[3] Wm. Beeckman to Stuyvesant, April 28, 1660. Ibid. 307.
[4] Ibid. 355, 357, 358-60.

the belongings left by Jacob Jongh, who was indebted
to the company to the extent of two hundred and forty
guilders,[1] but Lock appealed to Stuyvesant for pardon
and a remission of the fine, as his offense was due to
ignorance. His self-marriage had been performed with
out any bad intention and he would have willingly submitted to the usages of the Reformed Church, if they
had been known to him.[2] Acrelius states that Lock,
who had been suspended from the exercise of his ministry some time, finally obtained a confirmation of his divorce from Stuyvesant, who also approved his second
marriage. He was then again permitted to exercise
his ministerial office among the Swedes.[3]

Another Lutheran minister came to the colony, a
year after the conquest of the Province, in the ship
Mercurius, which had sailed with eighty-eight emigrants
from Gottenburg before the cessation of the Swedish
rule.[4] Although Stuyvesant was unable to prevent
the emigrants from disembarking, he had Herr Matthias
returned to Sweden in the same ship.[5] The vice-director did not allow his two sons, born during his administration on the South River, to be baptized by the
Lutheran minister,[6] but he continually urged the
appointment of a Dutch Reformed minister in that
region as a means of promoting immigration thither.

[1] Minutes of Court at Altona, April 14, 1662. Col. Decs N. Y.
xii. 366.
[2] Lock's petition to Stuyvesant, April 30, 1662. Ibed 367.
[3] Acrelius, History of New Sweden. Historical Society of Pennsylvania. Memoirs, xi. 100-101.
[4] Sprinchorn, History of the Colony of New Sweden, Pa. Mag.
of History and Biography, viii. p. 145.
[5] Acrelius, History of New Sweden. Historical Society of Pennsylvania. Memoirs xi. p. 92.
[6] Col. Docs. N. Y. xii. 410. Beeckman to Stuyvesant.

Like his predecessor, he was also bound under oath "to promote the Reformed Religion, as the same is taught and preached in the Fatherland and here according to God's Word and the Synod of Dortrecht."[1] In the absence of an ordained minister, a layman was appointed to read to the Dutch on Sundays from the Postilla. This had been done immediately after the Dutch conquest,[2] and in a letter of January 14, 1660, to Stuyvesant, Beeckman wrote that Jan Juriaens Becker was reading the sermon on Sundays.[3] The limited toleration extended to the Swedes did not include the toleration of other forms of dissent. When a fugitive Quaker from Maryland, Captain Woeler (Wheeler?) did not show the vice-director any sign of respect on the plea that his conscience did not allow it, Beeckman bluntly told him that his conscience could not tolerate such a persuasion or sect. Nevertheless; he was ready to tolerate him until further orders from Stuyvesant, provided no other Quakers would follow him into the Dutch jurisdiction; otherwise, he would enforce at once the orders of the provincial government against this sect.[4]

Meanwhile; a new jurisdiction had been introduced on the South River, which, however, was not entirely removed from the control of the Director General of New Netherland. The expenses incurred for the recovery of the South River had put the company deeply in

[1] Col. Docs. N. Y. xii. 220. Council minute, October 28, 1658.
[2] Megapolensis and Drisius to Classis of Amsterdam. August 5, 1657. Eccl. Recs. N. Y. i. 395-6.
[3] Wm. Beeckman to Stuyvesant. O'Callaghan, Cal. Hist. MSS. N. Y. (Dutch), i. 340.
[4] Wm. Beeckman to Stuyvesant, February 15, 1661. Col. Docs. N. Y. xii. 336.

debt to the City of Amsterdam. To liquidate this debt
and at the same time to strengthen the southern boundary of the Province, the Directors of the Amsterdam
Chamber and the Burgomasters of the City carried on
negotiations, which finally resulted in the cession of
Fort Casimir and the territory on the west side of the
river, from Christina Kill to the mouth of Delaware Bay,
to the City of Amsterdam. The Burgomasters, in their
draft of the conditions for the settlement, did not
neglect to provide for religion. They proposed to erect,
in the market-place or some other convenient spot of the
colony; a public building suitable for divine service, a
house for the minister, and also a school, which might
serve at the same time as the residence of the schoolmaster, whose office included the duties of sexton and
psalmsetter. The salaries of both were to be paid provisionally by the City, unless the Company decided
otherwise.[1] In a later draft, the City of Amsterdam
only offered to send there a schoolmaster, who was also
to read the Holy Scriptures and set the Psalms,[2] but the
States General, in its ratification of the report of its committee on the conditions for this settlement, insisted on
the installation of a preacher and consistory as soon as
the colony should number about two hundred families.[3]

By the spring of 1657, from one hundred and
twenty-five to one hundred and eighty immigrants had
settled at Fort Casimir, which now received the name
of New Amstel. Here the vice-director of the City of
Amsterdam Jacob Alrichs, took pu his residence.

[1] Col. Docs. N. Y. i. 620.
[2] Ibid. 631.
[3] Ibid. 637.

In the absence of a clergyman, Evert Pietersen, who had accompanied the settlers in the capacity of Schoolmaster and Comforter of the Sick, "read God's Word and led in singing." When the Directors of the City's colony had collected about three hundred more colonists, they requested the appointment of a minister to accompany them to New Netherland.[1] The Classis of Amsterdam hastened to fulfill their request, as these ministers realized how much diligence and labor were "required to prevent false opinions and foul heresies from becoming prejudicial to the pure truth" in New Amstel, where there were already many "of all manner of pernicious persuasions." They, therefore, seized the opportunity and earnestly urged the Mayor and Commissioners at Amsterdam "to establish some order in opposition to general license." The Mayor and Commissioners readily promised that, as soon as they received information that the sects carried on the exercise of their religion in the colony, they would look into the matter and adopt the measures necessary to prevent such license. At the same time, they protested that they could not force the consciences of men, which the ministers expressly stated they did not desire.[2] About this time, the vice-director, Alrichs, who considered it a scandal for the neighboring people and new-comers not to have either church or minister in New Amstel, insisted in a letter to his superiors in Amsterdam, on the necessity of the presence of a minister in the colony, "that those, who have little knowledge or light, may not

[1] Council minute of Amsterdam. March 9, 1657. Col. Doc. N. Y. ii. 4.
[2] Classis of Amsterdam to Consistory of New Netherland, May 25, 1657. Eccl. Recs. N. Y. i. 378.

become backsliders, and those, who are still weak in the faith, may be further strengthened."[1] Before this letter reached Holland, the Classis of Amsterdam had already called and ordained the Reverend Everardus Welius for this post.[2] On the arrival of the new clergyman at the South River, a church was organized with Alrichs and Jan Williams as elders and with two deacons, one of whom, Pietersen, also performed the duties of a precentor and Comforter of the Sick. Everardus Welius, to the sorrow and grief of the colony, only officiated a short period, as he died on December 9, 1659. During his ministration, the church, which formerly counted only nineteen members, had increased to the number of sixty.[3] A few months before this, the Commissioners of the colony at Amsterdam had an opportunity to make good their promise to repress dissenting worship in New Amstel. The Swedish parson had dared to preach there without permission. On August 22, 1659, they wrote to their vice-director, Alrichs, that he "must by proper means, put an end to or prevent such presumption on the part of other sectaries," "as yet no other religion but the Reformed can or may be tolerated there."[4]

The official orthodoxy of the colony began to give way in 1662 to the urgent necessity of obtaining colonists to repel English encroachments from Maryland. A company of Mennonites projected a settlement within the jurisdiction of the City's colony at the Whorekill on

[1] Alrichs to Commissioners, April 13, 1657.   Col. Docs. N. Y ii. 7.
[2] Acts of Classis of Amsterdam.   Eccl. Recs. N. Y. i. 371.
[3] Col. Docs. N. Y. ii. 111-112.
[4] Ibid. 61.

the South River, and on January 10, 1662, adopted a very curious constitution, consisting of one hundred and sixteen articles, to regulate the affairs of the colony. They unanimously agreed to exclude from the society all clergymen "for the maintenance of peace and concord," as the appointment of one minister would not harmonize so many opposing sects, and the appointment of a minister for each sect was not only impossible, but "an inevitable ruinous pest to all peace and union." Furthermore, they had no need of a clergyman, inasmuch as "they were themselves provided with the Holy Scriptures, which all ministers agreed in pronouncing the best, and which they considered the most peaceable and most economical of preachers." The ministry brought nothing but "an almost endless chaffering and jangling," on the proper interpretation of the Scriptures, which after all were only "efforts to interprete other men's interpretations." They, therefore, believed it wiser "to arrive, by certain and sound reasoning, beyond all uncertain cavil about Scripture, at a right rule for the establishment of good morals and the direction of civil affairs," which might be attained by plenty of schools and sound laws. Nor did they feel the need of the clergy for the administration of the sacraments, as Baptism and the Lord's Supper were to them only "signs or ceremonies becoming rather weak children than men in Christ." Nevertheless, public worship was not to be neglected. On every Sunday and holiday, the inhabitants were to assemble in the morning to sing a psalm and listen to the reading of a chapter from the Bible by some one of the society, appointed in turn. This simple service was then to be concluded by another hymn, after which the court was to assemble for the transaction of public business. Although the society was to be composed of persons of different creeds, each member of the community had to declare his religious persuasion, for "all intractable people, such as those in communion with the Roman See, usurious Jews, English stiffnecked Quakers, Puritans, foolhardy believers in the millenium, and obstinate modern pretenders to revelation" were not admitted into the colony.[1]   In April, twenty-five Mennonite families declared their willingness to settle in the City's colony in New Netherland, if the City would loan each family two hundred guilders in addition to the passage money, for the repayment of which the whole body was to be bound.   The authorities only granted each family a loan of one hundred guilders, including their passage money.[2]   A few months later, the contract[3] between the Burgomasters and Regents of the City of Amsterdam and Pieter Cornelius Plockhoy, the leader of the Mennonite settlers for the South River, was concluded for the tract of land at the Whorekill, which was to be exempt from all taxation for a term of twenty years.   Twenty-five hundred guilders were raised by the City of Amsterdam and loaned to this association, which was also bound in its entirety for the repayment of this debt.

In the summer of the same year, Hinyossa, the successor of Alrichs, who had died in 1659, offered

---

[1] O'Callaghan, New Netherland, ii. 465-9.   Kort Verhaal van Niewe Nederlandt, Gelegenthiet, Natuurlyke Voorrechten byzondere Bequaemheyt tur Vervolkingk, etc.
[2] Col. Docs. N. Y. ii. 176.
[3] Ibid. 176-177.

sixteen or eighteen families, most of whom were
Finns, residing in the jurisdiction of the company,
the free exercise of their religion with other inducements
to attract them to the City's colony.[1] A year later the
colonists of New Amstel, who professed the Augsburg
Confession, with the consent of the Director and Council
of the colony called a Lutheran Swede, Abelius Zetscoorn, to the exercise of the ministry, although he was
not yet ordained at the time. He was accused of baptizing children, while not in sacred orders, but the
testimony of Beeckman, the Company's vice-director,
acquitted him of this charge. The Swedes in the
Company's jurisdiction were also anxious to have his
services as their schoolmaster, for which they offered
him as high a salary as their minister Lars Carlson
Lockenius received, but the Swedes of New Amstel
refused to allow him to accept the offer. There was also
some opposition on the part of Lock, and the Commissaries had to force him to allow Zetscoorn to preach in
the Swedish Church at Tinnicum on the second day of
Pentecost.[2] However, Acrelius states that Abelius
Zetscoorn never presided over any congregation on the
South River as an ordained minister,[3] and Domine
Selyns, in his letter of June 9, 1664, speaks of him as a
person who has changed the Lutheran pulpit for a
schoolmaster's place. Two reasons are advanced by
this minister in the same letter for the speedy appointment of a Reformed minister in the place of Domine

[1] Wm. Beeckman to Stuyvesant, June 21, 1662. Col. Docs.
N. Y. xii. 384.
[2] Ibid. 431-432, 438, 447, 466.
[3] Acrelius, History of New Sweden. Historical Society of
Pennsylvania. Memoirs xi. 101.

Hadson, who had died on his passage to America, both of which manifest the condition of the orthodox faith on the South River at the time. The children had not been baptized since the death of the Reverend Welius, five years ago, and there were many persons in this region with "abominable sentiments," "who speak disrespectfully of the Holy Scriptures."[1] Meanwhile, the Directors of the Company had conceeded to the Burgomasters of Amsterdam all the territory on the west side of the river and a tract three miles wide along the entire east bank. Thus the friction that existed between the magistrates of the City's colony and the authorities of the Company's colony at Altona was happily terminated. Since the death of Alrichs, the whole policy of his successor, Hinyossa, was to claim independence from the control of the Company's authority. He refused to have the proclamations of thanksgiving days sent by Stuyvesant published, and appointed days of thanksgiving in his own name instead.[2]   A settlement of the question became urgent. The cession of this territory was also made in the hope that thus a barrier would be placed to the encroachments of Maryland, by active colonization on the part of the City of Amsterdam as the Burgomasters were bound to transport four hundred settlers thither every year. Although the City had even thought of restoring to the Company the territory previously obtained, the Burgomasters now persuaded themselves to continue and even increase their colonial enterprise, as "there is now as good an opportunity as

[1] Selyns to Classis of Amsterdam. June 9, 1664.   Eccl. Recs. N. Y. i. 550.
[2] Col. Docs. N. Y. xii. 390.

ever can offer for increasing the population with numbers of men, mechanics, etc., from home and from Germany, Norway, East and Westphalia and those countries, to which those of the *Faith* throughout the entire of France, also the Waldenses, have been subjected."[1] The Burgomasters had already received applications from some families residing in the vicinity of Rochelle, who only desired to make sure before their departure that they did not need to be in fear of the Indians. Thus the control of the South River passed into the hands of the Burgomasters of Amsterdam more than a year previous to its surrender to the English.

[1] Col. Docs. N. Y. ii. 201.

CHAPTER V

The Religious Factors in the English Immigration

A constant stream of English immigration into the Province of New Netherland began when the West India Company, under pressure from the States General surrendered, in the fall of 1638, its monopoly of the fur trade, opened to free competition also the other internal trade of New Netherland to colonists of the Province, and extended all these privileges not only to the inhabitants of the United Provinces, but also to their allies and friends who might be inclined to sail thither to engage in the cultivation of the land.[1] Although this English immigration was at first composed only of individual settlers from Virginia and New England, the Provincial government in the year following felt the necessity of assuring itself of their allegiance. The English settlers were, therefore, ordered to subscribe to an oath of fidelity "to their High Mightinesses the Lords States General, his Highness of Orange, and the Noble Director and Council of New Netherland; to follow the Director or any of his Council, wherever they shall lead; to give instant warning of any treason, or

[1] O'Callaghan, History of New Netherland, i. 200-3 (The proclamation is here printed in full.) Broadhead, History of New York, i. 288.

(136)

other detriment to this country that shall come to their knowledge; to assist to the utmost of their power in defending and protecting with their blood and treasure the inhabitants thereof against its enemies."[1]

Meanwhile, the States General continued to demand from the Company a new charter for these settlers, which would correspond to the conditions resulting from this change of its colonial policy. The States General wished to have measures adopted, that would lead to an increase of the population of the Province, so that all danger of its loss through a foreign invasion might be eliminated. At this time, the patroons had made an unsuccessful attempt to obtain greater independence from the Company and a greater restriction of private enterprise in the colony. This was the burden of the new project of colonization which they had submitted to the States General.[2] The West India Company had also submitted a draft of the articles and conditions which were to regulate the future colonization and trade of New Netherland.

The religious legislation of this new charter marks the beginning of a new era in the religious history of the colony. The first charter of this kind made the maintenance of the ministry of the Reformed Church obligatory on the part of the patroons and colonists, which thus obtained a legal recognition as early as 1629, a year after the arrival of the first min-

[1] O'Callaghan, o. c. 208; Alb. Recs, ii. Council minute, August 11, 1639, in O'Callaghan. Cal. Hist. MSS. (Dutch), i. p, 68-69. A month later Captain Underhill and a few families received permission to reside in New Netherland on taking the oath of allegiance. Ibid.
[2] O'Callaghan, History of New Netherland, i. 198-9.

ister of the Dutch Reformed Church.[1] With the extension of the rights of trade and property to foreigners,
there might naturally be expected an increase of dissent. This may be the explanation of the more detailed
religious legislation in the articles proposed by the West
India Company, which recognized the importance of
establishing the proper order for public worship in the
first commencement and planting of the population
according to the practice established by the government of the Netherlands. The decree which followed
is of great interest, on account of the close resemblance
of its phraseology to the decree drafted by Stuyvesant
against the conventicles which later arose principally
amongst the English settlers of Long Island. Although religion was to be taught and preached in the
Province of New Netherland "according to the confession and formularies of unity . . . publicly accepted in
the respective churches" of the fatherland, no person
was thereby to be "in any wise constrained or aggrieved in his conscience," but every person was to be
"free to live in peace and all decorum, provided he take
care not to frequent any forbidden assemblies or conventicles, much less collect or get up any such; and further abstain from all public scandals and offenses
which the magistrate is charged to prevent by all fitting
reproofs and admonitions, and if necessary to advise the
Company from time to time of what may occur there
herein, so that confusion and misunderstanding may
be timely obviated and prevented." The Company

---

[1] Cf. Art. xxvii. The union of minister, schoolmaster and
Comforter of the sick, evidently refers to the Dutch Reformed
Church. Col. Docs. N. Y. ii. 551-7.

then defined the religious duties of the inhabitants still more in detail. Every inhabitant was bound not only to fulfill his civic duties, but also to attend faithfully to any religious charge that he might receive in the churches, without any claim to a recompense. Further each inhabitant and householder was to bear such tax and public charge as would be considered proper for the maintenance of preachers, Comforters of the Sick, schoolmasters and similar necessary officers.[1] This charter with the "New Project" was again referred to the Chamber of the West India Company at Amsterdam and a reconsideration of the entire case of New Netherland with the deputies of the States General recommended.[2] No definite result was immediately attained, and, in the spring of 1640, the deputies of the States General were again instructed to assist in the deliberations of the West India Company and to take special care that no abuse might be introduced under cover of the fifth article, which decreed the administration of justice "in all civil and criminal matters according to the forms of procedure and the laws and customs already made or to be enacted."[3] Two months later the attention of the States General was again called to the affairs of New Netherland, when complaint was made that the West India Company had refused the offers of the Count of Solms, who wished to plant a colony in New Netherland with some of his vassals, who had been driven out of the County of Solms by the war. The patience of the States General was almost exhausted.

[1] Cf. Arts 6 and 8. Col. Docs. N. Y. i. 112.
[2] Ibid. 114-15.
[3] Ibid. 117.

Their deputies to the Assembly of the XIX were to urge free access to New Netherland for the Count of Solms and other inhabitants of those countries. They were also instructed to return with the conditions of such colonization, which the West India Company had been ordered to enact. If the Company failed to submit the new charter for approval and ratification to the States General, their High Mightinesses threatened to grant such a charter independent of the Company through the plentitude of its own power.[1] Finally on July 19, 1640, the new charter of Freedoms and Exemptions was promulgated, of which "all good inhabitants of the Netherlands and all others inclined to plant any colonies in New Netherland" might take advantage. The provisions of this revised charter in regard to religion are much less liberal in tone than the articles that had been proposed before by the Company. The subjection of the Church to the civil authority, which is expressed in all the Confessions of the Reformed Churches, also found its expression in this charter. It reserved to the Company the founding of churches, and to the Governor and Council the cognizance of all cases of religion.[2] The decree renewing the establishment of the Dutch Reformed Church in a negative form emphasizes the hostile spirit of the new constitution of the country towards dissent. *"And no other religion shall be publicly admitted in New Netherland except*

---

[1] Proceedings of States General, May 31, 1640, in Col. Docs. N.Y. i. 118. The house of Solms had a county of about four hundred square miles, situated on the banks of the Lahn, near Nassau, Hesse and Wetzlar. Cf Bouillet, iv. 319   Calvinism was prevalent in that region.

[2] Cf. two last Arts. of the Freedoms and Exemptions. Ibid. 123

the Reformed, as it is at present preached and practiced by public authority in the United Netherlands; and for this purpose the Company shall provide and maintain good and suitable preachers, schoolmasters, and comforters of the sick."[1]

The effect of the concession of this new charter on the religious character of the population of the Dutch Province is well summarized in the description drawn by Father Jogues a few years later. "On this Island of Manhate and its environs there may well be four or five hundred men of different sects and nations; the Director General told me that there were persons there of eighteen different languages." Although the Dutch were very generous in their treatment of Father Jogues, and later of other Jesuit missionaries, they were evidently bent on impressing him with the idea that dissenters from the established religion were only present in the colony on the sufferance of the local authorities, as he had been informed in all likelihood by the Director General himself that the colony had "orders to admit none but Calvinists." However, the Jesuit had observed that there were "besides Calvinists in the colony Catholics, English Puritans, Lutherans, Anabaptists, here called Mñistes, etc."[2] Ten years later, the diversity of religious opinion amongst the inhabitants of the Province is still more emphasized in the remonstrance which Domine Megapolensis sent to the Classis of Amsterdam as a protest against the admission of the Jews into the Province of New Netherland. "For as we have here Papists, Mennonites and Lutherans among the Dutch;

[1] Col. Docs N. Y. i. 123.
[2] Doc Hist. N Y. iv. 15. Jes. Rels. ix.

also many Puritans or Independents, and many athe-
ists and various servants of Baal among the English
under this government, who conceal themselves under
the name of Christians; it would create still greater
confusion, if the obstinate and immovable Jews came
to settle here."[1] It may be interesting to note that the
religious situation remained practically the same even
after the cessation of Dutch rule. Governor Andros
reported in 1678 that there were "religions of all
sorts, one Church of England, several Presbyterians and
Independents, Quakers and Anabaptists, of several
sects, some Jews, but Presbyterians and Independents
most numerous and substantial."[2] Eight years later
Governor Dongan affords a still clearer insight into the
diversity of belief and the prevalence of religious indifference. "Here be not many of the Church of England; few Roman Catholics; abundance of Quakers;
preachers, men and women especially; singing Quakers;
ranting Quakers; Sabatarians; Antisabatarians; some
Anabaptists; some Independents; some Jews; in short
of all sorts of opinion there are some, and the most of
none at all."[3] This religious indifference was not
merely a later development under English rule, but a
part of the heritage received from the Dutch.

The concession of the new charter of Freedoms and
Exemptions for New Netherland coincided with the rise
of a migratory movement in New England, where the
poverty of the soil gave the settlers little inducement to
remain. In the words of Winthrop, "many men began

---

[1] Eccl. Recs. N. Y. i. 336.
[2] Col Docs. N. Y. iii. 262.
[3] Ibid. 415

to enquire after the Southern parts."[1] Some began to move into the Dutch jurisdiction; others settled in territories claimed by the Dutch, but placed themselves under English jurisdiction, which, by successive encroachments, had been extended almost to the North River itself. The government of New Netherland was too feeble to do much more than protest against this invasion of its territories. These encroachments were not extended across the Sound to Long Island until the spring of 1640, when some inhabitants of Lynn, "straightened at home," attempted to begin a new plantation at Cow Bay on Long Island under a grant from "a Scotchman named Farrett, the agent of Lord Stirling," who had received a grant of the whole of Long Island in 1635 from the Plymouth Company at the request of Charles I. On their arrival, the arms of the High and Mighty Lords the States General were torn down from the tree to which they had been affixed, and a "fool's face" drawn in their place. Information of these highhanded proceedings led to the arrest and final expulsion of the English settlers, who now laid the foundations of a new plantation, Southampton, on the east end of the Island, unknown to the Dutch authorities.[2] In the year following, several families from Lynn and Ipswich sent agents to Long Island to select a suitable site for a plantation. Challenged by the Dutch, they were led to treat with the Governor of the Province of New

[1] Winthrop's Journal, i. 333. Cf. Frank Strong. "A Forgotten Danger to the New England Colonies." Report of Am. H. A, 1898, p. 77-94

[2] Winthrop's Journal, Hist. of New England, ii. 4-5. (Origin. Narratives of Am. Hist.) Cf. Cotton Mather, Magnalia Christi, and Lechford, Plain Dealing or Nevves from New England.

Netherland about the conditions for a settlement of the English under Dutch jurisdiction. Kieft no doubt thought that settlements of Englishmen, bound by an oath of allegiance to the States General and to the West India Company, would prove a good barrier to further encroachments on the part of New England governments. The English were, therefore, permitted to settle in Dutch territory on equal terms with the other colonies of the Province[1] in accordance with the provisions of the charter of 1640, which became the basis of all future grants from the Dutch to the English. This guaranteed them practically "the very same liberties, both ecclesiastical and civil, which they enjoyed in the Massachusetts."[2] They were not granted, as some historians seem to think, freedom of religion, but freedom of *their* religion. The pronoun is essential and saves the "fair terms" to the English from being a violation of the colonial charter just promulgated by the West India Company. Both the Dutch of New Netherland and the English of New England felt that their religion did not differ "in fundamentals." Robinson himself, the founder of the "New England Way," had declared as early as 1619 "before God and men, that we agree so entirely with the Reformed Dutch Churches in the matter of religion, that we are ready to subscribe to all and every one of the articles of faith of those churches, as they are contained in the Harmony of Confessions of

[1] Journal of New Netherland (1641-1646). Col Docs, N. Y. i. 181; For the conditions of an English colony, Cf. Council minute, June 6, 1641, in Col. Docs. N. Y. xiii. 8.
[2] Winthrop's Journal, ii. 35 (ed. Orig Narratives of Early Am. Hist.)

Faith."[1] In the following year, the New Netherland
Company submitted a memorial to the States General
with the request that Mr. Robinson might be permitted
to depart with four hundred families from Holland and
England to settle under Dutch protection in North
America and "to plant forthwith everywhere there the
true and pure Christian religion."[2] The petition was
denied, as the States General was planning to replace
the old provisional Company by the West India
Company. The consciousness of the "close union and
the congruity of the divine service of the two nations"
found expression even in the year in which these fair
terms were offered to the English of Ipswich and Lynn.
The Reverend Mr. Hugh Peters of Salem, who was sent
to England to negotiate with Parliament in regard to
New England affairs, was also instructed to go, if possible, to the Netherlands to treat with the West India
Company for a peaceable neighborhood with its colony
of New Netherland. According to the fifth article of
the propositions which he was to submit to the Company in the name of Massachusetts and Connecticut, he
was to request "that the company, knowing that the
English in America amount to about fifty thousand
souls, may be pleased to inform us in what manner we
can be employed in advancing the great work there,
being of the same religion with themselves."[3] This
feeling of solidarity in religion was also manifested by
the Dutch in the Netherlands. When the Dutch heard

[1] The Canons of the Synod of Dort. Robinson, Apology 6, in
Brodhead, Hist. of N. Y. i. 119-120.
[2] Col. Doc. i. 94-95, cited by O'Callaghan, Hist. of New Netherland, i. 84.
[3] Col Docs. N. Y. ii. 150-1.

that the Westminister Assembly "had agreed upon a
certain plan of church government, practically the same
in most points as that of the Reformed Church of this
country, and had laid the same before the Parliament of
England . . . for approval," they experienced great
gladness and singular "satisfaction" in "the assurance
that between the English Church and our Church there
should be effected a similar form of government."[1]
Even the triumph of Independency over Presbyterianism in England did not change this friendly feeling of
the Dutch towards the English Puritans. Upon the
restoration, the States General of the United Provinces
permitted "all Christian people of tender conscience in
England and elsewhere, oppressed, full liberty to erect
a colony in the West Indies between New England and
Virginia in America..on the conditions and privileges
granted by the committees of the respective chambers
representing the Assembly of the XIX..Therefore, if
any of the English, *good Christians*..shall be rationally
disposed to transport themselves to the said place
under the conduct of the United States, (they) shall
have full liberty to live in the fear of the Lord."[2]
Thus both English Congregationalists and English
Presbyterians found a welcome in New Netherland,
although the authorities, civil and ecclesiastical, of the
Province naturally favored the latter, whose agreement
with the Reformed Church was not limited to "fundamentals," but also extended to church polity in detail.

When the Court of Massachusetts learned of the
intention of these families in Lynn and Ipswich to set-

[1] Synods of North and South Holland, Eccl Recs. N. Y. i. 192.
[2] Doc. Hist N Y. iii. 37-39.

tle in Dutch jurisdiction, the magistrates did not object to their departure from their present place of residence, nor did they try to dissuade them from their project on religious grounds. The matter was discussed from a purely political point of view. "The court were offended and sought to stay them, not for going from us, but for strengthening the Dutch, our doubtful neighbors, and taking that from them which our king challenged and had granted a patent of..to the earl of Sterling, especially for binding themselves by an oath of fealty."[1] The court of Massachusetts was successful in its remonstrance, and the leaders of this movement of immigration "promised to desist." In spite of this, the discussion in the court of Massachusetts was of great importance in the history of New Netherland, as it doubtlessly widely diffused a knowledge of these fair terms for an English settlement under the Dutch throughout New England. Religious persecution on the part of New England authorities would make the argument of the Massachusetts Court less cogent in the minds of the oppressed. In fact, the emigration from New England into the Dutch settlements on Long Island and the mainland was chiefly Presbyterian in character, occasioned by the controversy between the Presbyterians and Congregationalists of New England as to the extent of the Abrahamic covenant in the matter of baptizing the children of those who were not church members. However, also a goodly number of Independents in course of time settled in the English towns in the Dutch jurisdiction.

[1] Winthrop's Journal, ii. 35 (ed. Orig. Narratives.)

Early in 1642, the Rev. Francis Doughty, Presbyterian minister, and his associates obtained a patent from the Director General and Council of New Netherland for a settlement at Mespath on Long Island. Doughty had been a Church of England clergyman. Silenced for non-conformity, he emigrated to Massachusetts in 1637, and settled at Cohannet, now Taunton, where he soon "found that he had got out of the frying pan into the fire."[1] According to the account of Lechford, there was a church gathered in Taunton, comprising ten or twenty to the exclusion of the rest of the inhabitants. Doughty "opposed the gathering of the Church there, alleadging that according to the Covenant of Abraham, all mens children that were of baptized parents, and so Abraham's children, ought to be baptized." In obedience to the request of the ministers of the church, the magistrate ordered the constable to expel him from the Assembly on the plea that he was raising a disturbance. He was then forced to leave the town with his wife and children.[2] Doughty evidently had a following amongst the inhabitants of the town with Presbyterian tendencies who were not church members. Francis Doughty first went to Rhode Island, to which also Mr. Richard Smith, "a most respectable inhabitant and prime leading man in Taunton in Plymouth Colony" came, on leaving Plymouth "for his conscience's sake,

[1] Remonstrance of New Netherland to the States General, July 28, 1649. Care must be exercised in the use of this document, as the author Dr. van der Donck is pleading the case of his father-in-law the Rev. Doughty.

[2] Lechford, Plaine Dealing, p. 91 (ed. J. H. Trumbull).

many difficulties arising."[1]   In the following year, some
English residing at Rhode Island, at Cohannock, and
other places commissioned Doughty as their agent to
negotiate a charter for a settlement under the Dutch
jurisdiction that they might "according to the *Dutch
Reformation* enjoy freedom of conscience."[2]   Kieft
readily granted Doughty and his associates freedom of
conscience *according to the Dutch Reformation* in the
clause of the Mespath patent, which gave them power
"to exercise the *Reformed* Christian Religion and church
discipline, which they profess."[3]   The members of this
colony, which soon numbered eighty persons, employed
Doughty as their minister. As "he had scarcely means
enough of his own to build a hut,"[4] his associates prepared a bowery for him in the colony, upon the proceeds
of which he was to live, while he discharged in return
the duty of preacher among them.[5]

In the autumn of the same year, John Throgmorton,
who had left Massachusetts on account of religious persecution, of which "fiery" Hugh Peters judged him as
worthy as Roger Williams, requested Kieft for permission to settle under his jurisdiction with thirty-five families and to live in peace, "provided they be allowed to

[1] This is the testimony of Roger Williams in 1679. Cf. Riker,
Annals of Newtown, 25, note 1; also Flint, Early Long Island, p. 164,
note 1.
[2] Tienhoven's answer to the Remonstrance of July 28, 1649, Col.
Docs. N. Y. i. 424-31.
[3] Book of Patents GG. p. 49, Riker, o. c. 413, O'Callaghan, Hist.
of New Netherland, i. 425.
[4] Lechford in the earlier draught of his account of the Cohannet
strife of Doughty added: "And being a man of estate, when he
came (to) the country, is undone." M. H. S. MS Cf. note 136 of
Trumbull's edition, p. 91.
[5] Tienhoven's answer to the Remonstrance of July 28, 1649. Col.
Docs. N. Y. i. 424-31.

enjoy the same privileges as other subjects and to freely exercise *their* religion." The Director General and Council, in virtue of the desires of the Company, granted the petitioners permission to settle in the County of Westchester, which was then known as "Vredeland" or "the land of Peace."[1] The following summer, the patent was issued for the territory that he and his companions had occupied, but it makes no mention of religion.[2] Mrs. Anne Hutchinson, with Collins, her son-in-law, and all her family,also moved, in the summer of 1642, into Dutch territory and settled only a few miles east of the Throgmorton settlement on Pelham Neck near New Rochelle. The memory of her residence there is still preserved in the name of Hutchinson's River, the small stream that separates the Neck from the town of East Chester. The New England authorities understood very well the signification of this secession. Winthrop tells us that "these people had cast off ordinances and churches, and now at last their own people, and for larger accommodations had subjected themselves to the Dutch."[3] The New England mind was inclined to see the hand of God in the calamities which the Indian war brought upon these settlements of wayward Englishmen.

Kieft had provoked a general uprising of the Algonquin tribes against the Dutch by the massacre of the River Indians, men, women and children, who had taken refuge at Vriesendael, Pavonia and Manhattan from the Mohawks in search of the tribute from these

[1] Council minute, October 2, 1642. Col Docs. N. Y. xiii. 10.
[2] Ibid.
[3] Winthrop's Journal, ii. 138.

Indians. The Presbyterian settlement of Mespath was invaded and the settlers "were all driven from their lands with the loss of some people and the destruction of many cattle, of almost all their houses and whatever they had."[1] The colonists now found a refuge during the war on Manhattan Island, where Doughty, supported by the voluntary contributions from the English and Dutch of the City, administered to his flock, who were even allowed the use of the Dutch church in the fort, as they were in agreement with the Dutch Reformed Church "in everything."[2] The English colonists of Westchester County were less fortunate than the people of Mespath. The Indians "came to Mrs. Hutchinson's in way of friendly neighborhood, as they had been accustomed, and taking their opportunity, killed her and Mr. Collins, her son-in-law, and all her family," with the exception of a little grand-daughter, eight years old, who was taken captive. After four years, on the conclusion of peace, she was delivered to the Dutch Governor by the Indians and then restored to her friends in New England. Winthrop states that "she had forgot her own language, and all her friends, and was loath to have come from the Indians."[8] Feelings of pious exultation were expressed at the destruction of Mrs. Anne Hutchinson in the "Rise, Reign and Ruin of the Antinomians," which Charles Francis Adams in the able introduction to his scholarly edition in the Prince Society Publications

[1] Remonstrance of New Netherland to States General. Col. Docs. N. Y. i. 305.
[2] Remonstrance and Answer of Tienhoven, Ibid
[8] Winthrop's Journal, ii. 138; 276-277.

attributes not to Rev. Th. Welde, but to the
pen of Governor Winthrop, with the exception of the
introduction. "God's hand is the more apparently
seen herein, to pick out this woeful woman, to make her
and those belonging to her an unheard-of heavy
example of their cruelty above others."[1] The Indians
then attacked Throgmorton's settlement and killed
"such of Mr. Throgmorton's and Mr. Cornhill's families as were at home; in all sixteen, and put their cattle
into their houses and there burnt them." Fortunately
a boat touched at the settlement at the time of the
Indian attack, to which some women and children fled
and were saved, but two of the boatmen going up to the
houses were shot and killed. The few settlers who
escaped removed again to Rhode Island.[2]

The fate of Captain Daniel Patrick was also considered by Winthrop as a punishment from God.
Patrick had been brought from Holland, where he was
a common soldier of the Prince's guard, and given a
Captain's commission by the Massachusetts Bay
Colony. Although there was little religion or
morality in the soldier, he was admitted a member of
the church of Watertown and made a freeman. Patrick soon "grew proud and very vicious, for though
he had a wife of his own, a good Dutch woman and
comely, yet he despised her and followed after other
women."[3] On the discovery of his evil life, Captain
Patrick removed to Connecticut and, in company with
Robert Feake, began in 1639 the settlement of Green-

[1] Adams, Charles Francis, ed. Antinomianism in the Colony of
Massachusetts Bay, 1636-38.
[2] Winthrop's Journal, ii. 138.
[3] Ibid. 153.

wich on the coast, within twenty miles of the Dutch.
The settlers later bought a title to this region from one
of the neighboring sachems, but the purchase was soon
protested by the Director General Kieft, who had
already secured a formal cession of this territory from
the Indians. For two years, these Englishmen refused to submit to Dutch authority, "having been
well assured that his majesty of England had pretended some right to this soil." However, when
they could no longer "presume to remain thus, on
account of the strifes of the English, the danger consequent thereon, and these treacherous and villainous
Indians, of whom we have seen sorrowful examples
enough," they placed themselves "under the protection of the Noble States General, His Highness the
Prince of Orange, and the West India Company,
or their Governor General of New Netherland."[1]
Now Patrick became guilty of a grave infraction of
New England church discipline, as he "joined to their
church, without being dismissed from Watertown."
When the Indians arose against the Dutch, Captain
Patrick took refuge in the neighboring town of Stamford, to which later a company of one hundred and
twenty Dutchmen came on his promise to direct
them to the Indians. When he failed to fulfil his
promise, he was accused of treachery by the Dutch,
but Patrick replied with "ill language" and finally
spat in the face of a Dutchman. Stung by this insult,
the Dutchman shot Patrick behind in the head as he
turned to go out of Captain Underhill's house, and

[1] Oath of fidelity, April 9, 1642. O'Callaghan, Hist. of New
Netherland. i. 252-3, note. 2.

"so he fell down dead and never spake." The mur-
derer was imprisoned but escaped out of custody.
"This was the fruit of (Captain Patrick's) wicked
course and breach of covenant with his wife, with the
church, and that state who had called him and maintained him, and he found his death from that hand
where he sought protection. It is observable that he
was killed upon the Lord's day in the time of the afternoon exercise, (for he seldom went to public assemblies.)"[1]

In the spring of 1644, another English colony of
Presbyterians settled on Long Island under the
Dutch jurisdiction. When the church of Wethersfield
had been so rent by "contention and alienation of
minds" that the two mediators, sent out by the parent
church of Watertown, "could not bring them to any
other accord than this, that the one party must remove
to some other place,"[2] the seceders obtained from New
Haven the lands that the colony had bought from the
Rippowan Indians, and founded the town of Stamford.
Over thirty families were settled by the fall of
1641. A feeling of dissatisfaction also developed in
some inhabitants of this town, which led to a migration
from Stamford to Long Island. This in all probability
was occasioned by a change in the right of suffrage,
necessitated by the incorporation of Stamford into the
Colony of New Haven, which limited its right of suffrage to church members. The Presbyterians, who had
amongst their number two ministers of their persuasion,
Richard Denton and Robert Fordham, sent a commit-

[1] Winthrop's Journal, ii. 154.
[2] Ibid. i. 307-8.

tee[1] to Long Island in 1643 to purchase lands from the
Indians. Early in the following year, the English were
settled "in the great plain, which is called Hempstead,
where Mr. Fordham, an English minister, had the
rule."[2] The reference to Mr. Fordham very likely is
due to his civil position in the new settlement, as the
ministerial office was not then exercised by him, but by
Richard Denton, who is later described by the Dutch
ministers of New Amsterdam as "sound in the faith, of
a friendly disposition, and beloved by all."[3] It is not
strange, therefore, that the settlement of Hempstead
received a patent with the same religious provisions as
were contained in the patent of Mespath. Thus the
settlers received full power and authority "to exercise

[1] This committee was composed of Robert Fordham and John
Carman.
[2] Broad Advice. N. Y. Hist. Soc. Col. 2d. Ser iii. 257 (1857.)
In 1642 Lechford speaks of him as a minister out of office.
[3] Megapolensis and Drisius to Classis of Amsterdam, October 22,
1657. Eccl. Recs. N. Y. i. 410-11. Cotton Mather writes: "The
apostle describing the false ministers of those primitive times calls
them clouds without water, carried about of winds. As for the true
men of our primitive times, they were indeed 'carried about of
winds', though not winds of strange doctrine, yet the winds of hard
suffering did carry him as far as from England into America: the
hurricanes of persecution wherein doubtless the 'Prince of the
powers of Air' had its influence, drove the heavenly clouds from
one part of the heavenly church into another. But they were not
clouds without waters, when they came with showers of blessings
and rained very gracious impressions upon the vineyard of the Lord.
Among those clouds was our pious and learned Mr. Richard Denton,
a Yorkshire man, who having watered Halifax, in England, with
his fruitful ministry, was by a tempest there hurried into New
England, where first at Weathersfield, and then at Stamford, his
doctrine dropped as the small rain, his speech distilled as the dew, as
the small rain upon tender herb, and as showers upon the grass.
Though he were a little man, yet he had a great soul; his well accomplished mind, in his lesser body, was an Iliad in a nut shell. I think
he was blind of an eye, yet he was not the least among the seers of
Israel; he saw a very considerable portion of those things which the
eye hath not seen. He was far from cloudy in his conceptions and
principles of divinity, whereof he wrote a system, entitled Soliliquia

the *Reformed* religion, which they profess,[1] with the ecclesiastical discipline thereunto belonging." It may be of interest to note that the name of Richard Denton is not found in the list of the patentees.[2]

The history of the early church of Hempstead reveals no polity of the church apart from the government of the town. This close union of things spiritual and temporal is well symbolized in the use of the same edifice both as a church and as a town-house for the transaction of public business. It also was manifested in an order issued by the General Court with the consent

Sacra, so accurately considering the fourfold state of man, in his created purity, contracted deformity, restored beauty and celestial glory, that judicious persons, who have seen it, very much lament the churches being so much deprived of it. At length he got into Heaven beyond the clouds, and so beyond storms; waiting the return of the Lord Jesus Christ, in the clouds of Heaven, when he will have his reward among the saints." Magnalia Christi, i. 398.

His epitaph also gives a flattering estimate:

Hic jacet et fruitur Tranquilla sede Richardus Dentonius Cujus
    Fama perennis erit.
Incola jam coeli velut Astra micantia fulget.
Que multes Fidei Lumina Clara dedit.

Flint, Early Long Island, 126.

[1] Patent, November 16, 1644, printed in Thompson, History of Long Island, ii. 5-6.

[2] It would be of interest to have the question solved of the relation of the document on file in the Public Record Office, London, dated 1628, to the settlers of the village of Hempstead on Long Island The Lord Keeper Coventry has endorsed it: "this letter was set up on the church of Hamsted in County Hertford and delivered by Mr Sanders of the Star Chamber." It is addressed, "Michael Mean-well to Matthew Mark-well at his house in Muse-much parish," from Little-worth, which is the name of a parish in Berks. The letter gives the reasons why the author and some others have decided to go to New England. The objections urged against the Established Church refer both to polity and doctrine. Ceremonies, that have no express warrant in the Word of God, may not be used in the worship of God without sin. On appeal to the works of Cartwright, Penry and Knox, exception is taken to the teaching, that God's predestination resulted from his foreknowledge of good and evil, that Christ died for all men, that all children baptized are saved, that a man may fall away from grace, and that the Sabbath is not a divine institution. N. E. Hist. and Gen. Reg. 1. 398.

of a full town meeting, September 16, 1650, which confessed that "the Contempt of God's Word And Sabbaths is the desolating Sinn off Civill States and Plantations, and that the Publick preaching of the Word, by those that are called therevnto is the Chiefe and ordinarie meanes ordayned of God for the Converting, Edifying and Saveing of ye Soules of the Elect, through the presence and power of the Holy Ghost therevnto promised." The General Court, therefore, decreed "That All persons Inhabiting In this Towne or ye Limitts thereof shall duely resort and repaire to the Publique meetings and Assemblies one the Lords dayes And one the Publique dayes of fastings and thanksgivings appointed by Publique Authority, both one the forenoones and afternoones." Persons, who should absent themselves "w'thout Just and Necessary Cause approved by the particular Court," were to "forfeict, for the first offense, five guilders, for ye second Offense ten guilders, And for ye third Offense twenty guilders." Those who prove refractory, perverse and obstinate, were to be "Lyable to the further Censure of the Court, Eyther for the Agravation of the fine, or for Corporall punishment or Banishment." Finally, persons who would inform the magistrates or the particular Court about the neglect or contempt of this order were to be rewarded by one half of the fine, the other half of which was to be converted to public use.[1] Seven years later, on the growth of Quaker dissent, the Director General approved this order of the General Court of Hempstead and commanded the magistrates of the town to execute

[1] Hempstead Town Recs. i. 56-58.

its provisions against trespassers. This was no doubt done at the instance of the town authorities themselves. The united action of the town authorities and the Provincial Government is also indicative of the sense of the union of the Church of the town with the Reformed Church of the Province. This is also shown by the ministration of Richard Denton in the English Congregation, organized in the capital of the Province, which worshipped in the same church building within the fort as the Dutch and French Reformed. An hour was assigned to them, that would not conflict with the use of the church by the Dutch congregation. The distinction between English Church and Dutch Church is clearly drawn in an ancient book of records in the Briggs family. "Sarah Woolsey was born in New York, August ye 3d, in ye year 1650, August 7, she was baptized in y^e *English church* by Mr. Denton, Capt. Newtown godfather, George Woolsey was born in New York, October 10, 1652; October 12 he was baptized in the *Dutch church*, Mrs. Newton godmother. Thomas Woolsey was born at Hempstead, April 10, 1655, and there baptized by Mr. Denton. Rebeckar Woolsey was born at New York February 13, 1659, February 16 she was baptized in the *Dutch church*, Mr. Bridges, godfather and her grandmother godmother." [1]   This close communion with the provincial Church hardly admits any doubt in regard to the character of the Church of Hempstead, and its minister, who moreover is expressly designated by the Dutch clergyman as a "Presbyterian preacher, who is in agreement with our church in

[1] Briggs, C. A., Puritanism in N. Y. Mag. of Am. Hist. xiii, 42.

everything."[1] However, the inhabitants of the town were not all of the same religious persuasion, even before the manifestation of Quaker dissent. There were some Independents, who listened attentively to the sermons of Richard Denton until he began to baptize the children of parents who were not church members, when they rushed out of the assembly.[2]

In spite of the close union of spiritual and temporal matters, the minister of Hempstead had to complain that he was getting in debt through lack of salary. To the sorrow of the Dutch authorities, he left New Netherland to seek a better living in Virginia.[3] Mr. Robert Fordham seems to have now taken up the work of the ministry in the place of Richard Denton. He also left the town of Hempstead and gave up the exercise of the ministry without the wish and knowledge of the provincial government, which later refused to admit him "in such mennor of comminge againe."[4] Meanwhile, Richard Denton had returned to New Netherland, but the clergy of New Amsterdam was not more successful in inducing him to remain than the Director General who endeavored to ensure him his share of the tithes of the village, if he should again consent to exercise his calling there.[5] He finally went to England to claim a legacy of four hundred pounds, lately left by a deceased friend, which he and his wife could not obtain except

[1] Megapolensis and Drisius to Classis of Amsterdam, August 5, 1657. Eccl. Recs. N. Y. i. 397-8.
[2] Ibid.
[3] Megapolensis and Drisius to Classis of Amsterdam, October 22, 1657. Ibid. 410-11.
[4] Stuyvesant to Magistrates of Hempstead, July 17, 1657, Doc. Hist. N. Y. iii. 118-119; Col. Docs. N. Y. xiv. 396.
[5] Ibid.

by their personal appearance.[1]   The authorities of both
town and Province were anxious to obtain "an able and
orthodox minister."   In 1660, Stuyvesant took advantage of the departure of a New England minister,
Mr. William Leveretts (Leveridge) by boat from New
Amsterdam to acquaint the Directors with the needs of
the English, who had been deprived of religious instruction for some time.   In the spring of 1661, the Director
General was informed that there were many unbaptized
children in Hempstead in consequence of the long vacancy in the ministry of the town.   He promised to send
as soon as possible one of the Dutch ministers to administer the sacrament, "hoopinge and not doubtinge
that yow will use all possible meanes that the
towne may tymely be supplyed with an able and
orthodox minister to the edification of God's glorie
and your owne Salvation."   A few weeks later,
Samuel Drisius visited the town, preached a sermon,
and baptized forty-one children and an aged
woman.[2]   Finally, the services of the Rev. Jonah
Fordham, the son of the old minister Robert Fordham,
who had removed to Southampton, were engaged by the
town of Hempstead.   The minister's salary was fixed at
seventy pounds sterling a year, which was to be raised
by a rate levied on every man in town.   When some
refused "to contribute to the Maintenancy of a Protestant Minister," the magistrates were empowered by the
provincial council "not only to constrain those that are
unwilling, but by further denyal to punish them as they

[1] Megapolensis and Drisius to Classis of Amsterdam, October 22,
1657.   Eccl Recs. N. Y. i. 410-11,
[2] Col. Docs. N. Y. xiv. 497. Stuyvesant to Magistrates of
Heemstede, March 25, 1661.

in aequity shall think meete."[1] In 1663, Hempstead showed its appreciation of the work of Mr. Fordham by voting him, in addition to the ordinary allotments of the inhabitants, an estate valued at £200. On the death of his father, he returned to Southampton, where he labored in the ministry probably until the arrival of the Rev. Mr. Taylor in 1680.[2]

On the termination of the disastrous Indian war in 1645, two English settlements on Long Island succeeded in obtaining a charter. This was evidently formulated by the patentees to avoid a recurrence of New England persecution, to which they had been subjected prior to their removal to New Netherland. At this time, Kieft was ready to make any possible concession that would attract new settlers and retain in the country the old inhabitants, for there was no hope for the improvement of the Dutch Province without an increase of its population, that had been seriously reduced during the Indian war. As the settlers of these two towns were apparently not considered within the pale of the Reformed Church, the Director General was not in a position to grant them the exercise of the Reformed Religion, which alone could be publicly practiced according to the constitutional charter of the Freedoms and Exemptions of 1640. Although he did not guarantee them religious autonomy, he granted them "Liberty of Conscience," which was further defined as freedom from "molestacon or disturbance from any Magistrate or Magistrates, or any other Ecclesiastical Minister, that may extend jurisdiction over them." A precedent for

[1] Council minute, May 16, 1662. Col. Docs. N. Y. xiv. 513.
[2] Thompson, Hist. of Long Island, ii. 21-22.

162 RELIGION IN NEW NETHERLAND

this concession was found in "the Custome and manner of Holland." The settlers of the town of Flushing were the first to receive this concession in their charter. A few months later Gravesend received a charter with the same provision.

The Reverend Francis Doughty had returned to the colony of Mespath upon the termination of the Indian war. Now internal dissensions arrested the progress of the settlement. Doughty claimed the privileges of a patroon and demanded from the settlers payment of their lands and an annual quitrent.[1] His associates, Richard and William Smith, opposed these proceedings because the minister was only one of a number of equal patentees.[2] These contentions probably gave rise to a defamatory song concerning the minister and his daughter, for which William Gerritsen, on June 10,1645, was found guilty of libel and sentenced to stand bound to the May-pole in the fort with two rods around his neck and the libel over his head until the conclusion of the English sermon, and threatened to be flogged and banished, if he should dare to sing the song again.[3] Doughty was evidently then ministering to the English congregation of New Amsterdam, whither he had again returned after a half year's residence in the Mespath Colony. The case between Doughty and his associates was brought before the Provincial Court, and the Director General and Council decided that he had no control

[1] Tienhoven's answer to the Remonstrance, July 28, 1649. Col. Docs. N. Y. i, 424-31.
[2] Council minutes, February 7, March 7, 1646. O'Callaghan, Cal. Hist. MSS. (Dutch), i. 107-8
[3] Council minutes, June 10, 1645. Ibid. 95.

over any other land in the colony than his own farm.
His associates were therefore free to "enter upon their
property." When Doughty threatened to appeal from
the sentence of the Provincial Court, Kieft had the minister arrested, imprisoned for twenty-four hours, and
fined twenty-five guilders. Doughty now endeavored
to obtain permission to leave the Dutch Province, but
this was steadily refused, as he was indebted to the
Company to the amount of eleven hundred florins,
which had been advanced to the minister in goods and
necessaries of life.[1]

Stuyvesant was not the man to compromise the
authority of his predecessor, but he was favorable
enough to Francis Doughty,especially on account of the
destitute circumstances of the English towns, as far as
a religious ministry was concerned. The representatives of Flushing, intimidated by the threats of Stuyvesant,[2] signed a contract with Francis Doughty, who

[1] Remonstrance of New Netherland, July 28, 1649. Col. Docs.
N. Y. i. 341. Representation of New Netherland, Narratives of
New Netherland, pp. 334-335. Answer of Van Tienhoven, November 29, 1650. Col. Docs. N Y i. 424-31. Narratives of New Netherland, pp. 366-8.

[2] This transaction seems to be indicated in the vindication of
Captain Underhill, who gathered together, in 1653, his reasons for
renouncing "the iniquitous government of Peter Stuyvesant over
the inhabitants living and dwelling on Long Island, in America."
He urged against Stuyvesant, that "he hath in violation of
liberty of conscience and contrary to hand and seal, enforced
articles upon the people, ordering them otherwise against the laws of
God and man to quit the country within two months."
Col. Docs. N. Y. ii. 151-2. Underhill's accusations seems to rest
on the religious provisions of the charter granted by Kieft with
its guarantee of freedom of conscience, without molestation from
magistrate or minister and the forced signing of the Articles, as the
contract between Doughty and the church of Flushing is called
in the Court minutes of New Amsterdam. Recs. New Amsterdam,
i. 179. There is nothing else in the early years of Stuyvesant's
directorship that would give any foundation to Underhill's accu-

was thus assured a salary of six hundred guilders a year, to be raised from the voluntary contributions of the inhabitants of the town. Under these circumstances, a conflict might be expected to develop in Flushing. In fact, differences soon manifested themselves and many began to absent themselves from the sermon and refused to contribute their share to the maintenance of the minister.[1] In spite of Stuyvesant's intervention, the salary remained unpaid.[2] The differences even became more pronounced and disturbed the peace and unanimity of the town, which seems to have been rent into two factions.[3] William Harck, the sheriff of Flushing and his associates with the representatives of the opposite party: Thomas Sael, John Lawrence, and William Turner, presented their case to the Director General and Council with the request for a pious, learned and Reformed minister, who was to be supported by the contributions of each inhabitant according to his ability. The Director General and Council admitted the justice of their case and resolved to adopt the measures necessary to promote peace, union and tranquility in ecclesiastical and civil affairs. Doughty's restive nature could not suffer this to pass in

sation. O'Callaghan's insertion "of belief" after articles is misleading. Hist. of New Netherland. ii. 226.

[1] Megapolensis and Drisius to Classis of Amsterdam, August 5, 1657. Eccl. Recs. N. Y. i. 397. In the letter of October 22, they accompany their request for two English preachers with the petition "that direction may be given to the magistracy that the money be paid by the English to the magistrate, and not to the preacher, which gives rise to dissatisfaction."

[2] Mandeville, Flushing, Past and Present. When Doughty instituted a suit for the payment of his salary, it was discovered that the contract had been destroyed, William Lawrence's wife having "put it under a pye." Cf. Flint, Early Long Island, p. 174.

[3] Col. Docs N. Y. xiv. 82.

silence; he attacked the civil authorities from the pulpit. This brought him into conflict with the new Schout, Captain John Underhill, who, in his first official act, ordered the church closed, because the minister "did preach against the present rulers, who were his masters."[1] Doughty remained some years in New Netherland, vainly endeavoring to collect his salary.[2] Finally, he went to Virginia, with the permission of Stuyvesant, who was then accused of exacting a promise from the minister not to complain anywhere of the treatment he received in New Netherland.[3] A few years after Doughty's departure, the Dutch ministers complained to the Classis of Amsterdam that many of the inhabitants of Flushing became "imbued with divers opinions" and it was "with them quot homines tot sententiae."[4] However, the inhabitants were not molested on account of this divergence of private belief until they violated the charter of Freedoms and Exemptions by the public exercise of dissenting worship. In 1656, William Wickendam, a cobbler from Rhode Island, came to Flushing claiming a commission from Christ and found recognition amongst its people. The sheriff himself, William Hallet, placed his own house at the disposal of the preacher for his religious meetings. Here several times he expounded and interpreted God's Holy Word, went with the people into the river and baptized them, and even administered to the sheriff and

---

[1] Waller, Hist. of Flushing, 24-25.
[2] Recs. of New Amsterdam, i. 179.
[3] Col. Docs. N.Y. i. 341, Remonstrance of New Netherland, July 28, 1649
[4] Megapolensis and Drisius, August 5, 1657. Eccl. Recs. N. Y. i. 396-7.

others "the bread in the form and manner in which the sacrament is usually celebrated and given." This was done without any authority, ecclesiastical or secular, contrary to the ecclesiastical rules of the Fatherland and especially to the placards of the Director General and Council, " expressly forbidding all such conventicles and gatherings, public or private, except the usual meetings, which are not only lawfully permitted, but also based on God's Word and ordered for the service of God, if they are held conformably to the Synod of Dort as in our Fatherland and in other churches of the Reformed Faith in Europe."[1] As soon as information of these proceedings reached New Amsterdam, the Fiscal was despatched to Flushing to arrest the preacher and the sheriff. William Hallett was degraded from his office, fined fifty pounds Flemish for neglect of duty, and banished from the Province of New Netherland. A few days later, he petitioned for the remission of the sentence of banishment, which was granted on the payment of the fine and the costs of the trial.[2] William Wickendam, in accordance with the provisions of the placard against conventicles, was condemned to a fine of one hundred pounds Flemish. After the payment of the fine and the costs incurred in his case, he was also to be banished from the Province, but as he was very poor, with a wife and children, and a cobbler by trade, his fine was remitted on the condition that, if he were caught within the province again, he was to pay the fine.

No appeal was made to the charter of the town by

[1] Col Docs. N. Y. xiv. 369-70   Megapolensis and Drisins to Classis of Amsterdam.   Eccl. Recs. N. Y. i. 396-7.
[2] O'Callaghan, Calender of N. Y. Hist. MSS. (Dutch), i. p. 178.

the condemned prisoners for the manifest reason that the charter of Flushing did not guarantee freedom of worship, but freedom of conscience, It was only when this freedom of conscience seemed to be called into question by "an order from the Hon. Director General not to admit, lodge and entertain in the said village any one of the heretical and abominable sect called the Quakers," that the people of Flushing appealed to the right guaranteed in their charter.

Although Gravesend received its charter a few months after Flushing, it had been settled as early as 1643,[1] shortly after the outbreak of the Indian war. The same savages, who destroyed the English settlements on the mainland as far as Stamford, crossed the Sound and assaulted Lady Moody in her house, but they were repulsed repeatedly by the forty men, who had gathered there in the new colony.[2] She had also left fair possessions in New England for conscience' sake. Two years after her arrival in Lynn in 1638, she had received a grant of four hundred acres of land from the General Court.[3] In Salem, she was also the proprietor of a flat-roofed house, but one story high, which had its

[1] Before this there was a small English settlement on Dental (Turtle) Bay, called Hopton, which had been broken up by the Indians. These old settlers joined the followers of Mrs. Moody in founding Gravesend. The former were indifferent in regard to religion, while the latter had left New England precisely on account of their deeply religious convictions, for which they were persecuted there. Under these circumstances "it was resolved to relegate the matter of religion in the new settlement entirely to the individual as a matter with which the organized community had no concern. And so in the laying out of lots no reservation for church purposes was made or intended to be made." Cf. W. H. Stillwell, Hist. of Ref. Prot. Dutch Church of Gravesend, Kings County.
[2] Winthrop's Journal, ii. 138.
[3] Mass. Recs. i. 123.

roof carried off by a high wind in 1646 without injury to
any of the inmates.[1]   Lechford tells us that "the good
Lady was almost undone by buying Master Humphries
farme, Swampscot, which cost her nine or eleven hundred pounds."[2]   Towards the end of the year 1642,
Lady Deborah Moody, Mrs. King, and the wife of John
Tilton were presented at the Quarterly Court "for
houlding that the baptism of infants is not ordained of
God."[3]   The following year, she was also "dealt withal
by many of the elders and others, and admonished by
the church of Salem,whereof she was a member, but,per-
sisting still and to avoid further trouble," she removed
"from under civil and church watch" to the Dutch on
Long Island with many others likewise infected with
Anabaptism.[4]   Under these circumstances, it is not
strange that the inhabitants of Gravesend should also
obtain a charter that granted them "the free libertie of
conscience according to the costome and manner of Holland, without molestation or disturbance from any
Madgistrate or Madgistrates or any other Ecclesiastical
Minister that may ptend jurisdiction over them."[5]   The
patentees received the power and authority to build a
town or towns, which must have excluded any disquali-
fication for the office of a magistrate on the ground of
Anabaptism.   Nevertheless, the Director General Stuyvesant and his Council insisted on a religious qualification for office in their answer to the remonstrance, that

[1] Winthrop's Journal, ii. 289.
[2] Lechford, Plaine Dealing, 98-99.
[3] Lynn Recs. in Flint, Hist. of Early Long Island, 106, [notes
1-2.
[4] Winthrop's Journal, ii. 126.
[5] Doc. Hist N. Y. i. 411.

several acted as officers and magistrates without the consent or nomination of the people.[1] "The English do not only enjoy the right of nominating their own Magistrates, but some of them also usurp the election and appointment of such magistrates, as they please, without regard to their religion. Some, especially the people of Gravesend, elect libertines and Anabaptists, which is decidedly against the laws of the Netherlands."[2] There was, however, no forcing of the conscience in Gravesend until the arrival of the Quakers in the town. Shortly before this, the Dutch ministers of New Amsterdam still classified in their report to the Classis of Amsterdam, the people of Gravesend as Mennonites. "The majority of them reject the baptism of infants, the observance of the Sabbath, the office of preacher and any teachers of God's Word. They say that thereby all sorts of contentions have come into the world. Whenever they meet, someone or other reads to them."[3] In the light of the consistent religious policy of Stuyvesant and the Dutch clergy, this toleration of Mennonite worship, attested in these words of the Dutch ministers of New Amsterdam, is so surprising a fact that it is open to suspicion. Is it a slip of the pen of the writers, occasioned by a description of Mennonite tenets and practices, which were well known to them? In fact, Domine Megapolensis seems to have been as vigilant for the repression of the Mennonites as of other dissenters. The peculiar tenets of their religion in regard to an

---

[1] Remonstrance, O'Callaghan, Hist. of New Netherland, ii. 245.
[2] Deduction by Director General and Council, Col. Docs. N. Y. xiv. 233-35.
[3] Megapolensis and Drisius to Classis of Amsterdam, August 5, 1657. Eccl. Recs. N. Y. i. 396-7.

organized ministry made them as ready to attack a "hireling" ministry, as the Quakers later became. On February 12, 1652, Megapolensis requested the Director and Council to restrain the Anabaptist Anna Smits "from using slanderous and calumniating expressions against God's Word and his servants."[1] Meanwhile, the Quaker movement gained adherents in the town, who soon became the object of a religious persecution. Another party also arose in Gravesend, which appealed, on April 12, 1660, to the Provincial government for relief in their religious destitution. Ten of the inhabitants of the village, only two of whom were English, the sheriff Charles Morgan and Lieutenant Nicholas Stillwell, informed the Director General and Council that "the licentious mode of living, the desecration of the Sabbath, the confusion of religious opinion prevalent in the village made many grow cold in the exercise of Christian virtue, and almost surpass the heathens, who have no knowledge of God and his commandments." They requested, therefore, that "a preacher be sent here, that the glory of God may be spread, the ignorant taught, the simple and innocent strengthened, and the licentious restrained." Stuyvesant and his Council were well pleased with this remonstrance and promised to fulfill their request, as soon as possible, but the English put an end to the Dutch rule before the promise was realized.[2]

The old settlement of Mespath never recovered entirely from the calamities of the Indian war. Even after the reoccupation of the colony, the dissensions

---

[1] Council minute. Col. Docs. N. Y. xiv. 155-6.
[2] Council minute, April 12, 1660. Ibid. 406.

between the colonists and their minister, Francis
Doughty, impeded the increase of its population. In
1652, some New England settlers with some individuals
from Hempstead—all formerly inhabitants of the Connecticut shore—obtained permission from Stuyvesant
to plant a new colony in the vicinity of the old settlement on the lands not yet occupied, which was, therefore, commonly known as Newtown, although its official
name was Middelburg. The privileges of the charter of
1640 were also extended to the new settlement with the
free exercise of their Protestant religion.[1] Some of the
inhabitants were Presbyterians, but the great majority
of them were Independents.[2] Shortly after the foundation of the town, the permission and assistance of the
Director General was obtained to appropriate ground
and to erect a building, which was to serve both as a
church and a residence for the minister.[3] The services
of an Independent John Moore were engaged, who did
not administer the sacraments, as he declared that he
had received in New England only license to preach.
Dissatisfied with the meager and irregular payment
from his hearers, Mr. Moore in 1656 went to the Barbadoes to seek a better living.[4] The Dutch ministers of
New Amsterdam immediately showed their interest in
the religious welfare of Newtown. They wrote to Holland for a minister to supply the vacancy created by
the departure of Mr. Moore.[5] In the absence of a

[1] Riker, Annals of Newtown, 26-27.
[2] Megapolensis and Drisius to Classis of Amsterdam, August 5,
1657. Eccl. Recs. N. Y. i. 396-7.
[3] Riker. Annals of Newtown, 40.
[4] Eccl. Recs. N. Y. i. 396-7.
[5] Onderdonck, H. Jr. Queens County in Olden Times. Am. Hist.
Rec. i. 4.

preacher, "some inhabitants and unqualified persons ventured to hold conventicles and gatherings and assumed to teach the Gospel." Megapolensis and Drisius, therefore, petitioned the Director General and Council, on January 15, 1656, to intervene and provide for the continuance of legitimate religious worship during the absence of Mr. Moore by the appointment of a suitable person to read the Bible and some other orthodox work on Sunday, until other provisions were made. Stuyvesant entrusted the choice of a suitable reader to the two ministers with the advice of the magistrates and the best informed inhabitants of Newtown. At the same time, he expressed his decision to have placards issued against those persons who,without either ecclesiastical or secular authority, acted as teachers in interpreting and expounding God's Holy Word.[1] On February 1, 1656, all religious meetings, except the Reformed, were prohibited under severe penalties.[2] Meanwhile, the wife of John Moore, with her seven or eight children, apparently continued to dwell in the town minister's house. In the beginning of the year 1657, information was lodged with Stuyvesant that some of the inhabitants had in fact given Mr. Moore this house for his private use. The Director General promptly insisted that this house had been built "for a public use and successively for the Ministrij," and ordered the magistrates to submit an explanation of this strange proceeding.[3] Mr. Moore again returned to Newtown and doubtless took up again the work of the

[1] Col. Docs. N. Y. xiv. 336-7.
[2] Recs. New Amsterdam, i. 20-21; ii. 34-35.
[3] Col. Docs. N. Y. xiv. 384.

ministry in the town, but he died on October 13,1657, of a pestilential disease, which was then prevalent in the English settlements of New Netherland and in the towns of New England.[1] Newtown was thus destitute of its ministry at the very time that the "raving Quakers" began "to disturb the people of the province" and "to pour forth their venom."[2] The town feared "that some of the inhabitants might be led away by the intrusion of the Quakers and other heretics." A petition was, therefore, presented in 1661 to the Director General who was requested to aid in obtaining a minister in the place of the deceased John Moore.[3] The inhabitants evidently felt the need "off the publyck meanes of grace and salvation." Although their request for a minister could not be fulfilled, they engaged, doubtless with the consent of Stuyvesant, a schoolmaster for the education of their children "in Scholastical discipline, the way to true happiness," who was also to be their "souls help in dispencinge God's Word" every Lord's day. In return for his services, the town wished to give to Richard Mills the use of the minister's house and glebe, but the town's right to dispose of this house was disputed by Francis Doughty, who had married the widow of the former minister, Mr. Moore, whose salary does not seem to have been paid in full. There was imminent danger that the house and barn, neglected during the course of this dispute, would

---

[1] Megapolensis and Drisius to Classis of Amsterdam, October 22, 1657. Eccl. Recs. N Y i. 410-11.
[2] Megapolensis and Drisius to the same, September 24, 1658, Ibid. 432-33.
[3] Brodhead, Hist. of New York, i. 689-90.

go to rack and ruin for want of repair, to the great injury of religion in the town, which would thus be deprived of these resources for the continuance of a public ministry. Stuyvesant again insisted that the house and land "beeinge with our knowledge, Consent and helpe buildt for the publyck use of the ministry," could not be "given and transported for a private heerytadge." Francis Doughty was, therefore, commanded to give and grant peaceful possession of this house and land to the Schoolmaster Richard Mills, and the magistrates and the inhabitants of the town ordered on their part to give to the heirs of Mr. Moore what was their due.[1] Stuyvesant evidently tried to be very just towards Francis Doughty. On April 20 of the same year, Richard Mills was ordered to deliver to Mr. Doughty, trees, etc., planted and left on the lot of the deceased Mr. Moore.[2] After the surrender of the minister's house, the town thoroughly repaired the building. In the following year, the Reverend William Leverich removed from Huntington, where he had been pastor, to Newtown, which welcomed his advent. Measures were adopted by the town to raise a salary for the new minister. Later the town gave him two parcels of meadow "for his encouragement among them," to which were added twelve acres more at the east end of Long Traines Meadow. The inhabitants now felt the need of a more suitable place of worship, and on January 9, 1663, voted to build a meetinghouse, but the disturbances leading up to the surrender

[1] Col. Docs. N. Y. xiv. 496.
[2] Council minute, April 20, 1661. O'Callaghan, Cal. Hist. MSS. N. Y. (Dutch), i. 223.

of the Dutch Province to England prevented the realization of this design under Dutch rule.[1]

In the meantime, the English had again encroached on the Dutch territory on the mainland. In 1655, Thomas Pell of Fairfield claimed the Vreeland tract in Westchester in virtue of a purchase from the Indians and sold lands there to several persons from Connecticut. The English settlers refused to give heed to the protest of the Dutch, who, in the spring of the following year, sent an armed expedition against the English squatters. Twenty-three were taken as prisoners to New Amsterdam, where most of them submitted to the authority of the Dutch and were permitted again to return to their old settlement under the provisions of the charter of 1640.[2] The inhabitants of this settlement, which the Dutch called Oostdorp, were Independents.[3] The Dutch commissioners, who went there on December 29, 1656, to administer the oath of office to the newly chosen magistrates, witnessed their Puritan service, which was conducted by two laymen, Robert Basset and a Mr. Bayly, probably the ruling elders of the church. The gathering consisted of about fifteen men and twelve women. On the conclusion of a prayer by Mr. Bayly, a sermon of some minister in England was read by Robert Basset. After this, another prayer was said by Robert Basset and a psalm was sung by the congregation, which then dispersed.[4] There was probably no change in their worship while under Dutch

[1] Riker, Annals of Newtown, 53.
[2] Cf. Brodhead and O'Callaghan, passim.
[3] Megapolensis and Drisius to Classis of Amsterdam, August 5, 1657. Eccl. Recs. N. Y. i. 396-7.
[4] Doc. Hist. N. Y. iii. 557-8.

jurisdiction, which was terminated, on its annexation by Connecticut, in the fall of 1663.

In 1656, colonists, mostly from Hempstead, who desired "a place to improve their labors," received land and leave to settle beyond the hills by the South Sea at Canarise. This was the beginning of the village of Jamaica, which was known to the Dutch by the name of Rustdorp. The new settlement enjoyed the usual privileges possessed by the villages of Middelburg, Breuckelen, Midwout and Amersfort.[1] Although Quaker dissent manifested itself in the town of Jamaica a month after the arrival of the Quakers in New Amsterdam, the town at large was of one way of thinking in religion, so that church affairs were considered and transacted at the town-meetings.[2] Drastic measures were adopted by the Director General to stem the Quaker movement, which was also favored somewhat through the lack of an orthodox minister. It was in response to the urgent request of some of the townspeople, that Stuyvesant, in the beginning of 1661, sent Domine Drisius to baptize their children. On this occasion, the Dutch minister preached twice in Jamaica and baptized eight children and two aged women.[3] The position of the orthodox faith was strengthened in the town by the appointment of new magistrates: Richard Everett, Nathaniel Denton, and Andrew Messenger. These men had been informers against the Quakers in town, and Stuyvesant felt that they could be trusted to promote the Protestant cause,

[1] O'Callaghan, Hist. of New Netherland, ii. 323
[2] Onderdonck, H. Jr. Antiquities of the Parish Church, Jamaica. Am. Hist. Rec. i. 27.
[3] Col Docs. N. Y. xiv. 489-90.

that is, to see to the execution of the government's ordinances, prohibitive of the exercise, public and private, of any religion but the Reformed.[1]

In the spring of the following year, the town ordered a house to be built for the minister with the proceeds obtained from the rates levied on the meadows and house-lots. The town considered this to be the most just distribution of the burden, as "every man's right and proportion in the township did arise from the quantity of meadow land he did possess."[2] The services of the Reverend Zacharia Walker were then engaged. He had been educated at Cambridge, but had not been ordained,[3] for the town later agreed to give Mr. Walker five pounds "provided he should continue with them from year to year, and should likewise procure an ordination, answerable to the law, thereby to capacitate him not only for the preaching of the Word, but for the baptizing of infants."[4] This, however, occurred after the termination of the Dutch rule. The town showed a great deal of zeal for religion in 1663. On February 14, the salary of sixty pounds per annum was voted for the maintenance of the minister; this sum was also to be procured "by rates which are to be levied on lands and estates."[5] On March 2, the parsonage, with the "accomodations belonging to it", was given to Mr. Walker and his heirs. It was not an absolute gift. If the minister left the town without a just cause, the

[1] Col. Docs. N. Y. xiv. 491-2.
[2] Flint, History of Early Long Island, i. 203. Onderdonck, H. Jr. History Rec. i. 27.
[3] Thompson, History of Long Island, ii. 99-100.
[4] Ibid. p. 101.
[5] Onderdonck, H. Jr., History Rec i. 27.

house and land was to revert to the town upon paying
for such labor, as he had expended upon it, but if the
town was the cause of his departure, then he was to be
paid for what the house was worth. In the case of his
death, the town reserved to itself the right of pre-emp-
tion, if his wife should decide to sell.[1]   These liberal
conditions were no doubt intended to make more certain
this minister's continuance among them. The town
now felt the need of a separate meeting house,
which was built the same year. It was again
agreed at the town-meeting that all the inhabitants of the town should pay toward the maintenance of
a minister according to what they possess.[2]   There may
have been some growth of dissent with a consequent
refusal on the part of the dissenters to submit to the
church rates imposed by the town. Such a movement
was favored by the disturbed condition of the Island on
the encroachments of English authority.

A very significant movement of emigration from
New Haven began to manifest itself on the restoration
of Charles II. This colony only grudgingly acknowledged the King and in consequence had good reason to
fear that the plan of Connecticut to absorb New Haven
might be realized, as the King moreover bore no
friendly feeling to this colony on account of its readiness
to shelter the regicides Goffe and Whalley from
his vengeance. The incorporation of New Haven
was easily obtained by Governor Winthrop in the new
charter graciously conceeded to the colony of Connecti-

---

[1] Thompson, History of Long Island, ii. 100.
[2] Onderdonck, H. Jr. Antiquities of the Parish Church, Jamaica
Town Recs.

cut. There was no attempt made by New Haven to hinder this union. In fact, a large party had gradually developed within the colony, which was not content with the restriction of the franchise to church members, and was apparently satisfied to be placed under the government of Connecticut, which made no such restriction. As soon as some of the most ardent adherents of the strict theocratic system of New Haven became aware of the probability of this change, they sought a place of refuge under the Dutch government, where they could still administer justice according the strict code of Moses and restrict their franchise to the elect. They were encouraged in this design by the invitation extended by the States General to all the English of tender conscience, oppressed in consequence of the restoration, to settle in America under the jurisdiction of Governor Stuyvesant on the conditions established by the West India Company.[1] The negotiations for the establishment of this settlement illustrate most clearly the attitude of Stuyvesant and the West India Company towards the "New England Way," even in its most exaggerated form.

Stuyvesant had repeatedly recognized the spiritual kinship which the Dutch bore to the churches of New England. On the outbreak of the war between England and Holland in 1652, he bewailed the existence of this enmity, as "religion will become wounded and the gospell schandalised to the reioycing and triumphing of the enemies thereof, who will upon all occasions be ready to adde fuell to the fire." Even at this time, he

[1] Doc. History N. Y. iii. 37-39.

urged the continuance of all love and friendship between the two colonies, especially because of "our ioynt prfession of ourr ffaith in our Lord Jesus Christ not differing in fundamentalls."[1] The same idea is advanced in the course of the negotiations with the New Haven petitioners in still greater detail. Application was first made by John Stickland of Huntington in the name of a company of Englishmen for information whether the disposal of the land at Achter Kol was still free and whether encouragement would be given to these Englishmen, if they should persist in their project to settle there on an inspection of the locality.[2] In the beginning of June, 1661, Stuyvesant requested the English to send some of their number to view the land, after which the conditions for such a settlement might be established.[3] Every courtesy was shown to the English envoys. On their return to New Haven, a committee was empowered by the English to conclude the terms, under which they with their friends and posterity could gradually settle in New Netherland at Achter Kol "for the enlargement of the Kingdom of Christ in the Congregational way and all other means of comfort in subordination hereunto." They were in hopes that "the glory of God and benefit and welfare of the Dutch nation in America and the honor of their principals in Europe" would be promoted in a larger measure by their plantation than by any other settlement under Dutch jurisdiction. As they were "true

---

[1] Stuyvesant to Gov. Endicott. Col. Docs. N. Y. xiv. 179.
[2] John Stickland to Brian Newtown, April 29, 1661. Col. Docs. N. Y. xiii. 195.
[3] June 2, 1661. Ibid.

men and noe spies," who wished to obtain only good, righteous and honest things for themselves, their posterity and like-minded friends,[1] they requested a plain and clear answer to their proposals, which were submitted, dated November 8, 1661, from Milford, N. E.; with the signatures of the committee: Benjamin Ffen, Richard Lawe, Robert Treatt, and Jasper Gun.[2] The English were evidently bent on transferring all their civil and ecclesiastical institutions to the projected settlement. The newly planted church or churches of the English were "to enjoy all such powers, privileges and liberties in the Congregational way as they have enjoyed in New England . . . without any disturbance, impediment or impositions of any other forms, orders or customs." They insisted that this approval of their churches be acknowledged by some public testimony upon record. Thus far they had asked for nothing that had not already been conceded to others in the Dutch Province, because there was "no difference in the fundamental poincts of the worship of God betwixt [the Dutch churches] and the churches of New England as onely in the Rueling of the same."[3] The church-polity of the former was Presbyterian, while that of he latter was Congregational. Now the Provincial government was asked not only to allow a corporate existence to individual churches, but also to allow these English churches planted under the Dutch government, when they should consent "to consociate together for mutuall helpfullness," to call a Synod and establish

[1] Matthew Gilbert to Director General, November 8, 1661. Col. Docs. N. Y. xiii. 208.
[2] Ibid. 209-10.
[3] Stuyvesant to Milford, November 28, 1661. Ibid. 210.

"by common consent such orders according to scripture
as may be requisite for the suppressing of hairesies,
schismes and false worships and for the establishment of
truth with peace in those English churches." They
also demanded the Governor and courts of New Amsterdam to protect the English churches and Synods
"from any that oppose them or be injurious to them."
The realization of this projected colony was impeded by
the demand for practical autonomy in civil affairs,
which the new colonists wished to regulate without the
right of appeal to the Provincial government, "according to the fundamentalls receiued in New Haven Col-
lonie," as far as it should suit "Christ's ends" and the
conditions of the new settlement. Stuyvesant was
ready to give the petitioners the usual privileges of the
charter of 1640 in regard to the election of magistrates,
the administration of justice and all civil affairs,[1] but
this apparently did not satisfy the demands of the New
Haven people, who sent John Gregory in the following
spring to New Amsterdam to negotiate more favorable
terms. Stuyvesant was willing to make all possible
concessions in regard to religion and he again adverted
to the fact "that there is noe at the least difference in
the fundamentall points of religion, the difference in
churches orders and government so small that wee doe
not stick at it, therefore have left and leave still to the
freedom off your owne consciences."[2] In fact, Stuyvesant
had before expressed the hope that even these differences would be removed "by a neerer meeting and conference" between the Dutch and English ministers with

[1] Col. Docs. N. Y. xiii. 210-11.
[2] Ibid. 216, March 11, 1662.

the result of a "lovinge unity" between their respective churches. This feeling of religious solidarity was further attested in the words of the oath which the magistrates of the new English settlement were to take. They were to be bound to "maintain the true and Protestant religion soo as the same accordinge to the word of God is declared and in this Province is professed."[1] There was no mention of religion in the oaths of the settlers and the military officers in the township.

Stuyvesant was not so ready to accede to the demand of these English in civil matters, "which do not scruple the consciency," although he was ready to make some concessions, especially by raising the sum of the fine from which appeal might be taken. He also wrote privately to Robert Treatt that he would consider any just and weighty reasons in favor of further concessions which he would urge, if necessary, even on his superiors in Europe, so that all reasonable satisfaction might be given.[2] This led to further negotiations between the Director General and Council and the English deputies, Robert Treatt, Philip Grues and John Gregory, for the purpose of clearing up some details which the English considered not sufficiently outlined in the previous concessions of the Director and Council. The demands in religious matters had before been categorically conceded, but now a more detailed account of the nature of their demand for the right of organizing a Synod made Stuyvesant realize the gravity of the matter. He had no objection that the church or churches

[1] Col. Docs. N. Y. xiii. 217.
[2] Ibid. 218.

of this colony should take advice with some English
minister or churches within the Dutch Province, but he
now demanded that the approbation and consent of the
Governor and Council be obtained for the calling of a
Synod.[1] He readily yielded, however, to their demand
to restrict the right of suffrage to church members and
granted them power to make laws, which would be confirmed by the Director General and Council, if they
proved not to be repugnant to the laws of the United
Netherlands and the Province of New Netherland.[2]
All other demands were also granted. Negotiations
now ceased for some time, as the English were waiting
for the return of Mr. Winthrop in the hope of a settlement of the claims of the Dutch, disputed by Connecticut,
and also as no further concessions could be made without the consent of the Directors in Holland.[3] Meanwhile, Stuyvesant sent a report of these proceedings to
the Directors, who warmly approved the plan of the
English to settle under the Company's jurisdiction at
Achter Kol, as they would serve as a strong outpost
against the Raritan and Nevesink Indians. This was
of such importance to the Dutch Province that the
Company was ready even to make concessions in the
matter of appeal in criminal and capital cases. There
were grave reasons against the concessions, as the New
Haven colonists punished with death adultery, fornication, and similar offences according to the Law and Word
of God, while the laws of the Netherlands were much
more lenient in this regard. Nevertheless, the Company

[1] May 30, 1662. Col. Docs. N. Y. xiii. 221.
[2] Ibid. 222.
[3] Robert Treatt to Stuyvesant, June 29, 1663 Ibid. 267.

waived the right of appeal in all these cases, when the crime imputed was confessed by the criminal, and when the criminal was one of their own people. The right of appeal was to be granted in all dubious cases and when the criminal happened to be a Hollander, who had settled among the English.[1] A few months after the receipt of this letter, Robert Treatt again wrote to Stuyvesant to learn whether he had been empowered by the Directors in Holland to grant them "free liberty" to "be a free people of themselves to act subordinately for themselves both in all Civill and Ecclesiastical Respects."[2] Stuyvesant now granted them full liberty to plant churches in the Congregational way and to organize them into a Synod. Their laws would also be approved, if they were found to concur with the Holy Scriptures by the Director General and Council and no appeal was to be granted from "capital sentences, wherein the partys are Convinced by owne Confession, but in dark and dubious matters, especially in Witchcraft,"[3] the sentence of death was to be executed only on the approbation of the Governor General and Council. In civil matters, only cases over a hundred pounds Flemish could be appealed. All other demands were conceded without modification.[4] With this the

---

[1] Col. Docs. N. Y. xiii. 239-40.

[2] Ibid. 267.

[3] The reason of the special mention of witchcraft appears in the letter of Stuyvesant to the people of Hartford, December 13, 1662. ". .me brother-in-lawe (being Necessitated to make a Second Voyage for aide his distressed Sister, Judith Varleth Imprisoned as we are Informed uppon pretend accusation off Witcherye,we really beleeve & out her knowne education, Lyfe, Conversation & profession off faith we deare assure, that Shee is innocent of such a horrible Crimen & therefore I doubt not he will now as formerly fynde your honnrs favour & ayde for the Innocent." Col. Docs. N. Y. xiv. 518.

[4] Ibid. 281.

matter ended, doubtless on account of the rumors
that were prevalent in the New England colonies at this
time, that the Province of New Netherland was soon to
be subjected to English authority. In spite of the conquest of the Dutch Province, some of the New Haven
people persisted in their design to settle in those parts
on the presentation of a favorable opportunity. This
occurred on the creation of the Province of New Jersey,
which offered them permission to settle under a town
constitution, limiting the franchise to communing
church members. This settlement, under the leadership of Robert Treatt and the minister Abraham Pier-
son, was established between the years 1665-67, with
colonists from Guilford, Branford and Milford, on the
Passaic River. The town first received the name of
Milford, which was soon changed to Newark, the
English home of its pastor.[1]

[1] Cf. Fiske, Dutch and Quaker Colonies in America, ii. 12-15.

CHAPTER VI

THE PERSECUTION OF THE LUTHERANS

For many years the Lutherans in New Netherland joined in the public worship of the Reformed Religion. Some of the principal Lutherans even became church members and joined the Dutch Calvinists in the celebration of the Lord's Supper. The ecclesiastical and civil authorities of New Amsterdam were thus led to look for a realization, in the new world, of those fond hopes for a union of the two greatest Protestant confessions, which had long been disappointed in Europe. They felt that the fusion of the Lutheran element into the Calvinist body ensured "the welfare, prosperity and edification of the church in this place," where the full benefit of the Reformed faith had hitherto been enjoyed through its exclusive establishment, which the Director General and Council and the Burgomasters and Schepens were bound under oath to maintain.[1] When the separatist movement of the Lutherans began to manifest itself, the civil authorities of New Amsterdam did not show less zealous care for the defense and

[1] Letter of Megapolensis and Drisius to Classis of Amsterdam October 6, 1653, in Eccl. Recs. N. Y. i. 317-18. Report of the Burgomasters and Schepens on the petition of the ministers against the toleration of Lutheran services, July 14, 1657. Ibid. i. 389.

maintenance of the Reformed Religion than the ecclesiastical authorities, who, in obedience to the command of the Classis of Amsterdam, " employed all diligence to ward off the wolves from the tender lambs of Christ."[1]

On October 4, 1653, the Lutherans petitioned the Director General for permission to call a Lutheran minister from Holland and to organize a separate congregation for the public exercise of the Unaltered Augsburg Confession here in New Netherland. They had twice submitted a similar petition to the Governor, and had also addressed letters to the States of Holland and to the Directors of the West India Company to this effect.[2] A twofold pretext was advanced in these letters[3] to Holland for their separation from the Reformed Church. They objected to the second question of the formula of baptism, used in the Dutch Church of New Amsterdam, in which, according to their statement, they were asked whether they acknowledged the dogma taught in the Christian Church "there" as the true doctrine. This was equivalent to a denial of their Lutheran Confession. Then they also objected to the strictness with which the Dutch ministers demanded the parents and sponsors to be present at the baptism of their children.

As soon as the Lutheran petition came to the knowledge of the Dutch ministers in New Amsterdam, they appealed to Stuyvesant, who "would rather relinquish his office than grant permission in this matter, since it is

---

[1] Letter of Classis of Amsterdam to consistory in New Netherland, May 26, 1656. in Eccl. Recs. N. Y. i. 348-9.
[2] Letter of Megapolensis and Drisius to Classis of Amsterdam, October 6, 1653, Ibid. 317-18.
[3] Letter of the same to Director General and Council, August 23, 1658. Ibid. 428-30.

contrary to the first article of his commission, which
was confirmed by him with an oath not to permit any
other than the Reformed Doctrine." The ministers
were not only disturbed by the fear that this would
tend to the injury of the church and the increase of dissensions, but also by the thought that it would pave the
way for other sects, so that in time New Netherland
would become a receptacle for all kinds of heretics and
fanatics.[1]   They, therefore, hastened to enlist the services of their ecclesiastical superiors in Holland, the
Classis of Amsterdam, and also addressed themselves
directly to the West India Company.   The Classis or
Amsterdam was even less tolerant of ecclesiastical differences in New Netherland than the ministers in the
colony itself.[2]   In their eyes, the concession of the freedom of religious worship to the Lutherans would entail
the concession of a similar privilege to the Mennonites
and English Independents, and even to the Jews, who
had, in fact, made this request of the Governor and had
"also attempted to erect a synagogue for the exercise
of their blasphemous religion."[3]   The Classis expressed,
with deep emotion, its realization of the fact that under
such circumstances a pastor's work would have greatly
increased and his path would have been beset with
obstacles and difficulties, which would interfere with a
minister's good and holy efforts for the extension of the

[1] Letter of Megapolensis and Drisius to Classis of Amsterdam,
October 6, 1653, in Eccl. Recs. N. Y. i. 317-18.
    [2] The right of the English Independents to the free exercise of
their religion in public, though not always regarded with the greatest
favor, was never disputed by either Stuyvesant or the ministers of
New Amsterdam.
    [3] Letter of Classis of Amsterdam to consistory of New Amster-
dam, May 26, 1656, in Eccl. Recs. N. Y. i, 348-9.

cause of Christ. Under the influence of the Classis of
Amsterdam, the Directors of the West India Company
also classed with the Mennonites the English Independents amongst those who might urge claims for the
freedom of religious worship upon the concession of
such a privilege to the Lutherans. Some uneasiness
was experienced in regard to the States of Holland,
who might be inclined to grant the Lutheran petition,
but these fears of the Classis were set at rest by the
promise, by which the Directors of the West India Company bound themselves to resist any such concession.[1]
In this matter, the decision of the West India Company
was pronounced finally on February 23, 1654, when the
Directors resolved not to tolerate any Lutheran pastors
there, nor any other public worship than the true
Reformed. The Classis of Amsterdam was perfectly
satisfied and did not doubt but that henceforth the
Reformed Doctrine "would be maintained without
being hindered by the Lutherans and other erring
spirits."[2] When the Directors of the Company announced to Stuyvesant their absolute denial of the
Lutheran petition, "pursuant to the customs hitherto
observed by us and the East India Company," they
recommended him to deny all similar petitions, but
"in the most civil and least offensive way, and to employ all possible but moderate means in order to induce
them to listen, and finally join the Reformed Church,

[1] Classis of Amsterdam, Acts of Deputies, February 23, 1654,
in Eccl. Recs. N. Y. i. 322.
[2] Classis of Amsterdam to Megapolensis and Drisius, February
26, 1654. Ibid. 323.

and thus live in greater love and harmony among themselves."[1]

The Lutherans remained quiet for a short time, but the next year they found a leader for the promotion of their cause in the person of Paulus Schrick, who had just returned from Holland.[2] Although the public exercise of their faith had been interdicted, there was thus far no legislation in New Netherland to prevent the organization of private conventicles. They now began to hold divine services with prayer, reading, and singing, in the expectation of finally receiving a minister of their own persuasion from the fatherland.[3] The Dutch ministers felt justified in their opposition by the results of this separate organization of the Lutheran worship. The Lutherans in New Amsterdam were a poor, uneducated people without any proper acquaintance with the teachings of Dr. Luther; they could, therefore, give the Dutch ministers no other reason for the faith that was in them than that "their parents and ancestors were Lutherans, as Paulus Schrick their leader once in his wisdom declared."[4] They were Lutherans and would remain such. The ministers considered this blind opposition to the preaching of the Divine Word. Toleration was out of the question, as the separatist movement gave rise to great contention and discord not only among the inhabitants and citizens in general, but also in families. In fact, some husbands had forced their

[1] Col. Docs. N. Y. xiv. 250.
[2] Letter of Megapolensis and Drisius to Director General and Council, August 23, 1658, in Eccl. Recs. N. Y. i. 429.
[3] Petition of the Lutherans to the Director General and Council, October 24, 1656, Ibid. p. 359.
[4] Ibid, p. 429.

wives to leave the Dutch Reformed Church and attend their conventicles. There was imminent danger, therefore, of a large leakage in the membership of the Dutch Reformed Church of New Amsterdam. Thus the Lutheran movement "would prove a plan of Satan to smother this infant, rising congregation almost in its birth, or at least obstruct the march of truth in its progress."[1]

The Lutheran issue entered a new phase on the successful termination of Stuyvesant's expedition of conquest to the South River. Here a commercial colony under the authority of a company, composed originally of Swedes and Dutch, had become nationalized to the exclusion of the latter element.[2] As far as religion was concerned, this resulted in the establishment of the Lutheran Church on the Delaware, where divine service was to be "zealously performed according to the Unaltered Augsburg Confession, the Council of Upsala, and the ceremonies of the Swedish Church."[3] The out-

---

[1] Remonstrance of Megapolensis and Drisius to Burgomasters and Schepens, July 6, 1657, in Eccl Recs. N. Y. i. 387-88.
[2] Cf. Odhner, C. T., The founding of New Sweden, in Pennsylvania Magazine of History and Biography, iii. 1879.
[3] The position of the Lutheran Church in Sweden is well summarized in the Church Act of 1686 under King Charles XI, that also reflects the conditions obtaining in the earlier period, in question here. "In our kingdom and in the countries belonging thereto, all persons shall profess solely and simply the Christian doctrine and the Christian faith, which is contained in the Holy Word of God, in the prophetical and apostolic scriptures of the Old and New Testament, and which is comprehensively stated in the three chief symbols, the Apostolic, the Nicene, and the Athanasian, as well as in the Unaltered Augsburg Confession of the year 1530, adopted 1593 by the Council at Upsala and explained in the entire so-called Book of Concord. And all those who assume any office as teachers in the churches, academies, gymnasia or schools, shall at their ordination, or when they receive a degree under oath solemnly subscribe this doctrine and confession." Cf. John Nicum, The Confessional History

break of Indian hostilities at New Amsterdam, on the eve of the surrender of New Sweden to Stuyvesant, made it impossible to abolish entirely the public exercise of the Lutheran worship. According to the Articles of Capitulation, one of the three Lutheran ministers, the Reverend Lars Lockenius, was allowed to remain to minister to the Swedes and Finns, of whom at least two hundred lived on the river above Fort Christina. Thus the Lutheran religion enjoyed, within certain limits of the subjugated territory, official recognition and could be exercised in public.

This concession, however, did not result in an extension of this privilege throughout other parts of the Province of New Netherland. In fact, there a stricter policy of religious repression in regard to other confessions than the Reformed was indicated in the points of advice,[1] submitted by the Director General to avert such calamities as the Indian war in the future. He firmly believed that the war had been the punishment of the sins of the community. Such "common, private and public sins, as drunkenness, profanation of the Lord's Name and Sabbath, swearing in public and in private, done even by the children on the street, *meetings of sectarians* and other irregularities" were to "be forbidden by the renewal of good orders and placards, to be promptly executed and by the issue and strict observance of new orders, to prevent as much as possible such occurrences."

The Lutherans at Amsterdam continued still to

of the Evangelical Lutheran Church in the United States, in Am. Soc. of Church History, iv. 1892.
[1] Col. Docs. N Y. xiii. 53, dated November 27, 1655.

assemble for the private exercise of their worship. Nevertheless, the proximate occasion for the decree against conventicles was not given at Amsterdam but at Middelburg (Newtown). The inhabitants of this town were mostly Independents, with a few Presbyterians. The latter could not be supplied with a Presbyterian preacher, but a Mr. John Moore, who claimed to have been licensed in New England to preach, but not authorized to administer the sacraments, attended to their spiritual needs. On the departure of Mr. Moore, "some inhabitants and unqualified persons ventured to hold conventicles and gatherings and assumed to teach the Gospel." Other places in New Netherland were as destitute of an authorized ministry and there was imminent danger in the minds of the preachers of New Amsterdam that this bad example would find imitation and result in quarrels, confusion and disorders in Church and commonalty. On the receipt of a petition from the ministers of New Amsterdam for his intervention, Stuyvesant expressed his decision to have placards issued against those persons, who, without either ecclesiastical or secular authority, acted as teachers in interpreting and expounding God's Holy Word. Stuyvesant also felt that this was a violation of the political and ecclesiastical rules of the fatherland, and an occasion for an outbreak of heresy and schism. Consequently, all such conventicles, both public and private, were prohibited by the Director General and Council under heavy penalties in the ordinance of February 1, 1656.[1] Persons presuming to ex-

[1] Recs. of New Amsterdam, i. 20-21; ii. 34-35; Eccl. Recs. N. Y. i. 343-4.

ercise, without due qualifications, the office of preacher, reader or chorister in such meetings, were subject to a fine of one hundred pounds Flemish; a fine of twenty-five pounds Flemish was incurred by any other man or woman who took part in such an assembly.

The penalties established by Stuyvesant were an innovation, but the remainder of the ordinance was largely modelled upon the second provision of the "Proposed Articles for the Colonization and Trade of New Netherland,"[1] presented to the States General by John de Laet, a Director of the West India Company, August 30, 1638, of which the bare essentials were retained in its final form in the "Freedoms and Exemptions," granted by the West India Company to Patroons and other planters of colonies in 1640.[2] The latter decree admitted the public exercise of no other religion than the Reformed, as preached and practiced by public authority in the United Netherlands, for which the Company was to provide and maintain suitable ministers, preachers, schoolmasters and Comforters of the Sick; the former expressly stated, in addition, that no person "shall be hereby in any wise aggrieved in his consciencc..provided he avoid frequenting any forbidden assembly or conventicles, much less collect or get up any such." The Director General and Council also declared in their ordinance that the religious worship of the Reformed Church was alone authorized and extended this decree not only to the public meetings but also to private meetings, assembled for worship in the Province of New Netherland. Stuyvesant, like so

[1] Col. Docs. N. Y. i. 110-11; Eccl. Recs. N. Y. i. 121.
[2] Col. Docs. N. Y. i. 119-23.

many other ardent Calvinists of his day, eagerly desired the close union of the various national Calvinist churches, which had found an early expression in the presence of delegates from these churches in the National Synod of Dortrecht (1618-19). He, therefore, appealed to the religious service of the Reformed Church, conformably to the Synod of Dortrecht, practiced in the Fatherland and the other Reformed churches of Europe, as the rule which was to establish the character of divine worship in his province. Thus, even at this time, Stuyvesant was ready to grant patents to new colonists, conceived along the lines followed by Kieft in his patents to Mespath, March 28, 1642,[1] and to Hempstead, November 16, 1644,[2] which assured the colonists the "exercise of the Reformed Religion, which they profess with the ecclesiastical discipline thereunto belonging." The mind of Stuyvesant on this point is clearly manifested later in his long correspondence with the Milford inhabitants, who intended to found a settlement under his jurisdiction, with freedom of worship, although they were not Presbyterians, as the Dutch, but Congregationalists.[3]

Although the ordinance legislated for the repression of the freedom of religious worship in conventicles not within the pale of the Reformed Church, the Director General and Council were careful to include the more liberal provisions of the "Articles" that had been proposed by John de Laet in the name of the West India

---

[1] Book of Patents GG. p. 49; cited in Riker, Annals of Newtown, p. 413.
[2] Thompson, History of Long Island, ii. 5-6.
[3] Correspondence from April 29, 1661 to July 20, 1663. Col. Docs. N. Y. xiii. 197, et passim.

Company to the States General for their approval.
They did not "hereby intend to force the conscience of
any to the prejudice of formerly given patents." This
can only refer to the patents of Flushing[1] and Gravesend,[2] which had been granted in 1645 by Kieft immediately after the termination of the ruinous Indian war,
in all probability to raise the distressed condition of
the Province by attracting new colonists on such liberal
conditions. Both patents grant "Liberty of conscience
according to the Custome and manner of Holland, without molestacon or disturbance from any Magistrate or
Magistrates, or any other ecclesiastical minister, that
may extend jurisdiccon over them." Stuyvesant's
interpretation of this liberty of conscience did not
include freedom of worship either in public or private
conventicles. However, he expressly stated that he
had no desire to invade the sanctuary of the home with
this legislation, which did not affect "the reading of
God's Holy Word, family prayers and worship, *each in
his own house.*" Thus the ordinance distinguished
three kinds of worship: 1, worship in public conventicles; 2, worship in private conventicles; and 3, worship within the family. The first two were limited to
the adherents of the Reformed Religion; the last was
extended to all. This precisely constituted "Liberty
of conscience according to the Custome and manner of
Holland."[3] The publication and execution of the

---

[1] Laws and Ordinances of New Netherland, New York Deed
Book, ii. 178, i. Waller History of Flushing, Appenidx.
[2] Doc. History New York, i. 411.
[3] Cf. Hubert's learned investigation of the religious legislation of
Holland in his work: Les Pays-Bas Espagnols et La République
des Provinces Unies, etc., especially his conclusion on p. 97.

ordinance was entrusted to the fiscal and inferior magistrates and schouts throughout New Netherland, and its presence in some of the town records shows the fidelity with which these orders were fulfilled.[1] In this way, the Director General and Council believed that they had made ample provisions for "the glory of God, the promotion of the Reformed Religion and public peace, harmony, and welfare."

Although the decree against conventicles did not affect the position of the public worship of the Lutheran faith in the conquered territory of New Sweden, the Lutherans of New Amsterdam understood at once that their religious assemblies did come under the prohibitive ordinance.   They, therefore, discontinued the divine services, which they had been holding regularly, in private, during the past year.[2]   The West India Company was also under the impression that this decree had been directly aimed at the Lutherans.   Its Directors resented Stuyvesant's methods of repression, which were so alien to the spirit of conciliation, with which they tried to inspire his policy towards Lutheran dissent, but, in point of fact, they did not revoke the decree, and expressly conceded only that measure of religious liberty, that had already been granted by the Director General himself: the free exercise of their religion in

[1] Niemant vermach heimlike of openbare conventiculen of vergaderinghe houden t'sij int lesen, singen, of prediken op de verbeurte van 100 ponden vlaems, en voor te toehoorders van ghelike 25 ponden vlaems bij ijder een, wat Religie of Secten het oock mochten sijn volgens den Placcat van den 1 February 1656. Corte aenwijsinghe van enighe placcaten over beganene uisusen etc. Het Bouk Van Het Durp Utrecht Aọ 1657.
[2] Petition of the Lutherans to the Director General and Council October 24, 1656, in Eccl. Recs. N. Y. i. 359; and O'Callaghan, History of New Netherland, ii. 320.

the home.[1] They continued to insist on the lenient treatment of the Lutherans, and wished in the future to have such ordinances, submitted to them prior to their publication. This letter of the Directors must have soon come to the knowledge of the Lutherans, both in New Amsterdam and in Holland, as renewed agitation to promote the Lutheran cause became manifest in the colony as well as in the fatherland. At Amsterdam, the Lutherans again requested the Directors to concede the privilege of the public exercise of their religion in New Netherland and supported their request by an appeal to the customs obtaining in Holland, where they as well as others enjoyed this privilege.[2] The Classis of Amsterdam became very much disturbed by the rumors, which began to circulate in regard to the contemplated action of the Board of Directors, who, according to reports, had delegated a committee to confer with some of the magistrates of the City of Amsterdam[3] on the question of permitting, in all their colonies, "all sorts of persuasions . . . to exercise their special forms of worship."[4] The Classis immediately directed

[1] Letter of Directors to Stuyvesant, June 14, 1656, in Col. Docs. N. Y. xiv. 391.

[2] Classis of Amsterdam, Acts of Deputies, xx 361,¶ in Eccl. Recs. N. Y. i. 354. For the extent of toleration in the Netherlands at this time, cf. Blok, a History of the People of the Netherlands, and especially the monograph of E. Hubert, Les Pays-Bas Espagnols et La République des Provinces Unies (1648-1713). La Question Religieuse et Les Relations Diplomatiques.

[3] The West India Company, July 12, 1656, to relieve the strained condition of its finances, surrendered to the City of Amsterdam some of its territory on the South River from the west side of Christina Kill to Bombay Hook at the mouth of the river. Here the city founded its colony of New Amstel. Cf. the histories of O'Callaghan and Brodhead.

[4] Classis of Amsterdam. Acts of Deputies, vi. 33; xix. 25, in Eccl. Recs. N. Y. i. 357. October 10, 1656.

its deputies on Indian affairs to wait upon these Directors and magistrates of Amsterdam and insist on the
"injuriousness of the general permission of all sorts of
persuasions," but they could only learn that the matter
was still far removed from a settlement. [1]

Meanwhile, the Lutherans at New Amsterdam had
received word from fellow-believers in Holland that
they had obtained a decree from the Directors of the
West India Company, according to which the Unaltered
Augsburg Confession was to "be tolerated in the West
Indies and New Netherland under their jurisdiction in
the same manner as in the fatherland under its praise-
worthy government." They, therefore, petitioned [2] the
Director General and Council to allow them again to
celebrate with prayer, reading and singing, until the
arrival of a minister of their own persuasion, whom they
expected to receive from the Fatherland next spring.
Stuyvesant refused to alter his decree against conventicles and all public gatherings "except those for the
divine service of the Reformed Church prevailing
here," but he again declared that no one was to "suffer
for this belief, nor be prevented each in his family from
reading, thanksgiving, and singing according to their
faith." If there were to be any changes in this legislation, they were to be made by the Directors of the Company, to whom the petition was finally sent. Thus the
issue was again presented for settlement at Amsterdam,
where the Classis instructed its deputies on Indian
affairs "with all serious arguments . . . to check, at the

[1] Classis of Amsterdam, Acts of Deputies, vi. 39, i. 360 in Eccl.
Recs. N. Y. November 7, 1656.
[2] Petition of the Lutherans, October 24, Ibid. i. 656, 359.

beginning, this toleration of all sorts of religions, and especially of the Lutherans, lest God's Church come to suffer more and more injury as time goes on."[1]

The deputies of the Classis soon learned that the Directors of the West India Company had in fact resolved to connive at the free exercise of dissenting worship. Their representations against the adoption of this religious policy influenced the Directors finally to abide by the resolution of the preceding year.[2] The petitioners were told that the concession of religious worship to the Lutherans exceeded the powers of the West India Company and depended on the States General, to whom they were referred.[3] Stuyvesant was, therefore, officially informed that it was not the intention of the Directors to grant to the Lutherans any more liberty in their worship than "the permission quietly to have their exercises at their own houses."[4] The deputies were not so successful with the Burgomasters of the City of Amsterdam, from whom they could only extort the indefinite promise that they would attend to the matter at the proper time, when information should arrive that the sects carried on the exercise of their religions. The magistrates of Amsterdam declared that they could not

[1] Acts of Classis of Amsterdam, xix. 42.; v. 41, Eccl. Recs. N. Y. i. 372.
[2] Classis of Amsterdam. Act of Deputies, vi. 45, Ibid, 375. April 10, 1657.
Classics of Amsterdam to Consistory of New Netherland, May 25, 1657, Ibed. 378.
Col. Docs, N. Y. xiv. 386-88. The Classis writes in the lettera "We cannot interpret this in any other way than that every one must have the freedom to serve God quietly within his dwelling in such manner as his religion may prescribe, without instituting any public gatherings or conventicles. When this interpretation is recognized, our complaints will cease."

force the consciences of men, and the ministers denied that this was the purpose of their intervention. Under these circumstances, the Classis, not feeling entirely at ease, resolved to encourage "the consistory in New Netherland to continue in their good zeal to check these evils in every possible way; diligence and labor are required to prevent false opinions and foul heresies from becoming prejudicial to the pure truth." This is also the burden of the letter,[1] which the Classis of Amsterdam sent the consistory of New Netherland, to introduce the Rev. Everardus Welius, the first minister to the City's colony of New Amstel.

The departure of a Lutheran minister, John Ernest Goedwater, for New Netherland in the ship "De Molen" on a mission from the Lutheran consistory was a new cause of anxiety to the Classis of Amsterdam. The Dutch ministers recognized the inconsistency of the concession of freedom of worship to the Swedish Lutherans on the South River and of its denial to the Dutch Lutherans on the North River at New Amsterdam. The Classis, therefore, resolved that the Directors were to be urged to correct this abuse in the territory of the West India Company and the Burgomasters requested to instruct their vice-director Alrichs to oppose the Lutherans and other sects in the district subject to the authority of the City of Amsterdam.[2] Both promised to be on their guard, and not permit, but rather endeavor to prevent the public exercise of the Lutheran worship.[3] Stuyvesant, nevertheless, faith-

---

[1] Eccl. Recs. N. Y. i. 378.
[2] Classis of Amsterdam, Acts of Deputies, May 7, 1657, Ibid 377.
[3] Acts of Classis of Amsterdam, Ibid. 382.

fully fulfilled the stipulation of the treaty with the
Swedes, which guaranteed them the freedom of their
Lutheran worship, until the termination of his authority
by the English conquest, and there is no evidence that
the clergy of New Amsterdam made any attempt to
change his policy in this regard.[1] The Classis was
gratified with better results from the commissioners of
the City's colony, who, on August 22, 1659, resented
"the bold undertaking of the Swedish parson to preach
there in the colony without permission," and
ordered the vice-director "by proper means to put an
end to or prevent such presumption on the part of
other sectaries," because "as yet no other religion but
the Reformed can nor may be tolerated there."[2]

The arrival of the Lutheran minister at New Amsterdam called forth a vigorous protest from the Dutch
clergy of the town, who summarized, in a remonstrance
of six points,[3] directed to the Burgomasters and Schepens, the injurious consequences of the exercise of the
Lutheran confession not only to the religious, but also
to the political interests of this place, as the strife in
religious matters resulting therefrom would produce
confusion in political matters and thus a united and
peaceful people would be transformed into a Babel of
confusion.[4] The ministers no doubt had in mind the
Colony of Rhode Island, which they regarded as the
cess-pool of New England, full of erring spirits and

---

[1] This fact should not be forgotten by those historians who wish
to throw the full responsibility for the policy of religious repression
on Stuyvesant and the clergy at New Amsterdam. The matter was
not at all so local.

[2] Col. Docs. N. Y. ii. 61.

[3] Eccl. Recs. N. Y. i. 386-88.

[4] Ibid.

enthusiasts.[1]   The Burgomasters and Schepens immediately summoned the Lutheran preacher to appear
before them for examination.   He frankly confessed
that he had been sent by the Lutheran consistory of
Amsterdam to occupy the position of preacher here, as
far as it was now permissible, though he felt confident
that the ship "Waag" would bring the news of the
concession of freedom of worship, which the Directors
of the West India Company had under consideration at
the time of his departure from the fatherland.   The
Burgomasters and Schepens could not believe that the
Directors would tolerate any other worship than the
true Reformed in this place, as the oath, which they
took on the assumption of their office, "to help maintain the true Reformed Religion and to suffer no other
religion or sects," had received the approval of the
Directors. They, therefore, forbade the Lutheran minister to hold either public or private conventicles, and
also to deliver to the Lutheran body in the city the letters, that he had brought from the Amsterdam
consistory, until further orders.   Then, as the
matter concerned not only the city but the
whole Province, they reported[2] these proceedings
to the Director General and Council, who commended in every particular their action and ordered the Burgomasters of this city and also all
inferior courts strictly to enforce the ordinance of
February 1, 1656, against conventicles, as this was
"necessary for the maintenance and conservation not

---

[1] Megapolensis and Drisius to Classis of Amsterdam, August 14,
1657, etc., Eccl. Recs. N. Y. i. 400.
[2] Ibid. 389.

only of the Reformed divine service, but also of political and civil peace, quietness and harmony."[1] The Dutch ministers now experienced that it was easier to keep out an enemy than to expel an enemy once admitted. They petitioned the authorities to send back to Holland the Lutheran preacher, who had come to the colony in such a capacity without the consent of the Directors of the West India Company.[2] The Director General and Council, therefore, ordered him to leave in the ship "Waag," which was then ready to sail, considering "this necessary for the glory of God, for the success of the Reformed Religion, and the common peace and tranquillity of the colony."[3] This order created great dissatisfaction among the Lutherans, who, at Fort Orange, had collected one hundred beaver skins, valued at eight hundred guilders, for the support of their minister.[4] They earnestly petitioned the Director General and Council to revoke the order, while they were quietly and without offense waiting for the toleration of the Unaltered Augsburg Confession under the new orders, that they expected from their sovereigns, the States General and the Noble Directors of the West India Company.[5] Anxious to trouble the waters, Goedwater refused to obey the orders of the Director and

[1] Eccl. Recs. N. Y. i. 390.
[2] Megapolensis and Drisius to Classis of Amsterdam, August 5, 1657, Ibid. 393-4.
[3] Director General and Council to Lutherans, October 16, 1657, Ibid. 407.
[4] Megapolensis and Drisius to Classis of Amsterdam, October 25, 1657, Ibid. 409. The amount collected at New Amsterdam was unknown.
[5] Petition of Lutherans, October 10, 1657, Ibid. 405.

was resolved to persevere with his adherents.[1]   Stuyvesant became all the more determined in his demand, as the order of the Provincial Government had been treated with contempt. Goedwater was again commanded, on October 16, 1657, to leave in one of the two ships about to sail,[2] but he secretly carried off his books and bedding,[3] and concealed himself in the house of Lawrence Noorman, á Lutheran farmer,[4] to whom the Lutherans gave six guilders a week during the whole winter for the minister's support.[5]   The Fiscal was again ordered to place him under arrest for transportation to Holland at the earliest opportunity.   Meanwhile, the Lutherans informed the Director General that their preacher was sick and requested the privilege of bringing him to the city for the medical care that he required. Stuyvesant granted the petition, but, on the arrival of Goedwater, immediately put him under the surveillance of the Fiscal, who was empowered to send the Lutheran minister to Holland on his recovery. This was done in the spring on the ship "De Bruynvisch."   The Dutch ministers soon had the satisfaction of seeing the leader in the separatist movement of the Lutherans a punctual attendant at the Reformed service in his pew near the pulpit.[6]   Their joy was, however, soon marred by the

[1] Megapolensis and Drisius to Classis of Amsterdam, September 10, 1659, in Eccl. Recs. N.Y. 449.
[2] Director and Council to Goedwater, Ibid. 408.
[3] Megapolensis and Drisius to Classis of Amsterdam, October 25, 1657, Ibid. 412.
[4] Megapolensis and Drisius to Director General and Council, August 23, 1658, Ibid. 430.
[5] Megapolensis and Drisius to Classis of Amsterdam, September 24, 1658, Ibid. 433.
[6] Megapolensis and Drisius to Classis of Amsterdam, September 10, 1659, Ibid. 449. The statement of this letter, that Goedwater

change which they were compelled to make by the
Directors in the administration of the sacrament of
baptism.

While the Directors were determined to uphold the
Dutch religious establishment to the exclusion of other
forms of worship in the Province of New Netherland,
they were anxious to eliminate everything that might
deter the people of other persuasions from joining in
the Reformed service of the Dutch Church. Thus,
although the Directors at Amsterdam declared the expulsion of the Lutheran minister to be in accord with
their good intentions, they again expressed their dissatisfaction with the vigorous measures, adopted by
Stuyvesant in these proceedings, and insisted that he
was to adopt in the future the least offensive and most
tolerant means, so that in course of time such dissenters
might be induced to listen to the preaching of the
Reformed ministers and finally won over to the established church of the colony.   To effect this, it was necessary to do away with the grievances that occasioned
the separatist movement of the Lutherans.   The question addressed to parents and witnesses at baptism
might be so formulated as not to be offensive to
Lutheran ears, and less stress might be placed upon the
presence of the parents and witnesses at the administration of this sacrament.   A precedent for these
changes in the usages of the Dutch Church of New
Netherland was found in the practice of some of the
churches in Holland even in their own time, and in the

began to hold meetings and to preach, is evidently false in the light
of the earlier letters, the Lutheran petitions, and Stuyvesant's
answers.

customs prevailing at the beginning of the Reformation, when circumstances also made it imperative for the Church to attract people of a different belief.[1] The Directors, therefore, ordered that the old formula of baptism, being "more moderate and less objectionable to those of other denominations," be used in the churches of the Province, and the words "present here in the church" be entirely omitted.[2] Stuyvesant gave a copy of this ordinance to the ministers, as soon as it came into his hands, and requested them to draw up "a full and correct view of the case."[3]

The ministers declared their willingness to follow the example of the apostolic churches, who, though they gave freedom for the sake of the weaker brethren in minor matters, would not yield one iota to the obstinate and perverse, who came to spy out the liberty of believers and to bring Christians into bondage. They knew that the Synod of The Hague in 1591(Art. 28) put the question, proposed to parents and sponsors in the form—"Whether they acknowledge the doctrine contained in the Old and New Testaments, and in the articles of the Christian faith, and taught in conformity therewith, to be the true and perfect doctrine of salvation?" They were also aware that the Synod of Middelburg in 1581 (Art. 21) made the use or omission of the clause— " the doctrine taught here" —optional. Nevertheless, they did not feel that they could change the formula of Baptism that had been used so long in

[1] Directors to Stuyvesant, May 20, 1658, in Col. Docs. N. Y. xiv. 418.
[2] Directors to Stuyvesant, June 7, 1658, Ibid. 421.
[3] Director General and Council to ministers of New Amsterdam, August 19, 1658, in Eccl. Recs. N. Y. i. 427.

the churches of New Netherland without perhaps giving offence to their own people. They, therefore, placed the decision of the question in the hands of the Classis of Amsterdam, their ecclesiastical superiors, whose advice they would take in the matter.[1]

According to the report of the ministers, two years previously, Peter Jansen, "who was neither a Lutheran, nor of the Reformed Religion, and who had not intelligence enough to understand the difference between them, nibbled at these questions, but could not give any reason against them, or receive and try to understand a reason in their favor." The Lutherans also did not give a more satisfactory reason for their opposition during the last five or six years. They had accused the Dutch ministers of adding to the rite of baptism, the phrase: "According to the Synod of Dort." These words specified doctrines, which they were asked to acknowledge as true, but which were contrary to their belief. The ministers denied this charge, although they did believe the teaching of this National Synod to be the truth, and they contended against the suppression of the objectionable word "here" as useless, inasmuch as, in spite of its omission, they would mean by the church, not the papal church, but the "true Protestant and Reformed Churches." The ministers also denied the second charge of the Lutherans, who had accused them of strictly compelling parents and sponsors to be present at the baptism of their children. Though several Synods[2] of the fatherland

---

[1] Megapolensis and Drisius to Director General and Council, August 23, 1658, in Eccl. Recs. N. Y. i. 431.
[2] The National Synod of Dort in 1574, Art. 61; the Synod of Middelburg, 1583, Art. 40; the Synod of The Hague, 1591, Art. 51

had prescribed the presence of the parents at the baptism of their children, these provisions were not strictly enforced. This practice had also moved the ministers at New Amsterdam to be lenient in regard to this point until they noticed that young persons, who could hardly carry the child, and who had scarcely more knowledge of religion, baptism, and the vows than the child itself, presented children for baptism. To correct this abuse, the ministers had urged from the pulpit that none could so well fulfill the promises made in regard to the children at baptism, as the parents, who were, in fact, bound to do this by the Word of God.[1] They, therefore, directed that henceforth no half grown youths were to present children for baptism.

The Classis of Amsterdam supported the ministers of the colony in their opposition, and begged them not to make any alterations in the customary forms, but the Directors persisted in their demands,[2] and manifested so much displeasure, that the deputies of the Classis on Indian affairs delayed addressing them on the subject until further correspondence with the brethren in New Netherland.[3] The Directors were not satisfied with the fact, that the Lutherans were now again taking part in the divine service of the Reformed Church; they wished to exclude any possibility of another separation, that might arise if they should continue to

[1] Megapolensis and Drisius to Director General and Council, August 23, 1658, in Eccl. Recs. N. Y. i. 430.
[2] Classis of Amsterdam, Acts of Deputies, vi. 134; xix. 53. Ibid. i. 440; Col. Docs. N. Y. xiv. 429. Directors to Stuyvesant, February 13, 1659.
[3] Acts of Classis of Amsterdam, February 24, 1659, vi. 135; xix. 54, in Eccl. Recs. N. Y. i. 442.

employ such precise forms and offensive expressions, as
the Lutherans could very easily obtain from the
authorities in the fatherland the right of organizing separate divine service, which the Directors would then be powerless to prevent. Stuyvesant was, therefore, again directed, on December
29, 1659, to admonish the ministers to employ
the old formula of baptism without waiting for
further orders from the Classis of Amsterdam. Thus
all dissensions in the Church and State of New Netherland would cease.[1] The Directors of the Company had
lost patience "with scruples about unnecessary forms,
which cause more division than edification." Stuyvesant loyally defended the preachers of New Amsterdam, "whose zeal in teaching, admonishing and punish-
ing, whose peaceable and edifying life and conduct. . .
compel them and us to pray, that God may give them
long life for the best of his infant church here, and to
assure your Honors that neither of them can be suspected of any leaven of innovation or turbulence."
The Director General had, therefore, kept secret the
severe condemnation of the ministers by the Directors,
and he now requested them to send over some psalm-
books or liturgies of the Reformed Church, in which the
old formula of baptism was given without the objectionable words, as this would facilitate the execution of
their ordinance.[2] The Directors had already anticipated this request by sending two testaments and
psalm-books, containing the old formula, with the two

[1] Directors to Stuyvesant, December 22, 1659, in Col. Docs.
N. Y. xiv. 451.
[2] Stuyvesant to Directors, April 21, 1660, Ibid. 472.

newly appointed preachers, Blom and Selyns, who, before their departure from Holland, had also promised the Directors to make use of it in the exercise of their clerical office.[1] When Megapolensis and Drisius learned this, they also resolved to use the old formula, prescribed by the Directors, "with the design of avoiding any division in the churches of this country."[2] At this time, a feeling of unrest was noticeable among some Lutherans at Fort Orange, who began to take up a subscription for the salary of a Lutheran preacher, but this movement soon subsided.[3] Here some Lutherans had already joined the Dutch Church, and others were gradually being led to it. The Classis of Amsterdam, after consulting the Directors, instructed the Reverend Gideon Schaats, the minister of Beverwyck at Fort Orange, freely to inform those good people, "that they may dismiss their newly conceived hopes, since they may find abundant edification and comfort of soul through the blessing of the Lord in the Reformed worship, if they harken diligently and endeavor to walk before God and man with a good conscience."[4] This proved the end of the separatist movement of the Dutch Lutherans in New Netherland until the termination of the Dutch rule.

[1] Directors to Stuyvesant, April 16, 1660, in Col. Docs. N. Y. xiv. 461.
[2] Drisius to Classis of Amsterdam, October 4, 1660, in Eccl Recs. N. Y. i. 486.
[3] Gideon Schaats to Classis of Amsterdam, September 22, 1660, Ibid, 483.
[4] Classis of Amsterdam to Gideon Schaats, December 5, 1661, Ibid. 515.

CHAPTER VII

THE PERSECUTION OF THE QUAKERS

The ordinance, prohibiting dissenting worship, public and private, also inspired the measures enacted against the Quakers, who made their first advent into the Dutch colony the year following its adoption. Their arrival was not of the character to lessen the prejudices against this new sect, which had already been implanted in the minds of the civil and ecclesiastical authorities of New Netherland by the accounts of Quaker activity received from Europe. The clergy saw in the Quakers the instruments of Satan to disturb the churches in America as well as in Europe, "wandering to and fro sowing their tares" among the people of the Province, but they trusted that God would baffle the designs of Satan;[1] the Director General and Council regarded them as anarchists, whose doings tended not only to the subversion of the Protestant Religion, but also to the abolition of law and order, and to the contempt of civil authority. Under this conviction, Stuyvesant, when he noticed the growth of Quaker dissent, proclaimed a day of prayer against the spiritual as well as the temporal calamities, with which God

[1] Megapolensis and Drisius to Classis of Amsterdam, August 4, 1657, in Eccl. Recs. N. Y. i. 400.

was about to visit the Province for the thankless use of
temporal blessings, "permitting and allowing the Spirit
of Error to scatter its injurious passion amongst us in
spiritual matters here and there, rising up and propagating a new unheard of abominable heresy, called
Quakers, seeking to seduce many, yea were it possible
even the true believers—all signs of God's just judgment and certain forerunners of severe punishments."[1]

On August 6, 1657, a ship entered the harbor of
New Amsterdam, that carried no flag to reveal its character and fired no salute before the fort to announce its arrival. The Fiscal, who went on board, received no sign of
respect, and the Director General was not more favored,
when he received the visit of the master of the vessel,
who "stood still with his hat firm on his head, as if a
goat." Hardly a word could be gleaned in regard to
conditions in Europe, but finally it was learned that the
ship had Quakers on board. Although the Quakers
reported that the Governor was "moderate in words
and action," they departed the following morning as
silently as they had come and sailed eastward towards
Rhode Island, where the Dutch thought that they
would settle, as the Quakers were not tolerated in any
other place. However, several Quakers had secretly
remained behind, and endeavored to disturb and excite
the people by the testimony, to which they believed
themselves moved by the Spirit. Two young women,
Dorothy Waugh and May Witherhead,"began to quake
and go into a frenzy" in the middle of the street, crying
out in a loud voice, that men should repent, for the day

[1] Proclamation, January 21, 1658, in Recs. of New Amsterdam
ii. 346-7.

of judgment was at hand. A great tumult arose among
the inhabitants of the Dutch town, who, not knowing
what was the matter, ran to and fro, crying "fire" or
something else of like nature. The two women were
arrested and led to prison, where they continued to cry
out and pray. After eight days' detention, they were
taken from prison, their arms pinioned behind them,
and escorted between two negroes to a vessel at
the dock, which soon set sail for Rhode Island.[1]

Meanwhile, Robert Hodgson,with two other Quakers,
had made his way from the mainland to Long Island,
where his preaching found favor with the English settlers, amongst whom there were "many sincere seekers
after Heavenly riches . . . prepared to appreciate
those spiritual views of religion which these gospel mes-
sengers had to declare." At Gravesend and Jamaica
they "were received with gladness." At Hempstead
Hodgson also found settlers, who "rejoiced in the spread
of those living truths, which were preached among
them." Here the two Quakers who accompanied him
went on to the east end of the Island, while Hodgson
remained to preach in the English town. In the absence of a suitable building, he appointed an orchard for
a meeting, to which, on the Sunday after his arrival, he
invited all the inhabitants of the town. Richard Gildersleeve, a justice of peace, was determined to put a
stop to such a violation of the law and issued a warrant
for the arrest of the preacher. The constable found

[1] Megapolensis and Drisius to Classis of Amsterdam, August
14,; October 22, 1657, in Eccl. Recs., N.Y., i. 400, 409-10   Onderdonck, H., Jr., Old Meeting Houses of the Society of Friends in
the City of New York. Am. Hist. Rec. i. 117-118. Annals
of Hempstead, p. 5.

Hodgson "pacing the orchard alone in quiet medita-
tion." He was at once arrested and confined in the
house of Richard Gildersleeve. While the justice of
peace went to church, the Quaker attracted a large
crowd of people before the house, "who staid and heard
the truth declared." On his return, the magistrate,
annoyed at being thus outwitted, committed the prisoner to another house and immediately left for Manhattan to inform Stuyvesant of the arrest. The
Director General commended the zeal of the magistrate
in suppressing the "Quaker heresy," and sent the Fiscal
with a guard of twelve musketeers to bring Hodgson
and those who had entertained him in their homes to
the Fort in New Amsterdam. Meanwhile, Hodgson,
had renewed his tactics of the morning. "In the afternoon," he says, "many came to me, and even those that
had been mine enemies, after they heard the truth, confessed it."

On the arrival of the Fiscal and guard, Hodgson was
searched and his papers and Bible seized. He was then
bound with cords and remanded to prison. Meanwhile, diligent search was made "for those two women
who had entertained the stranger." As soon as they
were found, they were placed under arrest, although one
of them was burdened with a nursing infant. The two
women were placed in a cart, to the tail of which Hodgson was tied and thus dragged through the woods and
over bad roads, "whereby he was much torn and
abused." On their arrival at Amsterdam, the women
were put in prison, but soon after they were again
released and allowed to return to their homes. Hodgson, however, was cast into a "dungeon full of vermin

and so odious for wet and dirt, as he never saw before."
The Quaker no doubt proved defiant at the examination before the Council. He was fined six hundred
guilders, in default of which he was sentenced to serve
two years at the wheelbarrow with a negro. Hodgson
attempted to argue the matter with the court, but he
was not allowed to speak, and sent back to prison,
"where no English were suffered to come to him."
Some time later, he was taken out of this horrible dungeon, and brought pinioned to the Council, where his
hat was removed from his head and another sentence
read to him in Dutch, that he did not understand,
"but that it displeased many of that nation did appear
by the shaking of their heads."

Some days after this, Hodgson, early one morning
was chained to a wheelbarrow and ordered to work.
When the Quaker refused, a pitched rope, about four
inches thick, was put in the hands of a strong negro
slave, who beat the prisoner until he fell to the ground.
This brought no respite. The unfortunate man was
lifted up and again beaten until he fell a second time.
In spite of his miserable plight, Hodgson was kept in
the heat of the sun, chained to the wheelbarrow, until
he could no longer support himself and had to sit down.
A second and a third day he was chained as before with
a sentinel to prevent all conversation, but he refused to
work, as he "had committed no evil." The Director
General then again commanded him to work, as "otherwise he should be whipt every day," but the Quaker
merely demanded in reply, "what law he had broken
and called for his accusers, that he might know his
transgression." No answer was given, but Hodgson

was again chained to the wheelbarrow and threatened
with severer punishment, if he should dare to speak to
any person. When he refused to keep silent, he was
confined to his dungeon for several days, "two nights
and one day and a half of which, without bread and
water." Then he was taken to a room, where he was
stripped to his waist and hung to the ceiling by his
hands with a heavy log tied to his feet, "so that he
could not turn his body." He was then scourged with
rods by a negro slave until his flesh was cut into pieces,
after which he was kept in the solitary confinement of
a loathsome dungeon for two days, when he was again
made to undergo the same savage torture. Hodgson
now felt as though he were about to die and asked that
some English person might be allowed to come to him.
An English woman was then allowed to bathe his
wounds. She thought that he could not live until
morning. When she told her husband of the horrible
condition of the prisoner, he tried to bribe the Fiscal
with the offer of a fat ox to obtain permission for Hodgson's removal to his own house until he recovered.
This was refused and the payment of the whole fine
demanded. The Quaker would not consent to this and
was kept "like a slave to hard work." Other persons
also interested themselves in favor of the Quaker's
release. An unknown person sent a letter to Stuyvesant and counselled him to send the obstinate Quaker
to Rhode Island, as his labor was hardly worth the cost.
When Stuyvesant's sister Anna, widow of Nicholas
Bayard, interceded earnestly in behalf of the prisoner,

the unfortunate Quaker was liberated on the condition of leaving the Province.[1]

By this time, Quaker preaching had so infected the English towns of Gravesend, Hempstead, Jamaica and Flushing, that the Director General and Council thought it advisable to adopt even more drastic measures for the repression of these "seducers of the people, who are destructive unto magistracy and ministry." An ordinance was issued, which made vessels bringing Quakers into the Province subject to confiscation, and persons entertaining a Quaker a single night, liable to a fine of fifty pounds, of which one-half was to go to the informer.[2] The proclamation of this ordinance met with open resistence from the people of Flushing, who were unwilling to infringe and violate the patent of the town, granted in the name of the States General, which guaranteed "Liberty of Conscience, according to the custom and manner of Holland without molestacon or disturbance, from any magistrate or magistrates, or any other Ecclesiastical Minister, that may extend jurisdiccon over them."[3] The sheriff of Flushing, Tobias Feake, instructed the clerk Edward Hart to draw up a remonstrance against this violation of the privileges of the town of Flushing, to be submitted to the people for

[1] Onderdonck, H., Jr., Friends on Long Island and in New York, Annals of Hempstead, pp. 5-6; 93. O'Callaghan, Hist of New Netherland, ii. 347-350.
[2] Brodhead, Hist. of State of New York, i. 637. Thompson, Hist. of Long Island, ii. 74, note
[3] Remonstrance of the people of Flushing, December 27, 1657, Col Docs., N, Y., xiv. 402-404; Laws and Ordinances of New Netherland, New York Deed Book, ii. 178, printed in Appendix of Waller, Hist. of Flushing. The town of Gravesend has the same provision in its charter, and was not less infected with Quaker teaching. Nevertheless, Gravesend did not make a similar protest

their approval and then presented to the Director General and Council.[1]   A town meeting was assembled in the house of Michael Milner, where the clerk read the remonstrance to the people of the town.   Thirty-one signed this protest.   They cannot condemn the Quakers nor can they stretch out their hands to punish, banish or persecute them, when they are bound by the law to do good unto all men, especially to those of the household of faith.   If the alternative is placed before them, to choose between God and man, their conscience will not allow them to hesitate in the choice, as "that which is of God will stand, and that which is of man will come to nothing."   They further declare that "the law of love, peace and liberty in the state, extending to Jews, Turks and Egyptians, as they are considered the sons of Adam, which is the glory of the outward state of Holland, so love, peace and liberty, extending to all in Christ Jesus, condemns hatred, war and bondage." The Savior had pronounced woe unto those by whom scandal cometh; their desire "is not to offend one of his little ones in whatsoever forme, name or title hee appeares in, whether Presbyterian, Independent, Baptist or Quaker; but shall be glad to see anything of God in any of them; desiring to do unto all men as wee desire all men to do unto us, which is the true law both of Church and State."   They, therefore, conclude, that, if any Quakers should come to them in love, they cannot in conscience lay violent hands upon them, but give them free ingress into their town and houses according to the

[1] Cross-examination of Hart, Col. Docs., N. Y., xiv. 404-405; petition of Hart for pardon, January 23, 1658, Ibid. 409.

commands of their conscience and the provisions of
their charter.

This remonstrance was delivered to the Director
General by Tobias Feake himself, who was immediately
arrested by the Fiscal, Nicasius de Sille.[1] On the first
day of the new year (1658), the two other magistrates
who had signed the remonstrance, Edward Farrington
and William Noble, appeared at New Amsterdam in
answer to the summons of the Director General and
Council, and were also immediately placed under
arrest,[2] but, after their petition,[3] they were given the
liberty to go about on Manhattan Island on promising
to appear at any time on the summons of the court.
The clerk, Edward Hart, was subjected to a cross-examination, intended to reveal the circumstances of the
composition of the remonstrance, and then also placed
in confinement. The Fiscal, Nicasius de Sille[4], accused
the magistrates of having violated the articles of the
charter of "Freedoms and Exemptions", which permitted the public exercise of no other religion than the
Reformed, and also the placards issued by the Director
General and Council. Farrington and Noble at first
refused to acknowledge themselves guilty of any offense.
They declared that they had considered the remonstrance in the light of a request for the information,
whether the liberty of conscience might still be given,
which they had understood to be granted by their
charter "without molistacion of Maiestrate or Minis-

[1] Council minute, January 1, 1658, Col. Docs. N. Y. xiv. 404.
[2] Ibid.
[3] Ibid. 406.
[4] Noble and Farrington to Director General and Council in
answer to Fiscal, January 9, 1658, Ibid. 406-7.

ter." This had been their conclusion of a close study of the patent, which they called their charter, and if they were in the dark in this matter, they desired to be corrected, as they did not know the articles, which the Fiscal had called their charter. They also protested that they had put into execution to the full extent of their powers their "Honners perticular wrting an order concerning yᵉ Quakers." If they were, therefore guilty of any offense, it was at most the result of ignorance, which they pleaded as the excuse for having signed a writing offensive to the Director General and Council, presented by Tobias Feake. Their fault was graciously forgiven and pardoned on the written acknowledgment of their error and promise to be more cautious in the future and on condition of paying the cost and mises of the law.[1] The clerk, Edward Hart, also obtained liberal treatment at the hands of the authorities under the same conditions. His request for a pardon had been supported by several of the inhabitants of Flushing, where he always had been willing to serve his neighbors, whose circumstances he knew thoroughly, being one of the oldest inhabitants of the town. Finally, the Director General and Council pardoned him, as he had drawn up the remonstrance at the instigation of the schout, Tobias Feake, and as he had a large family dependent upon him for their support.

Thus all the responsibility was thrown upon the schout of Flushing. Tobias Feake could not deny that he had received "an order from the Hon. Director General not to admit, lodge and entertain in the said village

[1] Col. Docs N. Y. xiv. 408, 409.

any one of the heretical and abominable sect called
Quakers," and he was found guilty of having instigated
"a seditious, mutinous and detestable letter of defiance
wherein (he and his accomplices) justify and uphold the
abominable sect of Quakers, who vilify both the political
authorities and the ministers of the Gospel, and undermine the State and God's service and absolutely
demand, that all sects, especially the said abominable
sect of Quakers, shall and must be tolerated and admitted." He deserved to be made an example to others,
as he had not only violated the laws of the Province,
but had also been unfaithful to his oath, official position
and duty, as a subordinate officer of the government in
the village of Flushing. Nevertheless, the Director
General and Council decided to be lenient, as the prisoner confessed his wrong doing andpromised to avoid
such errors hereafter. He was degraded from his office,
and sentenced to be banished from the Province of
New Netherland, or to pay a fine of two hundred florins
in addition to the costs of the trial.[1] Stuyvesant could
well be content with the result of his vigorous proceedings in this matter. All the principal remonstrants had
been brought to retract the principles which they had
advanced in contradiction to Stuyvesant's policy of
government. Although they had espoused the cause
of religious liberty in defense of the persecuted Quakers, they had not the heroic fortitude that made the
Quakers seal their testimony with their blood.

The opposition was so completely crushed in Flushing that the magistrates, Farrington and Noble, did not

[1] Sentence, January 28, 1658, in Col. Docs. N. Y. xiv. 409.

even dare to attend to the cases pending in the court without further orders.[1] When William Lawrence, the oldest magistrate of the town, submitted a petition to this effect, it was resolved to suspend the meetings of the magistrates until the Director General and Council could personally visit the town or send a committee to give the orders, that were required by the conditions not only of Flushing, but also of the other neighboring English villages. Meanwhile, any extraordinary matter, requiring immediate attention, was to be referred to the Director General and Council.[2] At the time of this visit, the inhabitants of Flushing peaceably submitted to a modification of their municipal government, which Stuyvesant thought would prevent the disorders, "arising from town meetings." In the future, the sheriff, who was to be "acquainted not only with the English and Dutch language, but also with Dutch practical law," and the other magistrates were to consult in all cases a board "of seven of the most reasonable and respectable of the inhabitants, to be called tribunes and townsmen." The growth of Quaker influence was ascribed to the lack of an organized ministry in the English towns, and a tax of twelve stivers per morgen was imposed upon the inhabitants of Flushing "for the support of an orthodox minister." Six weeks were granted for the signature of a written submission to the provisions of this new charter. Upon the expiration of this term, recusants had the only alternative "to

[1] January 20, 1658, Col. Docs. N. Y. xiv. 408.
[2] January 22, 1658, Ibid.

dispose of their property at their pleasure and leave the soil of this government."[1]

While the Flushing remonstrants were on trial, Stuyvesant found support for his policy of repression amongst some of the inhabitants of Long Island. Twelve of the principal inhabitants of Jamaica had informed the Director General and Council that the Quakers had an unusual correspondence at the house of Henry Townsend, where they and their followers had also been "lodged and provided with meat and drink." The antecedents of the offender were not such as to merit favor with Stuyvesant. In August, 1657, he had arranged a conventicle in his own house for Robert Hodgson,[2] for which he had been condemned a month later to a fine of eight pounds Flemish, that had not yet been paid. When Henry Townsend appeared before the court, the Fiscal demanded that he be condemned to a fine of one hundred pounds Flemish, as he had again lately violated the ordinance of the government by "lodging and keeping with Quakers." On the confession of his guilt, Henry Townsend was sentenced "as an example for other transgressors and contumacious offenders" to a fine of three hundred florins, to be paid with the costs of the trial before his liberation from prison.[4] His brother, John Townsend, was also cited before the court on the suspicion of favoring Quakers

---

[1] Provisions of March 26, 1658. Thompson, Hist. of Long Island, ii. 291-2.
[2] Minute, January 8, 1658, Col. Docs. N. Y. xiv. 405-6.
[3] Onderdonck, H., Jr., Amer. Hist., Rec. i. 210. "Friends' Meeting Houses on Long Island."
[4] Council minute, January 15, 1658. Col. Docs. N. Y. xiv. 407-8.

and of being implicated in the Flushing remonstrance. The accusation was made that he had gone, in the company of the clerk of Flushing, to the house of Edward Farrington, whom he had persuaded to sign the remonstrance. John Townsend admitted, that he had been at Flushing, and visited Farrington as an old acquaintance, but he denied that he had persuaded the magistrate to sign anything. He was also accused of having been in the company of a banished Quakeress at Gravesend. Although he also denied this charge, the suspicions of the court were not allayed. He was, therefore, given the choice either to go to prison, until the Fiscal could obtain more evidence on the friendly relations of the accused with the Quakers, or to give bail to the amount of twelve pounds sterling to ensure his appearance at the court on the summons of the Fiscal.[1] On the same day, judgment was also pronounced in the case of John Tilton, formerly town clerk, who had been imprisoned on the charge of the Schout of Gravesend,[2] that he had lodged a Quakeress, who had been banished from New Netherland, with some other persons of her adherents, belonging to that abominable sect. Tilton declared that the Quakeress had come to his house with other neighbors during his absence, but, in spite of his humble petition and former good conduct, he was fined "twelve pounds Flemish with the costs and mises of justice, to be applied, one-third in behalf of the Attorney General, one-third in behalf of the sheriff of Gravesend, and the rest as directed by law."[3] The opposition to

---

[1] Council minute, January 10, 1658. Col. Docs N. Y. xiv. 407.
[2] Council minute, January 8, 1658. Ibid. 406.
[3] Council minute, January 10, 1658. Ibid.

the Quakers was not limited in Gravesend to this magistrate alone. Two years later ten of the inhabitants of this village, only two of whom were English: the Sheriff Charles Morgan and Lieutenant Nicholas Stillwell, informed the Director General and Council that "the licentious mode of living, the desecration of the Sabbath, the confusion of religious opinion prevalent in the village" made many grow cold "in the exercise of Christian virtue, and almost surpass the heathens, who have no knowledge of God and his commandments." They requested, therefore, that "a preacher be sent here that the glory of God may be spread, the ignorant taught, the simple and innocent strengthened, and the licentious restrained." Stuyvesant and his council were well pleased with the remonstrance, and promised to fulfill their request as soon as possible.[1]

Nowhere did Stuyvesant's policy coincide so thoroughly with the views of the local authorities as in Hempstead, where the closest union between the town and its church establishment had found its expression in an order, issued by the General Court with the consent of a full town meeting, which confessed that "the Contempt of Gods Word And Sabbaths is the desolating Sinn off Civill States and Plantations, And that the Publick preaching of the Word, by those that are Called thereunto is the Chiefe and ordinarie meanes ordayned of God for the Converting, Edifying and Saveing of ye Soules of the Ellect, through the presence and power of the Holy Ghost therevnto promised." The General Court, therefore, decreed "That All per-

---

[1] Council minute, April 12, 1660. Col. Docs. N. Y. xiv. 460.

sons Inhabiting In this Towne or yᵉ Limitts thereof
shall duely resort and repaire to the Publique meetings,
and Assemblies one the Lords dayes And one the
Publique dayes of fastings and thanksgivings appointed
by Publique Authority, both one the forenoones
And Afternoones." Persons, who absented themselves "w'thout Just and Necessary Cause approved by
the particular Court," were to "forfeict, for the first
offence, five guilders, for yₑ second Offence, ten guilders
And for yᵉ third Offence, twenty Guilders." Those
who proved refractory, perverse and obstinate, were to
be "Lyable to the further Censure of the Court, Eyther
for the Agravation of the fine, or for Corporall punishment or Banishment." Finally, persons informing
the magistrates or the particular Court about the
neglect or contempt of this order, were to be rewarded by one-half of the fine, the other half of
which was to be converted to public use.[1] This ordinance, which had been passed by the General Court of
Hempstead, September 16, 1650, was approved, ratified
and confirmed, October 26,1657, by the Director General
and Council of New Netherland, who authorized the
magistrates of the village to execute promptly its
provisions against trespassers. The authentication of
the copy and its record in the Town books by John
James, the clerk of Hempstead, bear the date of January, 16, 1658. These facts show that the approved ordinance was returned to the town precisely at the time
that the growth of the Quaker movement on Long Island
claimed the strict attention of the authorities at New

[1] Recs. of Towns of N. and S. Hempstead, Long Island, i.
56-57.

Amsterdam.[1]   The magistrates of Hempstead were
not in need of much exhortation to proceed against
trespassers, for they had learned "by woeful experiance,
that of late a sect hath taken such ill effect amongst us
to the seducing of certain of the inhabitants, who by
giving heed to the seducing spirits under the notion of
being inspired by the Holy Spirit of God, have drawn
away with their error and misguided light those which
together with us did worship God in spirit and in
truth, and more unto our grief do separate from us:
and unto the great dishonor of God, and the violation
of the established laws and the Christian order, that
ought to be observed with love, peace and concord,
have broke the Sabbath, and neglected to join with us
in the true worship and service of God, as formerly they
have done."   The inhabitants in the town and to the
uttermost bounds thereof were, therefore, ordered to
give no entertainment, nor to have any converse with
the Quakers, who at the very most "are permitted for
one night's lodging in the parish, and so to depart
quietly without dispute or debate the next morning."[2]
This proclamation was published shortly after Stuyvesant's visit to Long Island on April 13, 1658.   Five
days later, the wives of Joseph Schott and Francis
Weeks were fined twenty guilders each in addition to
the costs of the trial.   They had not only absented
themselves from the public worship of God contrary
to the law of God and the laws of the town, but they
had also profaned the Lords day by going to a con-

---

[1] Recs. of Towns of N. and S. Hempstead, i. 57-58.
[2] Proclamation of the Magistrates of Hempstead, April 13,
1658. Thompson, Hist. of Long Island, ii. 11-12.

venticle or meeting in the woods, where there were two Quakers. The two women refused to admit themselves guilty of any offence, as they had gone out to meet the people of God.[1] The opposition, which was early manifested in this way by the magistrates of the town towards the Quakers, was the policy pursued without alteration in Hempstead. When Thomas Terry and Samuel Dearing petitioned for leave to settle some families at Matinecock within the jurisdiction of Hempstead, the magistrates of the town drew up a contract, dated July 4, 1661, which bound the petitioners to observe the laws of Hempstead, to admit only inhabitants possessing letters of commendation and approbation from the magistrates, elders or selected townsmen of their former place of residence, and finally "to bring in no Quakers or any such like opinionists, but such as are approved by the inhabitants of Hempstead." This contract was confirmed and still more specified in some details as late as June 23, 1663.[2]

New measures were adopted by Stuyvesant for the repression of the Quaker movement on Long Island in January, 1661. Letters from Jamaica, Flushing and Middelburg (Newton) had informed him, that the Quakers had uncommonly free access to the house of Henry Townsend, who had, therefore, been placed under arrest. A good occasion to investigate the condition of religion in the towns known to be infected was offered, when some of the inhabitants of Jamaica earnestly requested one of the clergymen of New

[1] Court minute, April 18, 1658. Thompson, Hist. of Long Island, ii, 12.
[2] Recs. of the Towns of N. and S. Hempstead, i. 143-145; Col. Docs. N. Y. xiv. 528-529.

Amsterdam to come to their village to preach and to
baptize several of their children. Stuyvesant then
instructed the minister Drisius, the deputy sheriff
Resolved Waldron, and the clerk Nicholas Bayard to
go to Jamaica and obtain minute information on the
violation of the ordinances against private conventicles
by the Quakers and other sects.[1] Drisius preached
twice on Sunday, January 9th, and baptized eight children and two old women. Meanwhile, the deputy
sheriff had learned that a meeting of Quakers was being
held at Gravesend. When Waldron and Bayard
arrived there the next day, the Quaker George Wilson
had already escaped, but they returned in the evening
to New Amsterdam with the Quaker's cloak and a
prisoner, Samuel Spicer, who "with several others had
not only followed and listened to the Quaker in several
conventicles, but also entertained him in his mother's
house." At Jamaica, the work of investigation had
been facilitated by the assistance of two of the townspeople, Richard Everett and Nathaniel Denton, who
gave the commissioners a list of ten persons, who had
assembled in the house of Henry Townsend, on his
invitation from door to door to listen to a learned man
there.[2] On the arrival of the commissioners at New
Amsterdam, both Henry Townsend and Samuel Spicer
were put on trial, but they refused to incriminate themselves by acknowledging the charges of the Fiscal, and
claimed that they had only called on their friends and
that no law forbade friends to meet each other. They
were remanded to prison and ordered to answer without

[1] Council minute, January 8, 1661. Col. Docs. N. Y. xiv. 489.
[2] Council minute, January 9, 1661. Ibid. 490.

any equivocation to the charges of the public prosecutor, who demanded that the prisoners be condemned to a fine of six hundred florins each, according to the ordinance violated.[1] Henry Townsend finally acknowledged that he had lodged in his house some friends who are called Quakers, and that he had assembled a meeting at his house, at which one of them spoke, but he concluded with the protest, that, although they might squander and devour his estate and manacle his person, his soul was his God's and his opinions his own. He refused to pay the fine of twenty-five pounds to which he was sentenced on January 20th, and languished in prison, where he was daily supplied with food, which his nine-year-old daughter Rose passed to him through the gratings of the jail.[2] Samuel Spicer was fined only twelve pounds. An order was also issued for the banishment of John Tilton of Gravesend and John Townsend of Jamaica. Mrs. Micah Spicer was also prosecuted for entertaining the Quaker, but she was acquitted, as she did not know that George Wilson was a member of that sect.[3]

Stuyvesant was now determined to enforce the observance of the ordinance against private conventicles, especially in the village of Jamaica, where the movement of Quaker dissent was most prevalent at this time. Some of those who had been entrusted with authority had been so unfaithful to their office as to

[1] Council minute, January 9, 1661. Col. Docs. N. Y. xii. 491.
[2] Thompson, Hist. of Long Island, ii. 292-3; 295.
[3] Cal. of Dutch MSS., ed. O'Callaghan, i. 220-1; Col. Docs. N. Y. l. c., note. Thompson says, "The widow Spicer, mother of Samuel, was also arrested, accused and condemned in an amende fifteen pounds Flanders."

"connive with the Sect, giving entertainment unto
their scattering preachers, leave and way unto their
unlawful meetings and prohibited conventicles," which
all tended to the subversion of the Protestant religion,
to the contempt of authority and to the destruction of
law and order. He, therefore, appointed three new
magistrates, Richard Everett, Nathaniel Denton and
Andrew Messenger, whose zeal for the good of the
country and the Protestant cause would ensure the
observance of the ordinance against conventicles. He
also sent six soldiers to assist them in this, "if need and
occasion should require," who were to be furnished
with convenient lodging in the town.[1] In obedience
to the orders of the Director General, the magistrates
called the inhabitants of the town together and submitted to them a written statement to sign, by which
they bound themselves to inform the authorities about
any meetings and conventicles of Quakers within the
town and also to assist them against the Quakers in
case of need.[2] Only six refused to subscribe. These
were John Townsend, Richard Harker, Samuel Dean,
Samuel Andrews, Benjamin Hubbard and Nathaniel
Cole.[3] In their report, Everett and Denton had petitioned Stuyvesant to relieve the town from quartering
the soldiers, as the innocent were thus unjustly punished for the self-will of the guilty. The Director
General then ordered the soldiers to be lodged and

[1] Stuyvesant to Jamaica, January 24, 1661. Col. Docs. N.Y. xii.
490-1.
[2] Ibid. 492; Jamaica Rec. i. 120. O'Callaghan, Hist. of New
Netherland, ii. 451. note 1.
[3] Everett and Denton to Stuyvesant, February 11, 1661.
Col. Docs. N. Y. xiv. 492.

furnished with decent meat and victuals by those who still refused to concur in the desires of the government.[1] When these men remonstrated, they were informed that the soldiers would be withdrawn, as soon as they would sign the pledge to inform against the Quakers. Most of the recusants then sold out and removed to Oyster Bay beyond the jurisdiction of the Dutch government.[2]

In spite of all vigilance, the magistrates of Jamaica had to report, in August of the following year, to the Director General, that the majority of the inhabitants of the village were adherents of the abominable sect called Quakers. They themselves could do nothing to stop the increase of this sect, as the townspeople did not assemble in forbidden conventicles within their jurisdiction, but in a large meeting held every Sunday at the house of John Bowne in Flushing, where the dissenters gathered from the whole neighborhood.[3] Stuyvesant then ordered all the magistrates and inhabitants of the English towns in the jurisdiction of New Netherland to assist the sheriff, Resolved Waldron, to imprison all persons, found in a prohibited or an unlawful meeting.[4]

John Bowne[5] first visited Flushing on the fifteenth of June, 1651, in company with his brother-in-law, Edward Farrington. There he was married to Hannah

---

[1] Col. Docs. N. Y. xiv. 493
[2] Onderdonck, H., Jr., Amer. Hist. Rec. i, 210.
[3] Council minute, August 24, 1662; Col. Docs. N. Y. xiv. 515.
[4] Council minute, September 9, 1662, Ibid. 516.
[5] For biographical data cf. Mandeville, Flushing Past and Present, p. 96, etc.; Thompson, Hist. of Long Island, ii. 285-6; 388; Watkins, Some Early New York Settlers from New England, in N. E. Hist. and Geneol. Reg., lv. 300 (1901); Henry Onderdonck, Jr., Amer. Hist. Rec., i. 8, note 1. 49-50 (1872).

Field, May 7, 1656, and five years later he built the house, which, within a few years, became the meeting place for all the Quakers of the neighborhood. His wife had first become a member of the Society of Friends, who then usually assembled for worship in the woods and fields. Her husband accompanied her to some of these meetings, mainly from motives of curiosity in the beginning. The beauty and simplicity of their worship so pleased him, that he invited the Quakers to assemble for these meetings in his own house, where he also was soon admitted as a member. He declared that his conversion resulted "not merely from the kindness and affection of his wife, but his judgment also was convinced of the truth of the principles which they held forth." His faith was soon put to test in the persecution, which he had to bear at the hands of the civil authority for remaining faithful to its teaching.[1]

As soon as the sheriff Resolved Waldron had received his commission from Stuyyesant, he set out for Flushing with a company of armed men to arrest John Bowne.[2] When he arrived at the house, John Bowne, with his youngest child sick in his arms, was taking care of his wife, who was also seriously ill in bed. Nevertheless, the sheriff ordered him to proceed to New Amsterdam for trial, but John Bowne made the plea that his family were not in a condition to permit him to leave them. The sheriff declared that he must fulfill his orders, but the day was now so advanced that

[1] Thompson, Hist. of Long Island, ii. 385-6.
[2] These details in the Journal of John Bowne, partly printed in Amer. Hist. Rec. i. by Onderdonck, 4-8.

he decided to leave the prisoner under guard till next day. Meanwhile, Resolved Waldron went to the town and in the evening returned with the Schout of Flushing. Bowne then demanded the order of his arrest from the sheriff, who at first refused, but then handed it to him. When John Bowne saw that it was not a special warrant, but the general commission of Stuyvesant, which authorized Waldron to arrest any person found in an unlawful assembly, he refused to go on foot to New Amsterdam in virtue of that order, as the sheriff had found him in no assembly of any kind, but the sheriff threatened to carry him off bound hand and foot. The next day he was transported thither in a boat and imprisoned in the courthouse. He attempted to obtain a few words with the Director General, whom he saw mounting his horse, but Stuyvesant gave the sergeant to understand that he would speak with Bowne only on the condition, that he would put off his hat and stand bareheaded in his presence, which Bowne declared he could not do. Stuyvesant anticipated the same refusal on the following day, when Bowne was brought for trial to the court room. As soon as he heard the approach of the prisoner, even before he came into view, the Director General bade him to take off his hat, but, before John Bowne could refuse, he commanded the Schout to give him the necessary assistance to comply with the demand. Stuyvesant himself read the ordinance against conventicles to the prisoner, but Bowne denied that he had kept meetings of "heretics, deceivers and seducers", as he could not admit the servants of the Lord to be such. Stuyvesant refused to argue and bluntly asked if he would deny that he had kept conventicles in his house. Bowne refused at first to incriminate himself, but then declared that he would not ask the court to prove the charge, that he was in their hands ready to suffer whatever they were allowed by God to inflict upon him. Finally, the prisoner gave the court to understand the condition of his family and the cruelty of separating him from them in these circumstances, but Stuyyesant placed the responsibility of this on John Bowne himself, who had occasioned his arrest by his refusal to obey the ordinances of the government. John Bowne was now removed again to his place of confinement, while the court deliberated on the nature of the offence and the extent of the penalty to be imposed. The Court found that the prisoner had not only provided with lodgings some of that heretical and abominable sect named Quakers, but even permitted them to keep their forbidden meetings in his house, at which he assisted with his whole family. Thus the abominable sect, that vilifies the magistrates and preachers of God's Holy Word, that endeavors to undermine both the State and Religion, found encouragement in its errors and seduced others from the right path with the dangerous consequences of heresy and schism. He was, therefore, fined twenty-five pounds on September 14, with the costs of the trial, and warned to abstain in the future from all such conventicles and meetings under the penalty of paying double that amount for the second offence, and of being banished from the Province for the third offence.[1] The Schout then privately informed John Bowne of the fine imposed

---

[1] Council minute, September 14, 1662, printed in full in Thompson, Hist. of Long Island, ii. 77-78.

and told him that he must remain until the fine was paid. The next day official notice of the fine was served on the prisoner, but he refused to pay anything on that account.[1]

At Gravesend, John Tilton and Mary, his wife, were also taken prisoners and transported to New Amsterdam to be tried for having attended meetings and for having lodged persons of the abominable sect of the Quakers.[2] Goody Tilton was furthermore charged with "having, like a sorceress, gone from door to door to lure even young girls to join the Quakers."[3] Two days after these complaints were made before the court, the Director General and Council issued an ordinance which interdicted under severe penalties the public exercise of any but the Reformed Religion, "either in houses, barns, ships or yachts, in the woods or fields, the provision of heretics, vagabonds or strollers with accommodations, and the introduction and distribution of all seditious or seducing books, papers or letters." The ordinance also required the registration of all persons arriving in the province, within six weeks of their advent, at the secretary's office, where they were also then to take the oath of allegiance. The execution of the ordinance was to be ensured by the provision, that all magistrates conniving at the violation of this statute were to be deposed from their office and declared incompetent to hold any public trust in the future.[4] Two weeks after the proclamation of this ordinance,

[1] Journal of John Bowne, Amer. Hist. Rec. i. 4-8
[2] Council minute, September 19, 1662. O'Callaghan, Cal. Hist. MSS. (Dutch), i.240.
[3] Thompson, Hist. for Long Island, ii. 295.
[4] O'Callaghan, Hist of New Netherland, ii. 454-5.

John and Mary Tilton were sentenced to be banished
from the province. On the same day, Micah Spicer
and her son Samuel, were also ordered to leave the
province, as they were found guilty of harboring
Quakers and distributing seditious and seducing pamphlets to propagate their heresy.[1]

When John Bowne continued firm in his refusal to
submit to the Court's sentence, he was removed, on the
twenty-fifth of September, to the dungeon, where the
guard of soldiers received a strict charge to allow no
one by day or night to visit the prisoner, who was to be
permitted nothing but coarse bread and water. The
following month, he was again removed to the Stadt-
house, where this severity was relaxed, "the door being
open sometimes for a week together, sometimes more,
sometimes less, both day and night." During this
time, he received the visits of his wife and of his friends,
and sometimes even went abroad in New Amsterdam.
His liberty was again more restricted, when, on the
fourteenth of December, the Director General and Council "for the welfare of the community and to crush, as
far as it is possible, that abominable sect, who treat
with contempt both the political magistrates and
the ministers of God's Holy Word and endeavor to
undermine the police and religion, resolved to transport
from this province the aforesaid John Bowne, if he
continues obstinate and pervicatious, in the first ship
ready to sail, for an example to others."[2] John Bowne
was now anxious to obtain an opportunity to plead his

[1] Council minute, October 5, 1662; O'Callaghan, Cal. of
Hist. MSS. (Dutch), i. 240.
[2] Council minute, December 14, 1662. Thompson, Hist. of
Long Island, ii. 78

cause before the court, but Stuyvesant refused to grant this request of the prisoner and insisted that he either pay the fine or go into exile, but he allowed him to go home for a chest and clothes. Later William Leveridge was authorized to tell Bowne, that, if he would promise to go out of the Dutch jurisdiction within three months, he would be set free the next day, but John Bowne refused to give any answer to this proposition, except to the Director General in person. William Leveridge neglected to deliver the message to Stuyvesant, who now had the prisoner kept more closely than before in his place of confinement. On the last day of December, John Bowne was offered the liberty to visit, for the first days of the new year, his wife and friends, on the condition that he would promise to return to New Amsterdam on the evening of the third day. The Schout also told him that the Director General was still willing to set him free, if he would promise to remove with his family out of his jurisdiction within a month, but John Bowne refused to entertain this proffer of Stuyvesant. Faithful to his promise, Bowne returned to New Amsterdam before the expiration of his leave of absence, and then was allowed the freedom of the town. He could learn nothing of the intentions of the authorities, although his chest, clothes, and bedding were still retained in prison. When a ship was about to sail, Bowne met Resolved Waldron. Upon the enquiries of the Quaker, the Schout saw the Director General, and then told Bowne to bring his things from prison and to transfer them to the boat. John Bowne now succeeded in obtaining an interview with Stuyvesant, who was very moderate in his conversation with the Quaker. He refused to argue, but, on the request of John Bowne, willingly gave him a written statement that he was banished from the country for not submitting to the sentence of the Court. The Quaker was, however, not satisfied with the wording of the statement, which doubtless was not more complimentary to that sect than the other official documents on this case. The Director again offered Bowne his liberty, if he would promise to leave his jurisdiction in three months. Bowne would not yield, but protested his innocence of any crime and of any desire to obtain revenge for the evil that they had done him, which moved the Director General to thank him and to call him Goodman Bowne. Nevertheless, on January eighth, the Director General and Council commanded him to depart on the ship Fox, now ready to sail, while it was once more left to his choice either to obey and submit to the judgment of the court or at the sight of the order to depart.[1] In the evening of the same day, he was carried on board the ship, which set sail the following day for Holland. Stuyvesant sent a report of the case to the Directors at Amsterdam, in which he complained of John Bowne, as a disturber of the peace, who "obstinately persisted in his refusal to pay the fine imposed by the Court of the province of New Netherland, and who now was banished" in the hope that other dissenters might be discouraged. The Director General also declared that he was determined to adopt "more severe prosecutions," if this example

[1] Council minute, January 8, 1663, in full in Thompson, Hist. of Long Island, ii. 78.

should fail to deter these sectarians from further contempt of authority in Church and State.[1]

When the Directors at Amsterdam received Stuyvesant's letter, they felt that it was time again to restrain the religious zeal of the Director General within the limits which they thought would not injure the interests of their colony. While they were also heartily desirous of seeing the Province free from Quakers and other sectarians, their zeal for the religious unity of the Province was tempered by the fear that a too rigorous policy might diminish the population and stop immigration, which had to be favored at this early stage of the development of the colony. Stuyvesant was, therefore, told, in the letter[2] of the Directors of April 16, 1663, that he might shut his eyes to the presence of dissent in New Netherland, or at least that he was not to force the conscience, but to allow everyone to have his own belief, as long as he behaved quietly and legally, gave no offence to his neighbors, and did not oppose the government. The Directors referred Stuyvesant to the moderation, practiced towards all forms of dissent in the City of Amsterdam, which made it the asylum of the persecuted and oppressed from every country, with the result of a large increase of its population. The same blessing would follow an imitation of this policy of moderation in the colony of New Netherland. The letter of the Directors of the Amsterdam Chamber has generally been interpreted in the light of an edict of toleration extended to the Province of New Netherland, with which all per-

[1] O'Callaghan, Hist of New Netherland, ii. 456-7; Brodhead, Hist. of New York, i. 706.
[2] Col. Docs. N. Y xiv. 526.

secution of the Quakers ceased until the termination of the Dutch rule.[1] It is true that the acts of repression, executed by the Council of New Netherland during the month of May, in all likelihood preceeded the arrival of this letter in New Amsterdam. Thus on May 7th, the Fiscal was ordered to make an inventory of the property of John Tilton of Gravesend, who was then in prison.[2] Ten days later, a warrant was granted to remove the prisoner and his wife, Mary Tilton, from the province.[3] On the same day, a new ordinance[4] was issued by the provincial government, which inflicted heavy penalties upon skippers and barques, smuggling into the country any of those "abominable imposters, runaways and strolling people called Quakers." There is, however, no doubt, that the Dutch minister Polhemus of Midwout, who in all his correspondence keeps himself free from the persecuting spirit of his fellow ministers in New Amsterdam, referred to a common measure of repression adopted against Quakers, when he wrote to the Classis of Amsterdam only four months before Stuyvesant's capitulation to the English: "The Quakers also are compelled to go before the court, and be put under oath; but such compulsion is displeasing to God."[5] In fact, the letter of the Directors only requests Stuyvesant to connive at dissent within his jurisdiction, but, at the same time, entertains the thought that such connivance might not be possible, and, in this event, it merely reit-

[1] Brodhead, Hist. of New York, i. 707; O'Callaghan, Hist. of New Netherland, ii. 457.
[2] Council minute. O'Callaghan, Cal. Hist. MSS. (Dutch), i. 246.
[3] Council minute. Ibid. 247.
[4] Ibid. Thompson, Hist. of Long Island, ii. 295.
[5] Eccl. Recs. N. Y. i. 544.

erates the command given repeatedly by the Directors in previous letters on similar occasions, at least to admit freedom of conscience, to allow every inhabitant of the Province to have his own belief. A more liberal interpretation of the letter also makes the conduct of the Directors towards John Bowne unintelligible.[1]

When John Bowne arrived in Amsterdam, he went to the West India House and submitted a petition to the Directors, which they referred to a special committee. The festivities of the season delayed a hearing of the case for two weeks, after which Bowne, with a companion, William Caton, was summoned to appear before the members of this committee, who, at the time, were very moderate towards the Quaker, not speaking one word in approval of Stuyvesant's persecution. Nevertheless, when John Bowne demanded the revocation of the sentence of the Provincial Court, the committee declared that they had not the power to fulfill his request, but that they would refer the matter to the Company. New difficulties arose, when John Bowne attempted to obtain his personal effects from the warehouse of the West India Company. His petition to this effect had been granted by the committee, but the keeper of the warehouse with his subordinate officials, refused to deliver his goods, unless he paid for his passage from New Netherland, for which they received the approval of the Company.

Bowne also made an attempt to engage a passage back to New Netherland, and the merchant consented

---

[1] Journal of John Bowne, Amer. Hist. Rec. i. 4-8. The Journal substitutes numbers for the names of the month and begins the year in March, which is, therefore, the first month of the year in Bowne's system of chronology.

to give him a berth, if he could obtain a pass from the West India Company. When Bowne submitted his petition to the Directors, he was asked whether he intended to return to the colony to bring his wife and children to Holland. When he stated that his inten-- tion was to labor and maintain them there as he had done before, he was told that the Directors thought it would be best for him to stay in Holland and to send for his wife and children, as *the Company does not give liberty there*. Bowne then appealed to the liberty guaranteed in the Flushing patent, which had been granted by the Director General Kieft, but the Director Perkens claimed that this patent was granted, when nothing or little was heard in the colony of the people of his persuasion. Bowne urged that the Quakers were a peaceable people, but he was told that their opposition to the laws of the province proved the contrary to be the case. Although Bowne retorted that these laws were contrary to justice and righteousness and a viola- tion of the privileges of their patent, the Directors insisted that all those, who were unwilling to become subject to the ordinances of the colony, would not be permitted to live under their jurisdiction, but, at the same time, they were ready to draw up the conditions, on which they would allow him to return to New Nether- land. When Bowne received this paper to sign, he found the terms to be contrary to his conscience, faith and religion.[1] He immediately wrote a letter to the West India Company in reply. He had expected

[1] Letter of John Bowne to West India Co., in Thompson, Hist. of Long Island, ii. 387-88; Mandeville, Flushing Past and Present, 119-120.

justice from the Directors of the Company, but only beheld additional oppression. Although his persecutors had thus mocked at the oppression of the oppressed, and added afflictions to the afflicted, he still prayed that the Lord would not lay this to their charge, but give them eyes to see and hearts to do justice, that they may find mercy with the Lord in the day of judgment. As late as the ninth of June, he complained in his letter [1] to his wife, that the Company detained his goods and denied him a passage home except on conditions, so gross and unreasonable, that he chose to suffer want of the dear company of his wife and children, imprisonment of his person, the ruin of his estate in his absence there, and the loss of his goods here, rather than to yield or consent to such injustice. At length, Bowne did become quite free of the Directors, and he tells us in his journal that he again arrived at New Amsterdam early in the year 1664. He immediately proceeded to his home in Flushing, which was the first house he entered in the country. It is said that John Bowne again met the old Governor after the establishment of the English rule, as a private citizen, who then seemed ashamed of what he had done, and glad to see the Quaker safe home again. [2]

[1] Letter printed in full in Thompson, Hist. of Long Island, ii. 386-7.
[2] Besse, Sufferings of the Quakers, ii. 237. Besse's account of the Bowne case is inaccurate.

CHAPTER VIII

THE PERSECUTION OF THE JEWS

A few years previous to the outbreak of religious persecution in New Netherland, the Jews had begun to immigrate into this Province. They also had to suffer under the measures which the civil authorities adopted for the repression of dissent. However, the motives that influenced the persecution of the Jews were not merely of a religious nature, as economical reasons also entered even in a larger measure. This is evidenced in the nature of the civil disabilities to which the Jews alone were subject.

Stuyvesant seemed to have felt what Usselinx so eloquently urged, when the Portuguese Jews invited the Dutch West India Company to invade Brazil. "No trust should be placed in the promises made there by the Jews, a race faithless and pusillanimous, enemies to all Christians, caring not whose house burns so long as they may warm themselves at the coals, who would rather see a hundred thousand Christians perish than suffer the loss of a hundred crown."[1] The clergy of New Netherland manifested even less tolerance towards the newly arrived Jews than their brethren in

[1] Jameson, William Usselinx. Papers, A. H. A., ii. 76

Brazil, who, with the zealous support of the Classis of
Amsterdam, had forced the civil authorities, in 1638, to
forbid the free exercise of the Jewish religion in public,
that had been guaranteed them on the conquest of the
country by the Dutch.[1]

Stuyvesant's opposition to the Jews was not
prompted merely by inborn prejudice. It was doubtlessly influenced by his unfortunate experience with
the Jewish colony, established in 1652 on the island of
Curaçoa, which, with the adjoining islands of Aruba and
Bonaire, was subject to his authority under a vice-
director. The Directors of the Amsterdam Chamber
had entertained the thought of abandoning the island
of Curaçoa, which yielded no satisfactory revenue,[2]
when a new opportunity to develop the resources of the
island was presented in its colonization with Jews.
Jan de Illan, a Jew, was made a patroon of a colony on
making known to the Directors of the Amsterdam
Chamber his intention to transport a good number of
colonists of his own nation there to settle and cultivate
the land. Although the Directors suspected that he
and his associates were planning to trade from Curaçoa
to the West Indies and the Main, they were willing to
make the experiment and time would show whether
they could succeed with this nation, characterized by
them as "crafty and generally treacherous."[3] Stuyvesant, far from being hostile to this enterprise, ex-

---

[1] Netscher, Les Hollandais au Brèsil, 94-95; for the action of
the Classis of Amsterdam, cf. Eccl. Recs. N.Y. i. 196; 204; 206. In
both reference is also made to the persecution suffered by Catholics.
[2] Directors to Stuyvesant, March 21, 1651. Col. Docs. N. Y.
xiv. 135.
[3] Directors to Stuvyesant, April 4, 1652, Ibid. 172; also letter
cited above.

pressed his satisfaction at the establishment of the
Jewish Colony.[1] The Directors now granted a similar
privilege to a Portuguese Jew, Joseph Fonseca, alias
David Nassy, who was preparing to take a large number of colonists to the island.[2] The charter granted
to Jan de Illan contained the usual provisions found
in the charters for patroons in New Netherland except
in the matter of religion. The Directors granted
freedom of worship to the Jews, but the patroon was
forbidden to compel any Christian colonists under his
authority to work on the Christian Sabbath, on which
even the Jews were not permitted to labor. The
exercise of the Christian faith was still more safeguarded
by the clause which prohibited the Jews from disturbing

[1] Col. Docs. N.Y. xiv 172. : "You think we have done well in
treating with Jean Dillan about establishing a colony at Curaçoa."
[2] The plan of David Nassy also to establish a colony in Curaçoa
was not realized. Later he turned his attention to another field
of colonial enterprise. Guiana was claimed exclusively by the
Zealand Chamber for colonization, but some individuals petitioned
permission to erect a colony on the Wild Coast from the Chamber
of Amsterdam, which now asserted its right to send colonists
thither. The dispute, which ensued, was adjusted September 3,
1659, by the compromise to permit all the Chambers of the Company to send colonies to Guiana in places not preempted by others.
Nine days later, David Nassy, with his associates, received a charter
for a colony in Cayenne with the most liberal provisions, which
mark a large departure from the religious policy followed by the
Chamber of Amsterdam in its Province of New Netherland. Article
vii grants religious liberty to all denominations in these terms:
"It shall be permitted to the Jews to have freedom of conscience
with public worship, and a synagogue and school, in the same manner as is allowed in the City of Amsterdam, in accordance with
the doctrines of their elders, without hindrance as well in the
district of this Colony, as in other places of our Dominions, and that
they shall enjoy all Liberties and Exemptions of other colonists
as long as they remain there; but the aforesaid Patroon and his
partners shall be bound to preserve the said freedom of conscience
to all the other colonists of any nation whatever, and that with the
worship and public rites of the Reformed, or any other that may
happen to be in the country." However, the religious liberty
conceded in these terms was not absolute, as Article xiv
restricts the Governing Council to members of the Reformed

Christian worship or giving any offense to the Christian conscience.[1]

In spite of these liberal conditions of their charter, the Jewish colony proved rather detrimental than profitable to the Company, which had been deceived both in regard to the resources of the projectors of this Jewish colonization and also in regard to the intentions of the patroon himself and his associates. Jan de Illan was deep in debt for the horses furnished him by the Company for his colony, where there was nothing which might be seized as security for its payment. The Directors also then learned that his partners in Holland possessed nothing. The Company owed him about 3,000 guilders for flour and clothing, which he had delivered to its servants, but even after the deduction

Faith: "The Company shall appoint in the aforesaid Colony a Schout for the maintenance of Justice and Police, provided the state of the colony be such as shall justify the appointment of a Governing Council, in which case the patroon or patroons shall nominate two of the most able persons living in the Colony being Dutch Christians of the Reformed Religion, through whom the Schout, as representative of the Company, may have supreme control in the country." This charter was modelled on the privileges granted the year previous by the Zealand Chamber to the people of the Hebrew Nation that had gone to the Wild Coast. The Egerton MSS. No. 2395, Fol. 46 in the British Museum, discovered by Mr. Lucien Wolfe of London, has been rightly identified by Oppenheim as a translation of the grant of the Zealand Chamber to the Jews, which was sent by some agent, probably to Thurloe. It is mentioned by Charles Longland in his letter from Leghorn to Cromwell's secretary, John Thurloe. Cf. An Early Jewish Colony in Western Guiana. Supplemental data, by Samuel Oppenheim. Pubs. Amer. Jewish Hist. Soc., No. 17, p. 54. Pubs. Amer. Jewish Hist. Soc., No. 16; Oppenheim, Early Jewish Colony in Western Guiana. (The appendix contains important documents.) Cf. also Report of U. S. Commission on Venezuela-British Guiana Boundary.

[1] Cone, G. Herbert, The Jews in Curaçoa, Pubs. Amer. Jewish Hist. Soc., No. 10, pp. 148; Van der Kemp, Ms. Translation, Dutch Recs. N. Y. viii. 34; O'Callaghan, Cal. N. Y. Hist. MSS. (Dutch), i. 329.

of this sum, there was still a large balance due to the Company.[1] The conduct of the Jewish colonists also gave the authorities a just cause of complaint, which continually recurs in the letters of the vice-director and of the Company. The Jews neglected to cultivate the land, and employed all their time in cutting logwood, which, with horses, they exported to the Carribean Islands. The Directors realized that, if this trade were not restrained, soon nothing of either article would be left in Curaçoa. The vice-director was, therefore, commanded to adopt the measures necessary to prevent the destruction of logwood and its exportation, as these woods were reserved exclusively to the Company. The Company also prohibited the exportation of horses from Curaçoa, Bonaire and Aruba, as they were to remain in the islands to be used in time in the Province of New Netherland.[2] The Directors had reason to fear that the Jews would become a burden to the magazine of the Company,[3] because, through the neglect of agriculture, they did not provide themselves with the first necessaries of life.[4] They were, therefore, determined to enforce the contract with the patroon, which bound the Jews to cultivate the land they occupied under the penalty of its forfeiture. The Jews were also brought into bad repute by the sale of their wares

[1] Van der Kemp, Ms. Translation, Dutch Recs. N.Y. viii. 107, Letter of Vice-Director Rodenburch to Directors, April 2, 1654. In Cone, l. c. 172.
[2] Chamber of Amsterdam to Director of W. I. Co., June 7, 1653; Van der Kemp l. c., iv. 101; Cone, l. c,. 151.
[3] Directors to Stuyvesant, December 13, 1652, Col. Docs. N. Y. xiv. 193.
[4] Chamber of Amsterdam to Directors of W. I. Co., June 6, 1653, Van der Kemp, l c., iv. 101; in Cone, The Jews of Curaçoa, l. c., p. 151.

at an exorbitant price. They were selling old curtains
and other shreds at three times the price for which
they might have been obtained in Holland.   Jan de
Illan in fact had asked the vice-director to credit the
Indian chief with one hundred and fifty R. Dall.,
which he claimed to have delivered him in goods. On
enquiry, it was learned that the value of the goods
delivered would not exceed the sum of fl.25.17 in the
fatherland.   This was merely an example of a practise
common among the Jews.   However, the vice-director
hoped to put a stop to such extortion, as Jan de Illan
would lose the privileges of his patroonship because of
his failure to fulfil its stipulations, which amongst other
things bound him to have fifty settlers in his colony
within four years.   There were then not more than ten or
twelve, and these wished to leave him and become
planters under the direct jurisdiction of the Company.[1]
When the Directors of the Amsterdam Chamber received
a report of the conditions existing in the Jewish colony,
they decided to furnish the vice-director goods, with
which he might be able to supply the colonists at a
reasonable price and thus put an end to the extortion
of the Jews.   However, they refused to permit the
colonists to leave the settlement of Jan de Illan until
the expiration of the time of their service, when they
would be free to go.[2]   Two years later the vice-director Beck wrote Stuyvesant that three or four Jews
solicited permission to leave the island, to which he
readily consented, as their presence was more injurious

---

[1] Vice-Director   Rodenburch   to   Directors,   April   2,   1654
Van der Kemp, l. c , viii. 107, in Cone, l. c., 152.
[2] Directors to Vice-Director Rodenburch, July 7, 1654, Van
der Kemp, l. c., viii. cited in Cone, l. c., 152-3.

than profitable.[1] A knowledge of these occurrences
made Stuyvesant hostile to the Jews in New Netherland, where the first Jew arrived in 1654.[2] His opposition to the Jews increased on the arrival of a number
of this nation in extreme poverty, which occasioned
the first measures of repression against the Jews.
In September, 1654, twenty-three Jews were brought
in his ship by Master Jacques de la Motthe, who had
made a contract with his Jewish passengers, by which
each individual Jew was held jointly for the freight
and board of the whole company from St. Anthony in
the West Indies to New Netherland.[3] On their
arrival at New Amsterdam, there was still a balance of
fl.1567 due to the captain of the vessel, which the Court
ordered to be paid according to contract within forty-
eight hours from the date of its decision. Meanwhile,
the furniture and other property of the Jews on board
the ship were to be retained as security.[4] On the

[1] Letter, March 21, 1656, l. c.
[2] This was the Jewish merchant, Jacob Barsimson. His
passage money is recorded as paid August 22. The list of immigrants on the ship Pear Tree also contains the Jewish name of
Jacob Aboaf, but he stopped off in England, according to a memorandum in the list itself. Cf. the passage from N. Y. Col. MSS.
xiv. 83, printed by Oppenheim in his Early Hist. of the Jews in
New York, p. 3. The beginning of the Jewish immigration into
the Province of New Netherland has been placed in the year 1652,
when the Directors of the Company are said to have sent to New
Amsterdam some Jews to serve as soldiers for the term of one year.
This statement was based on a misreading of the word "few" in
the MS. translation as "Jew." The original Dutch has
"eenige weynich" "some few." Cf. Oppenheim, l. c., p. 2.
[3] The location of this Cape St. Anthony in the West Indies
has been the subject of much speculation. Cf. Hühner, Leon.
Whence came the First Jewish Settlers of New York. Pubs.
Amer. Jewish Hist Soc. No. 9 His whole argumentation is
called into question by Oppenheim in the work cited above.
[4] Court minutes, September 7, 1654, Recs. New Amsterdam,
i. 240.

expiration of this time, de la Motthe was authorized, in
case of non-payment within four days, to have the
goods of the two greatest debtors, Abraham Israel and
Judicq de Mereda, sold at public auction, and if the sum
thus realized proved insufficient, he was furthermore authorized to proceed in like manner with the
other Jewish passengers until the full acquittance of
the debt.[1] When the sale of these goods still left a
balance, the Court, at the request of the master of the
vessel, placed under civil arrest two Jews as principals,
David Israel and Moses Ambrosius, who were held
for the payment of the balance.[2] The sailors now
brought a suit against Asser Levy, from whom they
demanded the payment of fl.106 still remaining due,
but the Court upheld its previous decision, that the
two Jews, who had been taken as principals, were to be
held for the payment of the balance. Asser Levy had
made the plea that he was no longer bound to pay, as he
had offered to do so on the condition that his goods
should not be sold.[3] This plea did not save him from
condemnation, when Rycke Nounes tried to recover
fl.105.18 from Asser Levy, as her goods had been sold
by auction to pay his freight over and above her own
debt.[4] The Court ordered him to satisfy her claims
within fourteen days. When the sailors promised to
wait for the payment of the balance of the freight of
the Jews until the arrival of ships from the fatherland,

[1] Court minutes, September 10, 1654. Recs. New Amsterdam,
i. 241.
[2] Court minutes, September 16, 1654. Ibid. 244.
[3] Court minutes, October 5, 1654. Ibid. 249.
[4] Court minutes, October 19, 1654. Ibid. 254.

her attorney was able to obtain the money still in the hands of the secretary.[1]

Although the Jews wished to remain, Stuyvesant required them in a friendly way to leave New Netherland, as the Jews were repugnant to the Dutch inferior magistrates and people "on account of their customary usury and deceitful trading with Christians," and also as the deaconry anticipated that the Jews, in the poverty to which they had been reduced by the lawsuit of Jacques de la Motthe, would later become a public charge.[2] In fact, during the winter the Jews did come several times to the house of Domine Megapolensis, weeping and bemoaning their lot. When the Jewish merchant refused to lend them even a few stivers, they became a heavy charge to the Dutch community, which had to spend several hundred guilders for their support.[3] Meanwhile, Stuyvesant tried to forestall all future Jewish immigration into the colony and petitioned the Directors of the Amsterdam Chamber that "the deceitful race—such hateful enemies and blasphemers of the name of Christ—be not allowed further to infect and trouble this new colony." The Directors did "raise obstacles to the giving of permits

[1] Court minutes, October 26, 1654. Recs. of New Amsterdam, 259.
[2] Extract from a letter of the Director Peter Stuyvesant to the Amsterdam Chamber, September 22, 1654. MS. in Library of Hist. Soc. of Pennsylvania, printed by Oppenheim. Early Hist. of Jews in New York, pp. 4-5.
[3] This was Jacob Barsimson, who does not appear to have been rich at this time. Megapolensis wrote "cooplieden," then crossed out "lieden," and wrote over the correction "man." The pronoun following is singular, "hij " "Waneer ick haar totte jodensche coopman wees, soo seijden sij dat hij haar niet een eenigen stuijver wilde verschieten." Cf. Oppenheim, Early Hist. of Jews in New York, pp. 49-52. Text, pp. 73-74.

and passports to the Portuguese Jews to travel and to go to reside in New Netherland." The Jewish merchants of Amsterdam protested against this injury to their nation, which would also turn out to the disadvantage of the Company itself. The Jews, who in Brazil had risked their possessions and their blood in the defense of the country, were now dispersed here and there in great poverty and could only retrieve their shattered fortunes in some Dutch colony under the protection of the Company, as opportunities were not sufficient for all in Holland, and they could not go to Spain or Portugal on account of the Inquisition. There were powerful reasons urged in favor of a Jewish immigration to New Netherland by these Portuguese merchants. A Jewish immigration to New Netherland would increase the number of loyal subjects in the colony and result in an increase of its revenues. Then there were many Jews amongst the principal shareholders of the West India Company, who had always worked for its best interests and had even lost immense sums of money in its shares and obligations. The plea was successful, although the Directors confessed to Stuyvesant their desire to fulfill his request.[1] Formal permission was now given to the Jews to travel, reside and traffic in New Netherland, "provided they shall not become a charge upon the deaconry or the Company."[2] The following spring began the new immi-

[1] Directors to Stuyvesant, April 26, 1655. Col. Docs. N. Y. xiv. 315; Petition of the Jewish Nation, January 1655, MS. in the Library of the Hist. Soc. of Pa., printed by Oppenheim, Early Hist of the Jews in New York, pp. 9-13.
[2] This was done on February 22, 1655. Cf. Council minutes, March 14, 1656, vi, 321. O'Callaghan, Cal. Hist. MSS. (Dutch). i. 162, Directors to Stuyvesant, June 14, 1656. Col. Docs. N. Y. xiv.

gration of the Jews, among whom were the merchants
Abraham de Lucena, Salvator d'Andrada, and Jacob
Cohen, who announced that others of the same nation
would follow later. A rumor arose in the town that, as
soon as the Jews were sufficiently numerous, they would
erect a synagogue for the exercise of their worship.
The Dutch minister, Megapolensis, was immediately
alive to the dangers of such a toleration of the Jews,
"who have no other God than the unrighteous Mammon
and no other aim than to get possession of Christian
property, and to ruin all other merchants by drawing
all trade to themselves." He earnestly requested the
Classis of Amsterdam to use its influence with the
Directors of the Company to have "these godless
rascals, who are of no benefit to the country, but look
at everything for their own profit," removed from the
Province. He felt that there would be still greater confusion created, if the obstinate and immovable Jews
came to settle in New Netherland, where there were
"Papists, Mennonites and Lutherans amongst the Dutch,
also many Puritans or Independents, and various other
servants of Baal among the English under this government, who conceal themselves under the name of Christians."[1] The minister's wish had already been anticipated by the Director General and Council, who
resolved that the Jews, who had arrived last year and

351. Petition of the Jews to trade on the South River, Council
minute, November 29, 1655. Col. Docs. N. Y. xii. 117-118.
[1] Megapolensis to Classis of Amsterdam, March 18, 1655.
Eccl. Recs. N. Y. i. 335-6. The same ground was taken by the
Classis of Amsterdam in its efforts to have the toleration of Lutheran
worship refused, "for the Mennonites and English Independents,
of whom there is said to be not a few, might have been led to under-
take the same thing in their turn, and would probably have attempted to introduce public gatherings"

in the spring of this year, were to prepare to leave at once. When the Burgomasters and Schepens took cognizance of this resolution, they had no objection to urge, but decided that the resolution "should take its course." They had just begun the trial of a Jew, Abraham de Lucena, charged with the double offense of keeping open his store during the sermon and selling by retail, for which the Schout of the City demanded the Jew to be deprived of his trade and condemned to a fine of six hundred guilders.[1] The Directors foresaw the same difficulties from Jewish residents in New Netherland as Stuyvesant did, and "would have liked to effectuate and fulfill" his wishes, but they felt unable to approve his policy in this respect, which they considered somewhat unreasonable and unfair, as the Jews had suffered considerable loss from the reconquest of Brazil by the Portuguese, and as they also still had large sums of money invested in the shares of the West India Company, of which it stood sorely in need in its present bankrupt condition.[2] They were, therefore, determined to regulate their conduct towards the Jews in New Netherland according to the concessions made by the Company on February 22, 1655, "provided the poor among them shall not become a burden to the Company or the community, but be supported by their own Nation."

The Jews now endeavored to obtain several concessions from the provincial government. On July 27, 1655,

[1] Recs. of New Amsterdam, i. 290-291.
[2] Directors to Stuyvesant, April 26, 1655. Col Docs. N. Y. xiv. 315. Revised version in Oppenheim, Early Hist. of Jews in New York, p. 8. Manasseh Ben Israel in his Humble Address to Cromwell: "The Jews were enjoying a good part of the (Dutch) East and West India Companies."

Abraham de Lucena, Salvador D'Andrada, and Jacob
Cohen petitioned the Director General for the concession of a burial place for the Jews. They were given
the permission to bury their dead anywhere in ground
belonging to the Company, that had not yet been appropriated for any other purpose.[1] In February of the
following year, on the presentation of a new petition,
Nicasius de Sille and Cornelius van Tienhoven were
authorized to show the same petitioners a suitable
spot for a burial-ground outside of the city.[2] They
were less successful in urging the recognition of their
civil privileges. The increase of the Jewish population
in New Amsterdam gave rise to a discussion of their
military service, especially at the time of the expedition
against the Swedes. The question, whether the Jewish
residents should also train and mount guard, was
presented by the captains and officers of the trainbands
to the Director General and Council, who recognized the
disinclination and unwillingness of these trainbands
to be fellow soldiers with the aforesaid nation and to be
on guard with them in the same guard-house. It was,
furthermore, urged that no city in the Netherlands
admitted Jews to the trainbands or common citizens'
guard. However, to prevent discontent among the Christian population, the Director General and Council professed to follow the usages of the City of Amsterdam
and placed a tax of sixty-five stivers a month on each
male person over sixteen and under sixty years of age
to compensate for their exemption. The military

[1] Council minute, July 27, 1655, Van der Kemp, Translation
Dutch Recs. ii. 21 in Kohler, Phases of Jewish Life in New York
before 1800, ii. Pubs. Amer. Jewish Hist. Soc., No. 3, pp. 76-77.
[2] Ibid. ii. 240; Kohler, Ibid. 77.

council of the citizens was authorized to carry into
effect this legislation and to collect the tax once every
month and, in case of refusal, to institute legal process
for its payment.[1] Jacob Barsimson and Asser Levy
then petitioned for leave to stand guard like other
Burghers of New Amsterdam or to be relieved from the
tax paid by the Jews, as "they must earn their living by
manual labor." "The Director General and Council
persist in the resolution passed, yet as the petitioners
are of opinion that the result of this will be injurious to
them, consent is hereby given to them to depart whenever and whither it pleases them."[2]   A little later the
Jewish merchants submitted a petition for permission
to travel and trade on the South River, at Fort Orange
and other places, situated within the jurisdiction of the
Dutch government of New Netherland, in accordance
with the concessions, that they had received from the
West India Company in Amsterdam.   The council
adopted the suggestion of Cornelius van Tienhoven,
who was of the opinion, that the concession of trading
privileges on the South River and at Fort Orange to
the Jews would be very injurious to the population
residing in these districts.   He, therefore, advised that
the petition be denied for the coming winter and that a
full report of the matter be submitted to the Directors
in the fatherland.   Meanwhile, these Jewish merchants
were allowed to dispatch one or two persons to the
South River to dispose of the goods that they had sent
there, without thereby establishing a precedent, to

[1] Council minute, August 28, 1655. Col. Docs. N. Y. xii. 96.
[2] Council minute, November 5, 1655, O'Callaghan, Cal.
Hist. MSS. N. Y. (Dutch) i. 155.   N. Y. Col. MSS. vi. 147, in
Oppenheim, Early Hist. of Jews in New York.

which the Jews might appeal later.[1] Stuyvesant had
already tried to win the Directors of the Amsterdam
Chamber to his anti-Semitic policy by pointing out the
dangers connected with further commercial concessions
to the Jews. "To give liberty to the Jews will be very
detrimental there, because the Christians there will
not be able at the same time to do business. Giving
them liberty, we cannot refuse the Lutherans and
Papists."[2] Stuyvesant mixed together here the interests of religion and the interests of trade, but the Directors insisted that the privileges granted by the Company
to the Jews in New Netherland were restricted to civil
and political rights without giving them a right to
claim the privilege of exercising their religion in a
synagogue or at a gathering.[3] The Directors were,
therefore, greatly displeased that Stuyvesant had
refused the Jews permission to trade at Fort Orange
and the South River and also to purchase real estate,
which had been granted this Nation in the Netherlands.
To show that his anxiety had not been premature,
Stuyvesant informed the Directors that the Jews had
many times requested "the free and public exercise
of their abominable religion. . . . What they may
obtain from your Honors, time will tell."[4]

[1] Council minute, November 29, 1655. Col. Docs. N. Y.
xii. 117-118.
[2] Bontemantel's abstract of Stuyvesant's letter to Directors,
October 30, 1655, MS. in Lenox Library, printed by Oppenheim,
o. c., p. 30 The Classis of Amsterdam wrote, May 26, 1656, to
the Consistory of New Netherland: "We are informed that even
the Jews have made request of the Honorable Governor and have
also attempted in that country the exercise of their blasphemous
religion." Eccl. Recs. N. Y. i. 348.
[3] Directors to Stuyvesant, March 13, 1656. Col. Docs. N.Y. xiv. 341.
[4] Bontemantel's abstract of Stuyvesant's letter, June 10, 1656.
MS. in Lenox Library, printed by Oppenheim, o. c., p. 21.

A few months previous to this, Abraham de Lucena, Jacob Cohen Henricus, Salvador D'Andrada, Joseph D'Acosta and David Frera had requested the same rights in matters of trade and in the acquisition of real estate as the other citizens of the province on the plea that these privileges were included in the grant received from the Company and that they and their co-religionists were assessed the same as other citizens.[1]   One of these Jews, Salvador D'Andrada, had purchased a house in New Amsterdam at a public auction, but the sale was cancelled on the contention that the Jews were not allowed to hold real estate.[2]   The authorities of New Netherland refused to grant the requested right of property to the Jews and awaited further instructions from Holland.[3]   Although the Directors did order Stuyvesant to give the Jews the rights of trade and property, they did not give them full civil liberty, inasmuch as the Jews were not allowed to exercise any handicraft which they were prohibited to do in Amsterdam, and were not allowed to have open retail shops.   Meanwhile, the religious privileges granted the Jews were not greater nor less than those granted to other forms of dissent in the Colony.   They were allowed to exercise in all tranquillity their religion in their houses, which were, therefore, to be built "close

---

[1] Council minute, March 14, 1656. O'Callaghan, Cal. Hist. MSS. (Dutch) i. 162.
[2] Council minutes, December 17, 1655; December 23, 1655; January 15, 1656; March 14, 1656, O'Callaghan, Ibid. pp. 156, 157, 162.
[3] "Ambachten op te stellen" wrongly translated by Berthold Fernow as shall not "be employed in any public service." O'Callaghan, Laws and Ordinances of New Netherland, N. Y. p. 194, rightly translates "to exercise any handicraft," and also Oppenheim, Early Hist. of Jews in New York, p. 33, "to establish themselves as mechanics."

together in a convenient place on one or the other side
of New Amsterdam—at their own choice, as they have
done here."[1]

After this, the Jews must have acquired considerable
freedom in trade, as one of the points to be considered
in the meeting of the Director General and Burgomasters and Schepens in January, 1657, was the practice
of keeping open store and of selling by retail on the part
of Jews and foreigners to the great detriment of the
interests of the citizens of the Province.[2] Complaints
had been made that these men took the bread out of the
mouths of the good Burghery and resident inhabitants,
as they carried away the profits in time of peace and
abandoned the country in time of war. The Director
General and Council, therefore, decreed that henceforth
all traders, in virtue of the stapleright of New Amsterdam, were to set up and keep open store in the city,
after having obtained the common or small burgher
right, without which no public store-business or handicraft could be exercised there.[3] The ordinance makes
no express mention of the Jews, although their trade
was seriously menaced, if its provisions were to be
strictly enforced. When Jacob Cohen Henricus
appeared, April 11, 1657, before the Court of Burgomasters and Schepens of New Amsterdam to obtain

[1] Directors to Stuyvesant, June 14, 1656. Col. Docs. N. Y.
xiv. 351 Oppenheim, Early Hist. of Jews in New York, p. 33-34.
[2] Court minutes, January 8, 1657, Recs. of New Amsterdam
ii. 262. Before this, March 15, 1556: "On the proposition made
to the Court by some of the Bench that some order be concluded
for preparing the progress of this city in keeping open retail shops,
inasmuch as Jews and foreigners are as much encouraged as a
burgher or citizen, it is resolved that the same be taken into consideration in full court." Recs. New Amsterdam, ii. p. 63.
[3] Court minute, January 30, 1657. Ibid. ii. 287.

permission "to bake and sell bread within the city as other bakers, but with closed door," he was informed that the request was directly contrary to the privileges of the Burghery of this City and to the orders of the Directors of the Company.[1] The Jews now realized the necessity of obtaining the Burgher right to enable them to continue in business, Asser Levy appeared before the Court of the Burgomasters and Schepens and requested to be admitted a Burgher. The request was refused and the petitioner referred to the Director General and Council,[2] to whom the Jews Salvador D'Andrada, Jacob Cohen Henricus, Abraham de Lucena and Joseph D'Acosta now appealed. They established their right to be admitted to citizenship on the grounds, that this privilege had been guaranteed them in the concessions of the Company, that the Jews possessed the right of citizenship in the City of Amsterdam, where certificates of citizenship were issued to them, and finally that the Jews, from the beginning of their residence in the Province of New Netherland, had borne their share with others in every burden of the citizens and continued to do so even then.[3] The appeal was successful. The Burgomasters of the city were authorized and commanded to admit the remonstrants with their Nation among the citizens of New Netherland. Stuyvesant evidently no longer dared to antagonize the Directors of the Amsterdam Chamber who were favorable to the Jews. Although he still called the Jews

[1] Court minute, April 11, 1657. Recs. of New Amsterdam, vii. 154.
[2] Ibid.
[3] Council minute, April 20, 1657. Van der Kemp, Translations of Dutch MSS. viii. 531. Revised Translation, in Oppenheim, Early Hist. of Jews, p. 36.

"usurious and covetous," when he wrote, on December 26, 1659, to the Directors for a regulation of the slave trade on the favorable terms conceded to the Jews on the establishment of the colony of the Jew, David Nassy, at Cayenne,[1] he was careful not to offend the Jewish conscience, when the instructions for the sworn butchers were framed. A special oath was presented to the Jews, Asser Levy and Moses Lucena, that exempted them from killing hogs, which their religion did not allow.[2]

[1] Stuyvesant to the Directors, December 26, 1659, Col. Docs. N. Y. xiv. 454-5. This is the regulation for the slave trade in the Cayenne colony: "That on the aforesaid coast there shall be delivered as many negroes as every one shall need, which shall be paid for on the production of the receipts, through some one thereunto commissioned, the sum of 150 guilders in ready money for a man or woman; two children from eight to twelve years to be counted as a man or woman; below eight years three for one; unweaned children to follow the mother, etc."

[2] Court minutes, October 15 and 29, 1660, Recs. of New Amsterdam, vii. 259, 261. Some other religious customs of the Jews were respected before this. In June, 1658, two cases against Jacob Barsimson were called before the municipal court of New Amsterdam. "Though the defendant is absent, yet no default is entered against him, as he was summoned on his Sabbath." Ibid. ii. pp. 396-397.

CHAPTER IX

Indian Missions in New Netherland

I.—Missionary Labors of the Dutch

The conversion of the American Indian usually received at least some mention in the colonial projects formed by Europeans in the seventeenth century. Usselinx, in his plan for the organization of the West India Company, used the missionary opportunities offered in America as an argument to further the project. "In the course of time the saving faith and gospel of Jesus Christ might be planted there, whereby the heathen would be rescued from the darkness of idolatry."[1] The plans of William Usselinx were rejected and the charter finally drawn up for the West India Company made no mention of any design to convert the Indians. However, the first Minister of the Province of New Netherland, Jonas Michaelius, on his arrival in 1628, gave some thought to this matter, but the difficulties of the task so impressed him, that no results were attained during his ministry. He found the natives "entirely savage and wild, proficient in all wickedness and godlessness, thievish, treacherous,

---

[1] O'Callaghan, Hist. of New Netherland. i. 31; Brodhead. Hist. of State of New York. i. 23.

inhuman in their cruelty, serving no one but the devil,"
who, in the spirit Manitou, represented to them
everything that was "subtle, crafty and beyond human
skill and power." The ministers in the fatherland had
been led to believe that the Indian was docile and
naturally inclined to Christianity, as he manifested
right principles of religion and vestiges of the natural
law, but Michaelius failed to discover these favorable
traits in his character. After some preaching to the
Indians, Michaelius abandoned all thought of converting the adult savages and recommended the separation
of the children from their parents and from their whole
nation to prevent "heathenish tricks and deviltries"
from being implanted in their hearts. The obstacle
to this plan arose from the unwillingness of the Indians
to part with their children, for whom they entertained
a very strong affection, but the minister hoped to gain
their consent by means of presents and promises and to
have them placed "under the instruction of some experienced and godly schoolmaster, by whom they may be
instructed not only to speak, read and write in our
language, but also especially in the fundamentals of our
Christian religion, with the good example of virtuous
living." It was his hope that these children would
become instruments of evangelization to their whole
nation. Although Michaelius expressed his intention
to seek better opportunities for the instruction of the
savages, there is no evidence of further missionary
labor on his part.[1]

Indian missions were, in fact, little favored by the
West India Company's policy in New Netherland, as

[1] Letter of Michaelius to Smoutius, Eccl. Recs. N. Y. i. 55-61.

the Company did not direct its efforts to the colonization of the province. On the establishment of the
patroonships, the Company was even accused of trying
to paralyse the efforts of the patroons to populate their
colonies by its attempts to minimize the Freedoms and
Exemptions granted in the charter of 1629. Kiliaen
van Rensselaer in 1633 submitted a protest to the
Assembly of the XIX and petitioned the deputies of
the States General on this board for an extension of
privileges, by which would be promoted "above all
things the diffusion of the Christian Reformed Religion
in those regions."[1]   He felt that this ought to bring
God's blessing on his undertaking.[2]   In 1640, he instructed Arent van Curler to seize the opportunity,
offered by the presentation of some gifts to several
Indian chiefs from the patroon, to acquaint them with
God, "who each day lets his bountiful gifts come to man
through the fruitfulness, which he gives to the products
of the earth and to man's sinful body."[3]   Two years
later, at the instance of the patroon, John Megapolensis
was called by the Classis of Amsterdam to "perform
the duty of the Gospel to the advancement of God's
Holy Name and the conversion of many poor blind
men" in the colony.[4]   For the patroon did not merely
look "to the profits of his investment, but had in
especial view, by means of the settling of the country
and the practice of godliness, to have the Christian

[1] Memorial.   November 25, 1633.   Van Rensselaer Bowier
MSS. p. 249.
[2] Letter of Kiliaen Van Rensselaer to Planck,   April 24, 1635.
Ibid. p. 314.
[3] Letter.   July 2, 1641.   Ibid. 508-9.
[4] Commission of Megapolensis from Classis, March 22, 1642.
Eccl. Recs. N. Y. i. 149.

Reformed Religion proclaimed there, in order that the blind heathen also might be brought to the knowledge of our Saviour Jesus Christ."[1] The Reverend Bogardus, the successor of Michaelius in New Amsterdam, and his entire consistory were exhorted to unite hands with the new minister in this apostolic work,[2] which hitherto had been almost totally neglected in all but the Catholic colonies. "Although some of the Reformed Religion— English, Scotch, French and Dutch—have already taken up their habitations in those parts, yet hath their going thither (as yet) been to small purpose for the converting of those natives, either for that they have placed themselves but in the skirts of America, where there are but few natives (as those of New England) or else for want of able and conscionable ministers (as in Virginia) they themselves are become exceedingly rude more likely to turn heathen than to turn others to the Christian faith."[3] This last was the sad truth in the Dutch colony almost from its very beginning. De Rasières, in his visit to New Plymouth in 1627,[4] noted the stringent laws and ordinances obtaining there upon the subject of fornication and adultery, which were maintained and enforced very strictly, even among the Indian tribes living within its jurisdiction. Knowledge of the dissolute conditions obtaining in

[1] Van Rensselaer Bowier, MSS. pp. 686-7.
[2] Letter of the Classis of Amsterdam to the Consistory of New Amsterdam, April 22, 1642. Eccl. Recs. N. Y. i. 151.
[3] Castell, William. Minister of the Gospel at Courtenhall in Northamptonshire. A Short Discoverie of the Coasts and Continents of America from the Ecquinotiall Northward, and of adjacent Isles. London, 1644. N. Y. Hist. Soc. Coll. 2nd Series, Vol. iii. (1857), pp. 233-34.
[4] In regard to this visit cf. Bradford's History of Plymouth Plantation. pp. 223-227 (ed. in Orig. Narratives of Early Am. History).

New Netherland had come to these English from the Indians, and the Dutch, who "lived so barbarously in these respects and without punishment," were severely and angrily censured by their Puritan neighbors.[1] This evil had also become so bad in Rensselaerswyck that the patroon found it necessary to promulgate a placard against the sinful intercourse between the Dutch and the heathen women and girls. The first offense was punished by a fine of twenty-five guilders, which was increased to fifty guilders, if the woman became pregnant, and to one hundred guilders, if the woman gave birth to a child.[2] Habitual illicit intercourse entailed a yearly fine of fifty guilders and, "according to the circumstances," banishment from the colony. One third of the fines was to go to the officer, one-third to the commander at Rensselaers-Steyn, and the remainder to the patroon himself for the building of the church.[3] The execution of this placard must have been somewhat neglected, as the new minister, sometime after his arrival in the colony, stated that the "Dutchmen run . . . very much" after the Indian

[1] Letter of De Rasières, 1627. N. Y. Hist. Soc. Coll. 2nd Ser. ii. (1849) p. 352. Narratives of New Netherlands. ed. Jameson. p. 112.

[2] It is hard to see how the increase of the fine in these last two instances would not have led to race-suicide, if the ordinance could have been enforced. Mrs. Schuyler van Rensselaer intimates that this was the case. "The Dutch Records assert that, especially in the early days of traffic and incipient colonization, many traders lived with Indian women, yet they mention few half-breeds, and no visible tinge of dark blood survived in the veins of the New Netherlanders." Hist. of the City of New York. i. 56.

[3] Redress of the abuses and faults in the colony of Rensselaerswyck. September 5, 1643. Van Rensselaer Bowier MSS. p. 694. Cf. Letters of Kiliaen van Rensselaer to Johannes Megapolensis. March 13, 1643 and to Arent van Curler. May 13, 1639. Ibid. 442; 645-46.

women, who, being "exceedingly addicted to whoring, . . . will lie with a man for the value of one, two or three shillings."[1] The continuation of this "great abomination to the Lord God" led the patroon, John van Rensselaer, in 1652 to instruct in forcible terms the Schout Fiscal of Rensselaerswyck to execute the provisions of the ordinances against the unlawful mingling of Christians "with the wives and daughters of heathens."[2]

Another great abuse in the relations of the Dutch with the Indians was the profitable liquor traffic, with the example of the vice of intemperance among the Dutch themselves. The evil was not lessened later to any appreciable extent in spite of the regulations of Stuyvesant. A curious testimony for the prevalence of this abuse is given in the Jesuit Relation for the year 1645–1646. An Iroquois, visiting some Christian Algonquins in Canada, came with them to assist at the holy sacrifice of the mass. He refused to leave the church at the request of the Jesuit Father, as he believed in God and possessed a rosary as well as the other Indians. The Algonquins said that the Iroquois was a Christian, but the priest requested them to ask him, if he had been baptized. "What is that," he replied, "to be baptized?" A savage in answer told him that it was

---

[1] Megapolensis. "A Short Account of the Mohawk Indians, their country, language, figure, costume, religion, and government. Written and dispatched from New Netherland, August 26, 1644, by John Megapolensis, minister there. With a brief account of the life and manners of the Stapongers of Brazil." The tract was published in Alkmaer, by Ysbr. Jansz. v. Houten, pp. 32, 1651, without the consent of the author. Translations: Hazard's State Papers. i. 517-526; N. Y. Hist. Soc. Coll. 2nd Ser. iii. p. 155. Narratives of New Netherland. p. 174.

[2] Instructions to Gerrit Swart. May 8, 1652, O'Callaghan. Hist. of New Netherland. ii. 565.

"to receive a water of great importance which effaces all stains and impurities from our soul." The Iroquois immediately exclaimed, "Ah! the Dutch have often given me of that water of importance; I drank so much of it as to be so drunk, that they had to bind my feet and hands, lest I should do harm to some one."[1] The outbreak of hostilities on the part of the Indians was precisely often the baneful result of the sale of liquor to the savages by the Dutch, who, through this and through the trade in firearms, often sought to acquire wealth without labor.

On the organization of the church after the arrival of the new minister in Rensselaerswyck, divine service awakened some curiosity among the Indians, and ten or twelve of their number attended it with long tobacco pipes in their mouths. They could not understand why the minister talked so much, while no one else in the congregation had a word to say. When they were informed later by the minister, that he told the Christians not to steal, or drink or commit adultery, or murder, and that they also ought not to be guilty of these crimes, the Indians only replied: "Why do so many Christians do these things?"[2] Although Megapolensis, on this occasion, promised the Indians to come to their country to teach them, when he understood their language better, the Dutch Reformed Church of New Netherland could only produce one Indian convert, who was "firm in his religious profession."[3] Indian

[1] Jesuit Rel. xxix. 152.
[2] Megapolensis. Tract on the Mohawks. Narratives of New Netherland, p. 178.
[3] Van der Donck. A Description of New Netherland. N. Y. Hist. Soc. Coll. 2nd Ser. vol. i. 214.

children were frequently taken into Dutch families as servants, "but as soon as they are grown up and turn lovers and associate again with the Indians, they forget their religious impressions and adopt Indian customs." Even the one Indian convert was no credit to the Dutch. The publication of Megapolensis's tract on the Mohawk Indians in the fatherland in 1651 probably gave the Classis of Amsterdam, as it still gives the uncritical historian, the impression that "the knowledge of the Gospel is making great progress among the Indians."[1] Megapolensis, who was then officiating in New Amsterdam, assisted by Domine Drisius, hastened to correct this erroneous impression. An Indian chief had indeed been under instruction for two years at the Manhattans, so that he was able to read and write Dutch tolerably well, and publicly to join in the recitation of the Catechism by the children. The ministers had hoped that the Indian would become an effective instrument in the evangelization of the savages, but he possessed even then only "a bare knowledge of the truth without the practice of godliness, as he was much inclined to drink."[2] Nevertheless, the convert was furnished with a bible and sent to christianize the other savages, but no results were attained. "He took to drinking brandy, he pawned the bible, and turned into a regular beast, doing more harm than good among the Indians". In the end, the clergy of New Amsterdam confessed that they saw no way to accomplish the conversion of the Indians, "until

---

[1] Megapolensis and Drisius to Classis of Amsterdam. July 15 1654. Eccl. Recs. N. Y. i. 326-7.
[2] Ibid.

they are subdued by the numbers and power of our
people, and reduced to some sort of civilization, and
also unless our people set them a better example than
they have done heretofore."[1] Van der Donck, the
only lawyer in the province of New Netherland, also
saw no hope of the conversion of the savages under the
conditions obtaining in the country. He 'advocated
the establishment of good schools in convenient places
for the instruction of the children, as the Indians
themselves declared that they were "very desirous to
have their children instructed in our language and
religion."[2] However, this could not be done without
some trouble and expense to the government. In
fact, the commonalty of New Netherland in the remonstrance, which it addressed to the States General on
July 28, 1649, had urged the conversion of the heathen,
and the remonstrance received this favorable comment
in that assembly: "The English and French have,
each in their way, already done their duty in this regard.
Nevertheless, we are older than they in that country,
and, therefore, ought also begin. Praestat sero quam
nunquam."[3] The patroon of Rensselaerswyck bound
his new minister the Reverend Gideon Schaets "to use
all Christian zeal there to bring up both the heathen and
their children in the Christian religion" and promised
to indemnify him "in case his Reverence should take
any of the heathen children there to board and edu-

[1] Megapolensis and Drisius to Classis of Amsterdam. August 5,
1657.   Eccl. Recs. N. Y. i. 398-99.
[2] Van der Donck. o. c. N.Y. Hist. Soc. Coll. 2d Ser. i. pp. 214-215.
[3] Additional Observations on the Petition of the Commonalty of
New Netherland to the States General, preceding the Remonstrance of July 28, 1649. Col. Docs. N. Y. i. 270.

cate,"[1] but the West India Company dismissed the matter with the cold remark, that "everyone conversant with the Indians in and around New Netherland will be able to say that it is morally impossible to convert the adults to the Christian faith," and that it was "a minister's business to apply himself to that and the Director's duty to assist him therein."[2] Stuyvesant wrote, in the following year, to the Classis of Amsterdam that he had conciliated the goodwill of the Indians from the beginning, and that he would be pleased to aid in carrying out any measures that they might suggest to introduce among these heathens the light of Christianity.[3] Nevertheless, fourteen years later, a few months before the English conquest of the province of New Netherland, the minister Polhemus could write to the same Classis, that "there is no communication among us . . . nor plans for propagating the Gospel among the savages and the English."[4] The Dutch could still repeat in all truth the words contained in the "Representation of New Netherland" of 1650. "Great is our disgrace now, and happy should we have been . . . had we striven to impart the Eternal Good to the Indians, as much as was in our power, in return for what they divided with us. It is to be feared that at the Last Day they will stand up against us for this injury."[5]

---

[1] Contract. May 8, 1652. O'Callaghan. Hist. of New Netherland, ii. 567.

[2] Digest of the Remonstrance of New Netherland to the States General. January 27, 1650. Col. Docs. N. Y. i. 340.

[3] Letter. September 7, 1650. De Witt Thomas, New Netherland. N. Y. Hist. Soc. Proceedings, 1844.

[4] Letter. April 21, 1664. Eccl. Recs. N. Y. i. 544.

[5] Representation of New Netherland. Narratives of New Netherland. p. 319.

While the Dutch failed to take an active interest in
the conversion of the savages within the province, they
used their influence with their Indian allies to obtain
the liberation of the Jesuit missionaries, who fell into
the hands of these inveterate enemies of the French.
In 1642, the Mohawks during a raid into French territory intercepted an expedition of Hurons, mostly
Christians, accompanied by Father Jogues and two lay
assistants Renè Goupil and William Coûture, with supplies for the distant mission of Ste. Marie.   During the
long journey to the Mohawk country, the Christian
prisoners suffered the painful tortures and mutilations
which savage cruelty suggested.   On their arrival,
Father Jogues sent word of their capture to the Dutch.[1]
Soon after this, Crol, the commandant of Fort Orange,
received an order from the Director General of the
province, William Kieft, to effect the ransom of these
prisoners,[2] but the Indians were not willing to accept
any ransom.   On the eighth of September, Arent van
Curler, the commissary of Rensselaerswyck, who had
gone into the Mohawk country with Labbadie and
Jacob Jansen, assembled all the chiefs of the three
castles and proposed the release of the Frenchmen.
The Indians professed all friendship for their Dutch
allies, but refused to discuss this question on the plea
that the French burned the Mohawks, who fell into

[1] Letter.   January 14, 1644, of Bartholomew Vimont, with
details obtained from Father Jogues.   Jes. Rel. xxv. 71.
[2] Letter.   September 11, 1642 of Kieft to Kiliaen van Rensselaer.   Van Rensselaer Bowier MSS. p. 625.

their hands.[1] Van Curler now offered a ransom of
six hundred guilders in goods, to which all the colony
was to contribute, but the chiefs could only be induced
to promise not to kill their prisoners and to convey them
back to Canada. The Dutch were convinced of the
futility of further negotiations for the present, although,
in response to the earnest requests of the French, they
were willing to do all in their power to obtain the liberation of the captives from their Indian allies.[2]

The murder of René Goupil, not long after the
departure of the Dutch, showed what little trust could
be placed in the promises of the savages. This zealous
lay missionary had excited the anger of a superstitious
old Indian by making the sign of the cross upon his
grandson.[3] According to the writings of the Jesuit
missionaries, the Iroquois and also other Indians bore
a deep hatred towards the Christian faith, which they
considered the harbinger of all the misfortune, famine,
disease, and death, so prevalent since the advent of the
Europeans among them.[4] The hatred of the Mohawks
towards the sign of the cross, the symbol of the Faith
preached by the Jesuit missionary, was nourished by
their enmity with the Indians under French protection

[1] This was done by the Indians converted by the French Jesuits
in spite of all the efforts of the missionaries to make these Indians
treat their prisoners more humanely. Later the Jesuits were able
to make the Indians give up this practice.

[2] Letter, June 16, 1643, of Arent van Curler to Kiliaen van
Rensselaer. O'Callaghan. Hist. of New Netherland. i. 463-4.
Letter. August 5, 1643, Jogues from Rensselaerswyck. Jes. Rel.
xxxix. 201.

[3] Cf. Jogues' letter from Rensselaerswyck, 1. c. 201, 203; also
Jogue's Notice sur Goupil. Jes. Rel. xxviii. 133-135; also the
Rel. by Hierosme Lalemant. Quebec. October 20, 1647 in Jes.
Rel. xxxi. 53-55.

[4] Rel. of 1647 by Hierosme Lalemant. Jes. Rel. xxxi. 121, 123.
Rel. of 1543-44. in Jes. Rel. xxvi. 279, 281.

and confirmed by the teaching of the Dutch, from whom
the Indians had learned that the sign of the cross was a
"veritable superstition," equally hateful to their
European neighbors.[1]   When the old Indian witnessed
the action of René Goupil, he ordered a young man of
his cabin, about to leave for the war, to kill the Christian sorcerer, as the sign of the cross would cause some
harm to the child.   The execution of the command was
not long delayed.   One day René Goupil and Father
Jogues had withdrawn outside the village to perform
their devotions with greater liberty.   Their prayers
were soon interrupted by two young men, who commanded them to return, but, at the entrance to the
village, one of them drew a hatchet and struck down
René Goupil, who fell half dead, invoking the Holy
Name of Jesus.   Jogues expected the same fate, but
the Indian, after making sure of the death of his victim,
told the Jesuit that his life was in the hands of another
family.   Somewhat later Jogues was called to eat in
the cabin of the old Indian.   When the Jesuit made the
sign of the cross before the meal, the old man said to

---

[1] Letter of Father Bressani from Isle de Rhè, Nov. 16, 1644. Jes.
Rels. xxxix. 85-87.

"Our Faith is accused of killing all who profess it . . they also
accused the Faith of the French of being responsible for all the ills
with which the whole people or individual persons seem to be
afflicted.   That is what an Apostate tried to make those Barbarians
believe, naming the Dutch as his authority for what he said.   He
asserted that the children of the Iroquois died two years after their
Baptism, and that the Christians either fractured their legs or
wounded their feet with thorns or became consumptive, or vomited
their souls with their blood, or were assailed by some great misfortune."   Preaching of the Faith to the Cayugas by Chaumonot and Ménard.   Relation.   1656-57.   Jes. Rels. xliii. 313-315.

"The Dutch, they (some Huron apostates) say, have preserved
the Iroquois by allowing them to live in their own fashion, just as
the black Gowns have ruined the Hurons by preaching the faith to
them."   Jes. Rels. xliv. 291.

him: "That is what we hate; that is why they have killed thy companion, and why they will kill thee. Our neighbors the Europeans do not do so." The Indians also made him feel their hatred of this symbol, and said "that it was hated by the Dutch," when in their hunting expeditions they found Jogues kneeling before a great cross, which he had carved on a large tree at some distance from the Indian cabin "where the Demon and the dreams were almost always adored."[1]

In the following spring, Jogues and another French captive were able to visit the house of Arent van Curler, where they were courteously received.[2] There seemed to be some hope, at that time, of procuring their release. As soon as the Indians returned from their hunting, Arent van Curler endeavored to obtain this but without any success. Nevertheless, the Dutch continued their efforts, but they could do nothing more than give various little gifts to the savages to obtain better treatment for Father Jogues,[3] who was now alone held captive in that region, as his fellow prisoner had been given to an Indian living in a distant village. The Indians now consented that he should go among the Dutch when accompanied by one of their number.[4] During one of these visits, Jogues received the intelligence that he would be burned on his return to the Indian village because of the failure of an expe-

---

[1] Letter.   August 5, 1643, Father Jogues from Rensselaerswyck. Jes. Rels. xxxix. 209.
[2] Cf. Letter.   June 16, 1643 of Arent Van Curler to Kiliaen Van Rensselaer.
[3] Letter of Jogues from Rensselaerswyck.   August 5, 1643. Jes. Rels. xxxix. 223.
[4] Letter of Megapolensis and Drisius to Classis of Amsterdam. September 28, 1658. Eccl. Recs. N. Y. i. 436-7.

dition against Fort Richelieu. A Huron Indian,
adopted by the Iroquois, previous to his departure, had
demanded a letter from Jogues, who hastened to take
the opportunity to inform the French governor of the
plot in spite of the risk of his life. Thus the Iroquois
were incensed against the Jesuit, upon whom they
placed all the responsibility for their misfortunes in the
expedition.[1] The Captain of the Dutch settlement,
knowing the evil designs of the savages, suggested some
means of escape, especially as the French Governor M.
le Chevalier de Montmagny had prevented the savages
of New France from coming to kill some Dutch.[2] To
the astonishment of the Captain, Father Jogues deferred
his decision until the next day. The Jesuit missionary
had, in fact, resolved to spend the remainder of his days
in captivity for the salvation of the Iroquois and their
captives, of whom he had been able to baptize seventy
in the past year. Now, however, the certainty of death
if he remained and the hope of a return to the Mohawks
under more favorable circumstances led him to consent
to escape with the help of the Dutch. On the next day,
Father Jogues told the Dutch Captain his intention to
take advantage of his proffered assistance. A ship
happened to be in the river at that time and the sailors,
on the representations of the Captain, pledged their
word that, if the Jesuit could once set foot on their
vessel, they would make his place of refuge secure and
would not have him leave the ship until he reached

[1] Letter of Jogues from Rensselaerswyck. August 30, 1643.
Jes. Rels. xxv. 47.
[2] Ibid. 49.   Charlevoix states that an order to obtain the
deliverance of Father Jogues had been sent to all the commandants
in New Belgium by the States General of Holland, from whom the
Queen Regent of France had urgently requested this.

Bordeaux or La Rochelle. A small boat was then left on the bank of the river, with which Jogues was to make his escape to the ship. This could only be done towards morning, when a farm-servant at the request of Jogues quieted the dogs, who had savagely torn his leg early in the night. The sailors concealed him in the hold of the vessel, where he spent two nights with such discomfort that he thought he would suffocate and die from the stench. Meanwhile, the Indians made some disturbance, so that the Dutch inhabitants of the country were afraid that they would set fire to their houses or kill their cattle. When Jogues learned this from the Dutch minister, he protested that he had no wish "to escape to the prejudice of the least man of their settlement," although his return to captivity meant certain death. Finally, the Captain decided to retain the person of Jogues in the settlement until the minds of the savages should be pacified. All the Dutch were convinced of the necessity of this step except the mariners, who felt that his removal from the ship to the house of the Captain at this critical moment was a violation of their word pledged to Jogues, on the strength of which he had imperilled his life by escaping from his savage captors.[1] For six weeks he was then placed in the custody of an old miser, who lodged him in a garret, exposed to the intense heat of the summer, with no other water than that, which this old man poured from week to week into a tub also used for making lye. The water after a few day became fetid and made Father Jogues feel intense pain in the stomach. Although

[1] Letter of Jogues from Rensselaerswyck. August 30, 1643. Jes. Rels. xxv.57-59-61.

plentiful provisions were sent for his consumption, the old miser barely gave him "as much as was necessary not to live, but not to die." Then the frequent visits of the Indians for purposes of trade to the room next to the garret, separated from it by planks with large intervening cracks, compelled Jogues to crouch behind casks, to avoid discovery, but at the price of great pain in the members of his body. Finally, gangrene began to manifest itself in the wound inflicted by the dog on his leg, but the kind ministration of the surgeon of the settlement saved his life also from this danger.

Meanwhile, the Director General of the province had learned that Father Jogues was not very much at ease in the vicinity of the Mohawks, who were induced by the Dutch towards the middle of September finally to accept some presents to the amount of three hundred livres. Then in accordance with the instructions of William Kieft, Father Jogues was taken by boat to New Amsterdam. The Dutch minister, who had shown him much kindness accompanied him down the Hudson River. "He was supplied with a number of bottles, which he dealt out lavishly,—especially on coming to an Island, to which he wished that my name should be given with the noise of cannon and of bottles." Jogues quaintly and naively remarks that "each one manifests his love in his own fashion." On his arrival at New Amsterdam, the Director General received him very humanely and furnished him with good raiment, of which he stood sorely in need. The inhabitants of the town gave the Jesuit missionary every token of regard and esteem. A Lutheran Pole, meeting him in a retired spot, fell at his feet, kissed his mutilated hands

and exclaimed "Martyr, martyr of Jesus Christ!"
Father Jogues was gratified to find, in a house near the
fort, two images on the mantelpiece, one of the Blessed
Virgin and the other of St. Aloysius, placed there by the
Portuguese wife of the master of the house.   The
Jesuit felt aggrieved that he could be of no assistance to
either of these two persons on account of his ignorance
of these languages, so that the "arrogance of Babel
deprived them of great benefits." However, he was
able to hear the confession of an Irish Catholic, arriving
at Manhattan from Virginia. In November, a bark of one
hundred tons was sent to Holland from New Amsterdam.   Father Jogues had much to suffer in the voyage
from the extreme cold of the winter, as he had no other
bed than the deck of the vessel or a pile of cordage, very
often washed by the waves of the sea.   The Dutch put
into an English port and left the vessel to refresh themselves on land.   Meanwhile, robbers entered the bark
and at the point of a pistol robbed Father Jogues of the
cloak and hat which the Dutch had given him.   He
finally succeeded in making his way to France on a
French collier, which happened to be in port at the
time.[1]

In the spring of the same year in which Jogues
reached his native country, another Jesuit missionary,
Father Bressani, was captured by a band of Iroquois,
who again succeeded in intercepting an expedition with
supplies for the missions in the Huron country.   He was
so cruelly treated that there was not a sound spot in his

---

[1] Letter of Father Jogues to Father Lalemant. January 6, 1644.
Jes. Rels. xxv. 63-65.   Rel. of Hierosme Lalemant.   1647 in Jes.
Rels. xxxi. 93-101.   Rel. of Bressani. 1653 in Jes. Rels. xxxix.
231-233.

body.[1] Finally, all the savages clamored for his death by fire, but an old woman, to whom he had been given in the place of her grandfather, killed some time before in an encounter with the Hurons, ransomed the missionary with a belt of wampum, worth about thirty-five livres. He was received into her cabin, but her daughters could not bear the sight of him on account of the horrible appearance of his mangled body.[2] Meanwhile, the Dutch gave him good reason to hope for his ransom, which was finally effected without much difficulty, as the Indians held him in little esteem, because of his want of skill for everything, and because they believed that he would never get well of his ailments.[3] The old woman ordered her son to take him to the Dutch and to deliver him into their hands after receiving some presents in return. The Dutch received the Jesuit, naked and with his fingers maimed and bleeding, in great kindness and satisfied the Indian with presents to the amount of about two hundred livres.[4] He was clothed, placed under the care of the surgeon, and almost daily fed at the table of the Dutch minister.[5] After he had been restored to health, he was brought to New Amsterdam, where he was finally placed on a ship, manned by Huguenots, sailing for Europe. He carried with him this letter of safe-conduct: "We, William Kieft, Director General, and the Council of New Netherland,

---

[1] Details given by Bressani himself in his Relation of 1653. Jes. Rels. xxxix.

[2] Rel. 1643-44 by Vimont. Jes. Rels. xxvi. 49.

[3] Letter of Bressani from New Amsterdam. August 31, 1644, Jes. Rels. xxxix. 77.

[4] Ibid. p. 78-79 with note 8.

[5] Letter of Megapolensis and Drisius to Classis of Amsterdam. Sept. 28, 1658. Eccl. Recs. N. Y. i. 437.

to all those who shall see these presents, greeting: Francis Joseph Bressani, of the Society of Jesus, for some time a prisoner among the Iroquois savages, commonly called Maquaas, and daily persecuted by these, was, when about to be burnt, snatched out of their hands, and ransomed by us for a large sum after considerable difficulty. As he proceeds with our permission to Holland, thence to return to France, Christian charity requires that he be humanely treated by those into whose hands he may happen to fall. Wherefore we request all governors, viceroys, or their lieutenants and captains that they would afford him their favor in going and returning, promising to do the same on like occasian. Dated in Fort Amsterdam, in New Netherland, this 20th of September, anno Salutis, 1644, Stylo Novo."[1]

Although Father Bressani, during the tiresome voyage of fifty-five days, had no other bed than a bare box, in which he could not stretch out at full length, he arrived in a sailor's dress at the Isle of Rhé in better health than he ever possessed in the eighteen years during which he had been in the Society.[2]

Both Father Bressani and Father Jogues again returned to Canada to continue their endeavors to convert the savages to Christianity. When some deputies of the Iroquois arranged a peace with the French, there was no one so well fitted to obtain the assent of the tribes as Father Jogues, who was thoroughly conversant with the language. When the Algonquins saw him

---

[1] O'Callaghan. Hist. of New Netherland. i. 337.
[2] Letter. November 16, 1644, from Isle of Rhé by Bressani. In his Relation of 1653. Jes. Rels. xxxix. 83, 85.

step into the canoe on this dangerous mission, they warned him not to speak in the beginning of the faith which was so repulsive to the Iroquois, as it seemed to exterminate everything that men held most dear. They also advised him to wear shorter apparel, as the long robe preached as well as the lips, and the warning was heeded.[1] On his arrival in the Mohawk country, his efforts to have the peace ratified by the Indians were successful. However, some savages with distrustful minds did not look with favor on a little box, which the Father left as a pledge of his return to the country, as they imagined that it enclosed some disastrous misfortune. Father Jogues opened the chest and showed these Indians that it contained no other mystery than some small necessaries, for which he might have use on his return.[2] This conclusion of a peace with the fierce Mohawks raised in the hearts of the Jesuits great hopes of their final conversion. In the following summer, Father Jogues was, in fact, appointed to begin among these Indians a new mission under the patronage of the Holy Martyrs. He planned to spend the winter in the Mohawk country to begin with solidity the instruction of those infidels.[3] Meanwhile, superstition had again poisoned the minds of the savages against the missionary in spite of all their former professions of undying friendship. Upon his arrival on the 17th of October, 1646, Father Jogues was stripped naked, loaded with blows and threatened with death on the following day. The savages kept their promise in spite of the opposition

---

[1] Rel. 1645-6 by Lalemant in Jes. Rels. xxix. 47, 49.
[2] Rel. 1645-6 by Lalemant in Jes. Rels. xxix 55, 57.
[3] Bressani's Relation of 1653. Jes. Rels. xxxix. 235-36.

of the Wolf and Turtle clans. In the evening, he was called to the lodge of the Bear to supper. As soon as he entered, a savage, concealed behind the door, stepped forward and split his head, which was immediately cut off and set upon the palisades of the village. The same fate awaited a companion of Father Jogues the next day, when both bodies were thrown into the river.[1] The Indians brought the Jesuit's missal and breviary, together with his underclothing and coat, to the Dutch minister, John Megapolensis, who diligently enquired of the principal men of the band the reason of this deed. They had no answer to make except that the Father had left the devil among some clothes, who had caused their Indian corn to be devoured.[2]

The war between the Iroquois and the French broke out anew with unabated fury. The savages again held French prisoners in bondage. Stuyvesant received intelligence that eight or nine Christian captives in the hands of the Mohawks would be cruelly tortured, unless they were ransomed with a large sum. Moved by compassion for these unfortunate Frenchmen, the Director General sent word of this fact to the Directors of the Company in Amsterdam. They confessed that the ransom of Christian captives from the savages was "the duty of all Christians, but every one is bound to care for himself and his own people." Frenchmen had been ransomed before "at the expense of the Company and by the contributions of the community, for which we

[1] Letter of Labbadie to M. La Montague. October 30, 1646. Jes. Rels. xxxi. 117.
[2] Wm. Kieft to M. le Chevalier de Montmagny. November 14, 1646. Ibid. 115. Megapolensis and Drisius to Classis of Amsterdam. September 28, 1658. Ecl. Recs. N. Y. i. 736-7.

have never been repaid, so that we think that, when complaints reach France, they will take care of their countrymen."[1]

Two years later on August 20, 1653, a band of marauding Iroquois, during an incursion into Canada, captured Father Joseph Poncet and another Frenchman, Maturin Franchetot, while the Jesuit was speaking to the latter in his field to induce him to garner the little harvest of a poor French widow. On the arrival of these Indians in the Mohawk country, their prisoners were stripped of their clothing and compelled to run the gauntlet under a shower of blows. Later in the day, Father Poncet lost the first finger of his left hand, which was cut off by a child at the bidding of a savage in response to the request of an Indian woman. Meanwhile, the Mohawks, who were besieging Three Rivers, met with greater resistance than they had anticipated, and began to sue for peace, but the French refused to begin any negotiations, unless the Jesuit Father and his fellow-prisoner were restored. The Indian chief pleaded ignorance of the capture of these Frenchmen and immediately ordered two canoes to return to the Mohawk country to prevent any harm from being done to the prisoners, and to procure their release if still alive.[2] Franchetot had already been burned to death on the eighth of September, while the life of Father Poncet had been saved through his adoption by a good old woman in the place of a brother, killed or captured some time before. The Indian, who brought the mes-

[1] Letter of Directors to Stuyvesant. March 21, 1651.   Col. Docs. N. Y. xiii. 28.
[2] Relation. 1652-53. Jes. Rels. xl. 171.

sage of his deliverance to Father Poncet, happened to be
a brother to the woman who had adopted him, and
showed the Jesuit great kindness. He brought him to
the Dutch settlement, where the Jesuit Father was
very kindly entertained by some of the inhabitants, but
very coldly received by Commissary Dyckman, the
commander of Fort Orange, although the French
Governor, M. de Lauzon, had given the Mohawk a letter
to present to the Dutch authorities to recommend the
Father to their care. The Jesuit was about to lie down
on the bare floor without bed or supper, when his Indian conductor obtained permission to take him to
some of his friends in the settlement. Here he was
received with much kindness by an old man, under
whose hospitable roof he spent three days. His host, a
good Walloon, and a good Scotch Lady, who had shown
herself on all occasions very charitable toward the
French, vied with one another in their efforts to find
clothes for the priest. Father Poncet thanked them
all, but would not accept anything but a hooded cloak,
and some stockings of the savage fashion with some
French shoes and a blanket that was to serve as a bed
on his return journey. He was also urged to accept
some provisions, but he contented himself with some
peaches from a Brussels merchant, a good Catholic,
whom he confessed before his departure. He had administered the same sacrament to a young man also, residing
with his host. This Frenchman had been captured by the
Iroquois at Three Rivers, and ransomed by the Dutch,
whom he now served as interpreter. When Father
Poncet took leave of his generous friends, he had to

promise them to return the next summer.[1] Meanwhile, the Indian Councils gathered the presents and selected the embassy for the solemn conclusion of peace with the French. Father Poncet with his conductor and the other Iroquois finally arrived at Montreal on October 24th, and on the sixth of November the great affair of peace, so ardently desired, was brought to a close in Quebec.[2] The Mohawks left four of their number as hostages with the French, while two young soldiers volunteered to go to the Mohawk country in the same capacity at the request of the savages. In the calculation of the Mohawks, the peace was only a preliminary step to obtain the removal of the Hurons to their own country, which had been secretly proposed to the latter at the very time that they were discussing the conclusion of the peace with the French.[3]

During the winter of 1654, the Onondagas came to Quebec to strengthen the peace that they had already negotiated in the preceding fall. They also made the same secret proposals to the Hurons, who did not dare to refuse in their anxiety for peace, but demanded first a dwelling for the black robes, their teachers, whom they would

[1] The Relation of 1656-7 gives a curious fact, which may be mentioned here in its own words. "A woman, who was very ill at Onontaghé, had dreamed that she required a black gown to effect her cure. But, as the recent cruel massacre of our Fathers by those Barbarians deprived them of all hope of being able to obtain one from us, they applied to the Dutch, who sold them at a very high price the wretched cassock of Father Poncet, who had shortly before been despoiled of it by the Annienhronnons. The woman attributed her cure to it, and wished to keep it all her life as a precious relic." Jes. Rels xliii. 273.
[2] Relation of 1652-53. Jes. Rels. xl. 119-157.
[3] Relation of 1653-54. Jes. Rels. xli. 47-49.

follow wherever they should decide to go.[1] The French
Governor, informed of the secret negotiations, had the
Hurons represent to the Onondagas that the French
themselves had proposed to build a new settlement on
the great lake of the Iroquois, so that there was no
reason to conceal anything from them. Thus at the
council, the Governor supported the proposals of the
Huron Indians with presents. In the following May,
the Onondagas returned to continue their negotiations,
which they opened favorably by obtaining the release
of a young surgeon, captured during the winter by a
wandering band of Iroquois of another tribe. Then the
Onondaga spokesman told the French that he wished
above all things to see in his country one of the black
robes, who had taught the Hurons to honor the one
God. The Indians promised to receive his teaching with
love, as it was their wish to worship Him, who is the
master of their lives.[2] Simon Le Moyne was, therefore,
allowed to accompany these Indians, who began their
homeward journey from Quebec on the second of July.
A few days later a Mohawk Captain, the son of an
Iroquois mother and a Dutch father, known as the
Flemish Bastard, appeared in Quebec with some other
Mohawks and the two French hostages, whom he had
promised to restore at this time. This chief had been
in Canada before, towards the end of the winter, when
he had brought letters from the Dutch commandant of
Fort Orange and from some Dutch tradesmen, who all
assured the French that now they really saw a disposition for peace on the part of their Indian allies. The

[1] Rel. 1653-1654. Jes. Rel. xli. 55-63.
[2] Ibid. 73-74.

Mohawks were disappointed by the fact that they had
been forestalled by the Onondagas. The chief in a
clever speech made their complaint known to the
French. "Ought not one to enter a house by the door,
and not by the chimney or roof of the cabin, unless he
be a thief, and wish to take the inmates by surprise?
We, the five Iroquois Nations, compose but one cabin;
we maintain but one fire; and we have, from time im-
memorial, dwelt under one and the same roof. Well,
then, will you not enter the cabin by the door, which
is at the ground floor of the house? It is with us
Mohawks, that you should begin; whereas you, by
beginning with the Onondagas, try to enter by the roof
and through the chimney. Have you no fear that the
smoke may blind you, our fire not being extinguished
and that you may fall from the top to the bottom,
having nothing solid on which to plant your feet?"
The French Governor assured the Mohawks that
Father Le Moyne would also go to their country and
gave him letters to deliver to the Jesuit missionary to
inform him to that effect, but the Father had gained
such a start that the Mohawk chief could not overtake
him.[1] Father Le Moyne, on his arrival in the Onondaga
country, received every evidence of good will on the
part of the savages, who at this time had great fear of
the issue of an impending war with the powerful Erie
tribes or the Cat Nation. The chief of the Onondagas,
speaking in the name of the Five Iroquois Nations,
again told Father Le Moyne that it was their wish to
acknowledge Him of whom he had told them, who is
the master of their lives, and who was unknown to them,

[1] Relation. 1653-54. Jes. Rels. xli. 87-89.

but the richest presents accompanied the words, in which he spoke of the courage inspired in their hearts by the French Governor for their new wars. The French were told to select a site for their new settlement on the shores of the great lake, to which the Onondagas promised to go to receive instruction.[1] On his journey back to Canada, the Jesuit missionary with his Indian guides arrived at the entrance to a little lake and tasted the water from a spring, which the Indians dared not to drink, as they believed that an evil spirit rendered it foul. He found it to be a spring of salt water, from which he procured some salt, "as natural as that which comes from the sea."[2]

Although the Onondaga chief pretended to speak in the name of the five Iroquois Nations, the Mohawks were not really comprised in these negotiations, of which they were, in fact, jealous. Some Mohawks on the St. Lawrence, meeting the canoe which, under the guidance of two Onondagas, was carrying Father Le Moyne to Montreal, killed one of the Onondagas, and bound the Jesuit missionary after slaying some Hurons and Algonquins. The surviving Onondaga protested so energetically against this outrage, which would be deeply resented by his tribe, that the Mohawks finally released their prisoner. He was then safely conducted to Montreal.[3] There were also other acts of hostility committed by the Mohawks, who showed themselves as "perfidious and treacherous as usual." In spite of the previous negotiations for peace, a Jesuit lay brother, Jean Ligeois, was shot by some Mohawks in ambush, while

[1] Rel. 1653-54. Jes. Rels. xli. 117-119.
[2] Ibid. 123-125.
[3] Ibid. 199-201

he was trying to discover the presence of the enemy for the sake of the Christian savages at work in the fields, whom he wished to warn.   Persons were killed and taken captive on either side.   Finally, the Mohawks, weary of the war, brought back the French captives and requested the restoration of their own Indians.   They agreed not to attack the French any longer, nor to bear arms below Three Rivers, but they refused to discontinue the war against the Algonquins and Hurons, whom they might find above that village on the river of St. Lawrence.   Father Le Moyne was now sent to the Mohawks to take back the prisoners, captured by the French, and "also to cement that peace, as well as it can be cemented with the Infidels who are allied to Heretics."[1]   The Jesuit left Montreal on this mission, August 17, 1655, with twelve Iroquois and two Frenchmen. A month later the party reached their destination, where the Father was received with "extraordinary cordiality."   A council was held, which passed in many exchanges of courtesy. Le Moyne then pushed on to the Dutch settlement where he was also received "with great demonstration of affection by the Dutch," from whom he learned of the attack of the River Indians upon New Amsterdam.   On his return to the Mohawks, he almost met death at the hands of a a madman, who finally was calmed by a quickwitted Indian squaw's suggestion to kill her dog in the place of the missionary.   However, a Huron Christian had his head split without ceremony upon a mere suspicion that he had revealed to the Father some of the designs,

[1] Introduction to Copies of two Letters sent from New France. 1656. Jes. Rel. xli. 201-223.

which the Mohawks wished to conceal from him. Nevertheless, Father Le Moyne and the two Frenchmen were allowed to set out for Canada under the guidance of three Iroquois. The Father had hardly left the country, when a body of one hundred of these Indians appeared at Fort Orange. They were on the point of setting forth on a war excursion against the Canada Indians, and, fearing "that the French had poisoned the ears of their Dutch brothers against them," they now asked the latter to remain neutral.[1]

Meanwhile, the Onondagas appeared again in Quebec, urging the foundation of the French settlement in their country and requesting some Jesuit Fathers to teach their children and to make of them a thoroughly Christian people. They also promised to use their influence with the Mohawks, who now alone prevented the reign of universal peace in the country. Two Fathers, Joseph Chaumont and Claude Dablon, accompanied the Indians to Onondaga to promote this important enterprise. They spent the whole winter at the Onondaga village, where a chapel had been erected for them by the savages, who gave them great hopes of success in their missionary work. The savages were charmed with the many discourses of the Fathers, which to some were the occasion of a comparison unfavorable to their other European neighbors. "The Dutch had neither sense nor tongues; they had never heard them mention Paradise or Hell; on the contrary, they were the first to incite them to wrong-doing."[2] However, the Onondagas

[1] Fort Orange Recs. O'Callaghan.   Hist. of New Netherland ii. 306.
[2] Rels. 1655-56. Jes. Rels. xlii. 111. Similar testimony is given in the Relation 1657-1658. "Very few of our savages come

were not content.   In a solemn council, on the 29th of
February, the Savages told the Fathers, that they were
tired of any further postponement of the French settlement, for which they had been waiting from year to
year.   In the event of further delay, they threatened to
break the peace, which they had concluded with the
French under this condition.   A few days later, Father
Dablon, realizing the urgency of the matter, set out
for Canada with some Indian guides, and, after a weary
journey through snow, ice and rain, arrived at Montreal
on the 30th of March.   All preparations for the new settlement were completed on the 17th of May.   A band
of about fifty Frenchmen, with Father Francis le
Mercier, Father René Menard and Father Jacques
Fremin, and Brothers Ambroise Broar and Joseph
Boursier, accompanied Father Dablon back to Onondaga, where they arrived on the eleventh of July.

News of this French settlement at Onondaga soon
reached the Dutch Province.   Although the Jesuits
believed that the Dutch were glad that they dwelt in
these places, and reported that the Dutch were even
willing to bring them horses and other commodities,[1]
the Directors of the Amsterdam Chamber, informed by
Stuyvesant of a French settlement among the Senecas,
expressed their dissatisfaction, as the matter could only
be to the disadvantage of the Province of New Netherland and its inhabitants.   There is no doubt that
their suspicions were well founded, for the Jesuits

back from Kebec without greater esteem and affection for our
mysteries, and without a desire to be instructed and to embrace the
Faith; they say that they experience quite different feelings when
they return from the Dutch settlements." Jes. Rels. xliv. 45.
[1] Relation of 1656-57.   Jes. Rels. xliii. 185.

themselves realized that an alliance between the French and the Senecas would bring the fur trade of these Indians to Canada, which was much easier of access by the river routes and devoid of the great danger from the Andastes, hostile to the Senecas, than the overland journey to the Dutch settlements through the country of the insolent and overbearing Mohawks.[1] The Dutch Directors, therefore, commanded Stuyvesant to investigate the matter more closely and not to neglect any measures necessary for the security of Fort Orange, "that no mishap befall us there."[2]

In the following year, there was promise of many conversions in all the villages of the Upper Iroquois and two Jesuit Fathers, Paul Raguenau and Francis Du Perron, some Frenchmen with some fifty Christian Hurons, men, women and children, left Montreal on the 26th of July to help their brethren in the new mission. Treachery was evidenced, not more than a week later, by the massacre of the Huron men and the enslavement of their women and children before the very eyes of the French,[3] who would have shared their fate, if the savages had not feared retaliation on the Onondagas, who remained behind in Quebec in the hope of inducing the rest of the Hurons to remove to their country. The Jesuit Fathers were able to send to Quebec intelligence of the secret designs entertained for their destruction by the Indians, who no longer had any need of French help after their triumph over the

[1] Relation. 1653-54. Jes. Rels. xli. 201-3. Relation. 1660-1661. Jes. Rels. xlvii. 111.
[2] Directors to Stuyvesant. December 19, 1656. Col. Docs. N. Y. xiv. 371-374.
[3] Letter of Paul Raguenau. August 9, 1657. Rel. 1656-57. Jes. Rels. xliv. 69-77.

Cat Nation. A number of murders committed by the Iroquois at Montreal confirmed the fears of the French, and resulted in the arrest of all the Iroquois found in Montreal, Three Rivers and Quebec.[1] War was inevitable. The destruction of the French settlers had already been determined, when they escaped in a body, while the savages were overcome by sleep after a generous feast given by the French. After a perilous journey, they reached Montreal on the 3d of April, but three Frenchmen had lost their lives in the rapids of the St. Lawrence.[2]

The Onondaga settlement had been the source of much jealousy to the Mohawks. However, a Huron clan had also been forced to settle in the Mohawk country, in the spring of 1655, to obtain the peace, for which the Hurons sued, after their enemies had surprised their village on the Isle of Orleans. On his visit to the Mohawks in the summer, Father LeMoyne found these Hurons reduced to a state of slavery. "The husband was separated from the wife, and the children from their parents; in short they were serving those Barbarians as beasts of burden." As in the preceding year the missionary's labors were mainly claimed by this suffering flock among the heathen Mohawks. Like a good shepherd, "he consoled the afflicted; he taught the ignorant; he heard the confessions of those who came to him; he baptized the children; he made all pray to God; he exhorted all to persevere in the Faith and in avoiding sin." Little success followed his efforts with the Mohawks themselves. Nevertheless, he never

[1] Rel. 1657-58. Jes. Rel. xliv. 155-6.
[2] Letter of Paul Raguenau. Ibid. 175-183.

allowed an Iroquois to go from his presence without
"a word of instruction on Hell and Paradise, or the
power of God who sees and knows all, who punishes the
wicked and rewards the good."[1]   The possibility of
missionary work with Mohawks themselves became
still less, when news arrived of the imprisonment of the
Iroquois found in the French settlements after the
murder of some Frenchmen at Montreal.   Some of these
Indians were Mohawks.   Le Moyne tells that the
detention of these prisoners nearly caused his death,
though, in point of fact, it was the salvatian of his life.[2]

In the preceding autumn, the missionary had made
a visit to New Amsterdam.   The Dutch minister believed that his visit was occasioned by the invitation of
the Papists, living in Manhattan, and especially of some
French privateers, who had arrived in the port with a
good prize.   To these Catholics, he administered the
sacrament of penance and granted whatever indulgences
he was empowered as a Jesuit missionary to impart to
the faithful.   One of the Dutch, who understood
French, overheard him telling them that they did not
need to go to Rome, inasmuch as "he had as full power
from the Pope to forgive their sins, as if they were to
go to Rome."   The report made of this visit to the
Classis of Amsterdam by Megapolensis is somewhat
caustic and does not reveal that kindly feeling, which
his past relations with the Jesuit missionaries might
lead one to expect, although Father Le Moyne was careful not to debate religion, even when provoked to do so
by the Dutch minister's question "whether he had

[1] Rel. 1656-7.   Jes. Rels. xliii. 215.
[2] Letter of Le Moyne, New Holland.   March 25, 1658.   Relation 1656-58.   Jes. Rels. xliv. 219.

taught the Indians anything more than to make the sign of the Cross and such like superstitions."[1] The missionary told the minister that he wanted only to chat. He informed him of the existence of wonderful mineral springs in the western part of the country inhabited by the Iroquois. There was a spring of salt water from which he had obtained excellent salt by boiling the water; there was an oil spring, which the Indians used to anoint their hair; and there was another spring of hot sulphurous water, in which paper and dry materials became ignited. The minister could not decide, whether all this was true, or whether it was a mere Jesuit lie, and so he mentioned the whole matter on the authority of the Jesuit to his ecclesiastical superiors in Holland.[2]

[1] The Dutch seem to have been under the impression that the conversion of the Indians to Christianity wrought by the Jesuits was superficial. Thus while Van der Donck admits that "the Jesuits have taken great pains and trouble in Canada to convert the Indians to the Roman Church," he believes that the Indians profess that religion only "outwardly," and so "inasmuch as they are not well instructed in its fundamental principles, they fall off lightly and make sport of the subject and its doctrine." Van der Donck's authority for this statement is the alleged experience of a Dutch merchant on a trading trip to Canada in 1639, who plied an Indian chief with liquor, loosening his tongue and imagiantion. "After he had drank two or three glasses of wine, . . . the chief said that he had been instructed so far that he often said mass among the Indians, and that on a certain occasion the place where the altar stood caught fire by accident, and our people made preparations to put out the fire, which he forbade them to do, saying that God who stands there is almighty, and he will put out the fire himself; and we waited with great attention, but the fire continued till all was burned up, with your Almighty God himself and with all the fine things about him. Since that time I have never held to that religion, but regard the sun and the moon much more, as being better than all your Gods are; for they warm the earth and cause the fruits to grow, when your lovely Gods cannot preserve themselves from the fire." Van der Donck. A Description of New Netherland. N. Y. Hist. Society Coll. 2nd. Ser. i. (1841), p. 214.

[2] "The Springs, which are as numerous as they are wonderful, are nearly all minerals. Our little lake (Onondaga) which is only

Father Le Moyne spent eight days in New Amsterdam. Before his departure, the Dutch told him of their
desire to open trade between Canada and New Netherland.   Le Moyne sent word of this proposal to the

six or seven leagues in circumference, is almost entirely surrounded
by salt springs. The water is used for salting and seasoning meat,
and for making very good salt. It often forms of itself in fine
crystals with which nature takes pleasure in surrounding these
springs. The salt that forms at a spring about two days' journey
from our residence, toward Oiogoen, is much stronger than that
from the springs of Gannentaa; for when the water—which looks as
white as milk, and the smell of which is perceptible from a great
distance—is boiled, it leaves a kind of salt almost as corrosive as
caustic. The rocks about that spring are covered with a foam as
thick as cream. The spring in the direction of Sonnontouan is no
less wonderful for its water-being of the same nature as the surrounding soil, which has only to be washed in order to obtain perfectly
pure sulphur—it ignites when it is shaken violently, and yields
sulphur when boiled. As one approaches nearer to the country of
the Cats, one finds heavy and thick water, which ignites like brandy,
and boils up in bubles of flame when fire is applied to it.   It is,
moreover, so oily, that all our savages use it to anoint and grease
their heads and their bodies."   Rel. 1656-7. Cap. xi. Jes. Rel. xliii.
259-261.
   "The first one has never been exactly identified.   By
land, it would probably be about thirty miles from the fort to
Auburn; but such a spring would be at least at the base of the lime-
stone rocks, farther north, and probably in the Salina group.   The
river route, two days' journey, would bring the travellers to the salt
springs at Montezuma; and the text seems to imply salt springs
highly charged with lime.   The sulphurous odor and the milky tinge
would be caused by the decomposition of sulphate of lime. There are
many small springs of this sort, continually forming calcareous tufa—
sometimes encrusting large masses of leaves or moss, and sometimes
forming masses of a light and spongy nature, yellow in hue.   When
wet, these are quite caustic to the touch.   The "burning spring"
near the Senecas" is in the town of Bristol, Ontario County,
halfway between Canandaigua and Honeoye, where Charlevoix's
map locates it as the "Fontaine brulante."   There are several
other carburated hydrogen gas springs in Ontario County.
The spring "toward the country of the Cats" (Eries) was probably the noted Oil spring in the town of Cuba, Alleghany County,
about fifty miles southwest of the "burning spring."   It is on the
Oil Spring Reservation, and is described as a dirty, stagnant pool,
twenty feet in diameter, and without an outlet.   A yellowish-brown
oil collects on the surface, which is skimmed off.   (Seneca oil,
formerly a popular remedy). This spring was so highly esteemed by
the Senecas that in their treaties they reserved it, with a square
mile of land.   The spring toward Cayuga cannot be satisfactorily

French Governor, who immediately took counsel with
the principal inhabitants of Canada in regard to this
matter. There was no objection raised to the commerce of the Dutch with Canada, as the Dutch had
long been received in French ports as friends and allies
of the Crown. The French Governor only stipulated
that their ships were to observe the same customs, as
the French vessels, which excluded all participation in
the Indian trade and the public exercise on land of
any religion that was opposed to the Roman faith.[1]
Father Le Moyne communicated this reply to the
Dutch from Fort Orange on April 7, 1658, and expressed
regret that he was unable to accompany the first ship
to Quebec, as he had planned to do, inasmuch as he
would have with him, on his journey to Canada, "his
sailors of the woods."[2]   The Mohawks, in their negotiations for the release of the prisoners held by the French,
had promised to bring back Father Le Moyne to
Canada in the spring. They stopped at Fort Orange
previous to their departure and the Jesuit took the
opportunity to send a long letter to the Dutch minister,
who had been a Catholic until his twenty-third year,
when he had left the Church of Rome to become a
follower of John Calvin. To win back the minister to

identified. There are several magnesian springs, but not located as
in the text. I think it was one of the common springs, highly
charged with sulphate of lime. John Bartram saw one of these in
1743, at Onondaga; but it was not oderous, being above the gypsum
rocks. Cf. allusions to the mineral springs of that region, in Robert
Munro's Description of the Genesee Country (N. Y. 1804; reprinted
in N. Y. Doc. Hist. ii. 679-689.")—W. M. Beauchamp. Note
21. Jes. Rels. xliii. 326.
    [1] Letter of Governor D'Aillebout to Father Le Moyne, Quebec.
February 18, 1658. O'Callaghan. Hist. of New Netherland. ii. p.
364.
    [2] Letter. Ibid.

the old Faith, Father Le Moyne sent him three trea-
tises, one on the succession of the popes, the second on
the councils, and the third on heresies.   He exhorted
the minister to carefully meditate upon them, as Christ
hanging on the Cross was always ready to receive the
penitent.   The Jesuit appealed to the apostolic succession in the Church of Rome from St. Peter, the vicar
of Christ on earth, the rock upon which the Church
was built, against which the gates of hell were not to
prevail, as the pledge of the truth of her teaching.   The
Faith, received by the Church from Christ, had been
preserved in its purity by the indwelling of the Holy
Spirit, the Spirit of Truth, who had never forsaken the
Church assembled in the great Councils in union with
the Holy See of Rome, while on the contrary the truth
had been corrupted outside of the Catholic Church
through the work of the heretics, beginning with Judas
and ending with Calvin.   The letter had as little effect
upon the religious belief of the Dutch minister, as the
letters which Jogues and Poncet had sent to work his
conversion.   Megapolensis denied the succession to be
a proof of the teaching of the Church of Rome and
accused Le Moyne of bad faith in not including in his
list of the popes the mythical Joanna, who, he believed,
was well attested in history.   He claimed that the
names of Christ and Peter could not be admitted into
the list of popes, as they could not endorse some of the
doctrines of the Church of Rome.   He did not deny
the presence of the Holy Spirit in the Church, the bride
of Christ, but he did not see the bride of Christ in the
church of Rome, "the Babylonian harlot . . . drunk
with the blood of holy martyrs."   He asserted that the

validity of a council did not depend on the approval of
the Pope, but on its conformity with the Word of God—
of course according to the Reformed interpretation—
which alone assured the presence of the Holy Spirit,
while Popes and Councils often contradicted one
another. Megapolensis could not deny Calvin's departure from the Christian belief obtaining in the world
before his day, but he represented Calvin's teaching as a
restoration of the Gospel of Christ in its "purity,"
inasmuch as Calvin had discerned anew "the pure doctrines" of election, founded solely on the good pleasure
of God, of Christ as the only sacrifice for sin and only
mediator with God, of good works, done out of gratitude
and for the glory of God, and not from the selfish
motive of reward. The Dutch, minister, therefore, did
not allow the charge of heresy against Calvin, "who
brought back the doctrine of Christ's merits," while
the Jesuits, putting off even the name of Christian,
took refuge "in the fictitious merits, indulgences, and
satisfactions" of Ignatius of Loyola and Francis Xavier.
He, therefore, tells Le Moyne to omit some names in his
list of heretics and insert in their place various Orders
of Monks and several Orders of Nuns. Finally Megapolensis implored the Jesuit in his advancing age to
ponder on his responsibility to Christ for his steward-
ship, as he was profaning the holy ordinance of Christ
in baptizing Indians, when they were willing to make
the sign of the cross, and sometimes even when half
dead. The Dutch minister promised to pray for
Le Moyne "that he may be delivered from his errors
and led to the true knowledge of Christ." The first
ship dispatched from New Amsterdam to Canada

carried this reply of John Megapolensis to Le Moyne, with which the Dutch minister was so satisfied, that he sent a draft to the Classis of Amsterdam. However, the Jesuit never received the letter, as the Dutch bark, St. Jean, under Captain John Petrel was wrecked at the entrance of the gulf and left her bones on the Island of Anticosti.[1]

For some time peace negotiations between the French and the Iroquois continued, although occasionally prisoners were made on both sides. On the arrival of Father Le Moyne with three Mohawk ambassadors towards the end of May, they made known the deliberations of the great council of the Mohawks assembled on April 19, in the presence of the most notable of the Dutch of Manhattan, whom the Indians had made witnesses of their peaceful intentions. They, therefore, asked the French Governor to put away the irons, with which he bound the Mohawk captive, and demanded finally that the French should not intervene in Indian conflicts. "Do like the Dutchman who interferes not in the wars of the Wolves."[2] When the Governor charged them with the murders committed recently by the Indians, the Mohawks threw the blame upon the thoughtless Oneidas, who also sometimes inflicted such injuries upon their Mohawk Father.[3] On the conclusion of the council, the savages were dismiss-

---

[1] Reply of Rev. Johannes Megapolensis, Pastor of the Church of New Amsterdam to a letter of Father Simon Le Moyne, a French Jesuit Missionary of Canada. 1658. New York. 1907. The original copy is in the Sage Library of the Theological Seminary at New Brunswick, N. J.

[2] The Mohegans were called the Wolf Nation by the French. Cf. Rel. 1659-60. Jes. Rels. xlvi. 87.

[3] Journal Des PP. Jésuites. 1658. Jes. Rels. xliv. 95-99.

ed with presents and also some prisoners and directed to invite the Elders to visit the Governor for the conclusion of a general peace with all the Nations. Good treatment was promised to the Mohawk prisoners, who were retained in captivity.[1] Shortly after the return of the Mohawks to their own country, fifteen of the oldest chiefs presented themselves at Fort Orange and requested the Dutch authorities to give them an interpreter,who was to assist them in the exchange of four French prisoners for Six Mohawk captives and in the conclusion of a peace with all the Indians of that region. The Dutch replied that they had no person who was able to act in such a capacity, but the Mohawks refused to allow such an excuse. "When ye were at war with the Indians, we went to the Manhattans and used our best endeavors to procure you peace. Ye are bound, therefore, now to befriend us on this occasion." The public crier was then sent around to offer one hundred guilders to any person, who would consent to act as interpreter to these Mohawks. One of the Company's soldiers, Henry Martin, volunteered and set out with the Mohawks, who promised to bring him back in safety at the end of forty days.[2]

On their arrival, the Mohawks, calling the attention of the French to the fact that the Captain of New Holland was their companion in this embassy, told the French Governor to seek the means of establishing a firm peace, but appointed the Mohawk village as the place of the council, in which all their nations would assemble. The Governor, speaking in the name of the

[1] Rel. 1657-58. Jes. Rels. xliv. 223.
[2] Cf. Letter. August 15, 1658. La Montague to M. De la Petrie. O'Callaghan. Hist. of New Netherland. ii. 366.

French, Hurons, and Algonquins, declared that he had
come from France precisely to procure peace throughout all these countries, so that the preachers of the
Gospel might have free access to them. Father Le
Moyne was, therefore, to go to the Mohawk country to
negotiate peace with all their nations, whom the Algonquins would also visit next spring, as they had no gifts
at present to give their ambassadors. However, as the
young Mohawks showed but little faithfulness, the Governor was compelled to keep four of their people in
Quebec as hostages for the life of the Jesuit Father,
who would go with them. At the end of November,
some of the Mohawks, with the prisoners then released,
began their homeward journey.[1] In the spring of the
following year, 1659, an embassy of three Oneidas
appeared in Quebec to demand again, in the name of
their own tribe, the Mohawks, and Onondagas, the liberation of the Oneida and Mohawk prisoners and to remind
the Governor of his promise, that Father Le Moyne and
the Algonquins were now to visit the Mohawk country
to arrange the peace. On May 7th, Father Le Moyne
and Jean de Noyon started from Three Rivers on an
embassy to Agnié, with two Algonquins, Tigarihogen,
four prisoners freed at Quebec and the three Oneida
ambassadors. One of the Algonquins, after remaining
two days in the Mohawk village, was overcome by fear
and fled back to Montreal, where he arrived towards the
end of June. A few days later, Father Le Moyne also arrived in Quebec with the remaining Algonquin and four
Mohawks, who came to get the remaining Mohawk
hostages. However, only two of these were sent back

[1] Journal des PP. Jésuites. Jes. Rels. xliv. 121-129.

to their country, while the two Oneidas were retained
until two Frenchmen taken by the Onondagas should
be restored.[1]   In spite of the promises made by these
Mohawks at the time of their departure, eight Frenchmen were taken captive a month later by a band of one
hundred Mohawks near Three Rivers, but, shortly before
this, some savages had killed nine Iroquois a day's
journey above Montreal.[2]   The Dutch requested the
Mohawks to release their eight French prisoners and to
restore them to their country, but the Mohawks
deferred the answer to this request until the assembly of a council of their castles. They complained bitterly that the French did not keep the
peace, as French savages attacked them, whenever
they were out hunting, and thrashed them with
the help of the disguised Frenchmen always among
them.[3]   On January 16, 1660, Abraham Staes of
Beverwyck wrote to Stuyvesant that the Mohawks had
declared that they would bring back to Canada the
French prisoners in the spring and then make a solid
peace with the French.   However, with the arrival of
spring, the Iroquois threatened all the French settlements on the St. Lawrence.[4]   Seventeen young Frenchmen of Montreal under Dollard, with forty Huron Warriors, decided to cut off the Iroquois returning from the
chase, but, in the month of June, they were hemmed in,
in an old dilapidated fort at Long Sault, by seven
hundred Iroquois, composed of two hundred Ononda-

[1] Journal des PP. Jésuites. 1659-1660. Jes. Rels. xlv. 81-95.
[2] Ibid. 107, 109.
[3] Minutes of the Court of Fort Orange. September 24, 1659. Col.
Docs. N. Y. xiii. 113.
[4] Journal des PP. Jésuites. 1660. Jes. Rels. xlv. 153.

gas and five hundred Mohawks. After a gallant defense, the few survivors, five Frenchmen and four Hurons, were captured and carried away to be tortured to death. Two Frenchmen were apportioned to the Mohawks, two to the Onondagas, and the fifth to the Oneidas, to give them all a taste of French flesh, and to whet their appetites to desire more in revenge of the death of a score of savages on this occasion. This heroic defense diverted the Iroquois from Montreal, which was thus saved from destruction.[1] Two months later, fifty Iroquois from Cayuga, who had come to Montreal and claimed to be neutral in the war rekindled between the French and the Iroquois, were suspected to be spies, as their spokesmen had none of the marks customary to ambassadors. They were, therefore, seized in the hope thus to gain freedom from attack during the harvest and to obtain the liberation of the Frenchmen in captivity amongst the Mohawks, The French knew that the Mohawks had invited the Onondagas to join forces with them in the following autumn for the destruction of the colony of Three Rivers.[2]

The French realized that the devastation caused by the Iroquois was the great obstacle to the security of Canada and to the propagation of the Gospel among the infidel savages. The struggling native churches, that they had established with such heroic zeal and with such sacrifices, were continually made desolate, so that the neophytes were forced "to seek caves and the thickest and most remote forests to drag out a miserable

[1] Journal des PP. Jésuits. 1660. Jes. Rels. xlv. 157. Relation of 1659-60. Jes. Rels. xlv. 245-261.
[2] Relation. 1659-60. Jes. Rels. xlvi. 117-121.

existence there in want of all things." This misery was the work of a handful of Iroquois, who all together did not equal the thousandth part of those whose salvation they prevented. The Jesuits estimated the force of the Five Nations at this period at twenty-two hundred warriors, of which the Mohawks constituted five hundred "in two or three wretched villages," the Oneidas one hundred, the Onondagas and the Cayugas three hundred each, and the Senecas one thousand. Even this number was not composed solely of pure Iroquois, of whom scarcely more than twelve hundred could be found in the whole of the Five Nations.[1] The soul of the hostility of the Iroquois to the French was the Mohawk, who, before the advent of the Dutch, had been overcome in a ten years war by the Andastes and sometime before by the Algonquins so that the nation had been almost rendered extinct. They were then so humiliated that the mere name of Algonquin made the Mohawks tremble. However, when the Dutch took possession of New Netherland, they furnished those people with firearms, with which it was easy for them to conquer their conquerors, who were filled with terror at the mere sound of their guns. They became victorious everywhere and aspired to sovereign sway over all the Nations. There was, therefore, no hope of peace and the Jesuits felt that the destruction of these Indian was necessary to open the approaches to at least ten

[1] Mrs. Schuyler van Rensselaer says: "Yet even in the days of their greatest strength and power, during the first half of the seventeenth century, when they had procured firearms from the white men, they numbered not more than four thousand warriors, twenty thousand souls in all. Twice as many of their descendants, it has been computed, now survive in and near the State of New York." History of the City of New York. i. 58.

Nations of savages, who were asking for Fathers of the
Society to instruct them. The Jesuits, therefore,
appealed to the chivalrous spirit of the French. "Are
not these sights touching enough to rekindle in the
French that zeal and ardor which, of old, made such
noble conquests among the infidels, and rendered
France so glorious through the crusades."[1] The same
thought arose in the minds of Father Gabriel Drueilletes
and Father Claude Dablon, when, in their mission to the
North Sea, they found the tribes dispersed by the
Iroquois who had preceded them.   Would not the
destruction of a people who are overthrowing Christianity everywhere "be a holy war and blessed crusade,
well fitted to signalize the piety and consecrate the
courage of the French against this little Turk of New
France?"[2]   The frequent hostile incursions of the
Iroquois throughout the spring of 1661, bringing death
and captivity to numerous Frenchmen at Three Rivers
and Montreal, strengthened the Jesuits in their conviction of the necessity of decisive action to save the
country, before the Iroquois drained the last drop of
its blood.

However, in the month of July, when the fate of the
French colony appeared most hopeless, an embassy
with four French prisoners as pledges of their sincerity
was sent by the Onondagas and the Cayugas to negotiate a peace, in which the Senecas also wished to
participate.   They demanded as preliminary conditions
the liberation of the eight Cayuga prisoners, and the
sending of the Black Gown with them, as "the lives of

[1] Relation of 1659-60. xlv. 189-191; 205-207; xlvi. 67 seq.
[2] Relation of 1660-61. Jes. Rels. xlvi. 291.

twenty Frenchmen in captivity at Onondaga depended on this journey." The demand was reinforced by the production of a leaf torn out of a book with the signatures of the twenty Frenchmen to guarantee the good faith of the ambassadors. When the four Frenchmen, former captives at Onondaga, gave testimony of the kind treatment received by the French at the hands of those savages, the Governor and his councillors, after mature deliberation, accepted the proposals of the Indians. Father Le Moyne accompanied the ambassadors with the liberated Cayugas, after they had pledged their word to return at the end of forty days with the French captives and with some of their elders to deliberate on matters of public interest.[1]

Father Le Moyne was received with great honor in Onondaga, where he found the twenty French captives under the protection of Garacontié. He reminded the savages of the promise to restore the French, but they consented to liberate only nine of them, seven at Onondaga and two at Cayuga, while the other Frenchmen were to remain at Onondaga with Father Le Moyne until next spring, when they also would obtain their liberty.[2] Garacontié headed the embassy, which left Onondaga towards the middle of September with the nine Frenchmen. Some of the Indians wished to abandon the enterprise, when they met an Onondaga chieftain, clothed in the cassock of Father Le Maistre, whom he had murdered shortly before, but Garacontié was able to overcome their fear of retaliation on their own per-

---

[1] Relation 1660-1661. Jes. Rels. xlvi. 223-241.
[2] Letter of Le Moyne. August 25, and September 11, 1661, to Lalemant. Jes. Rels. xlvii. 69-83.

son, as the French left with Father Le Moyne were
sufficient surety for their own safety. The embassy
reached Montreal on October 5. In the Council,
Garacontié broke the bonds of the nine French captives
and promised the return of Father Le Moyne with the
other prisoners in the following spring, who would
then ennoble the conclusion of a firm peace between the
French and the Onondagas, Cayugas and Senecas.[1]

Meanwhile, the towns of the three tribes were open to
the missionaries and also to the other Frenchmen, who
were invited to settle in large numbers among them.
The new Governor, M. d'Avougour, was now fully
determined to destroy the two small tribes of Mohawks and Oneidas, still hostile to the French, if
the King sent the soldiers needed for such an
expedition.[2] About the same time, Father Paul
Raguenau suggested to the Prince de Condé to
send a French Regiment, which might effectively
attack these Iroquois through New Holland, the
shortest and most convenient road to their country.[3]
There is little probability that this design would have
obtained the consent of the Dutch, as it would have cost
them the friendship of the Mohawks, which they always
had been most careful to maintain. If we are to
believe a Frenchman held captive by the Mohawks at
this time, "the Dutch are no longer willing to secure our
freedom, as it costs them too dearly; on the contrary,
they tell the Iroquois to cut off our arms and legs, and

---

[1] Relation. 1660-1661. Jes. Rels. xlvii. 93-103.
[2] Letter. October 20, 1661. Father Chaumonot to Father
Rippault of Dijon. Jes. Rels. xlvi. 157.
[3] Letter from Quebec. October 12, 1661. Jes. Rels. xlvi. 147-
149.

kill us where they find us, without burdening themselves with us."[1]

During the winter, Father Le Moyne consoled the
French in their captivity, strengthened the Huron
Christians in their faith and laid the foundations to the
conversion of the Iroquois. His life was not without
danger from the hands of savages under the domination
of the demon of dreams and of the demon of drink.
One, who in a dream had seen himself dressed in a cassock, broke into the chapel, determined to strip the
missionary of this garment. Another in a drunken fit
attempted to pounce on the crucifix over the altar.[2]
His hatchet was raised to strike the Jesuit, who was
resolved to give his life sooner than surrender the image
of the Crucified Saviour, but he was rescued by the
Elders of the village. Some of the Indians "threw the
blame on the Dutch, who (they say) furnish them a
certain drink that makes madmen of the wisest, and
deprives him of his reason before he knows it." For
the Indians brought brandy "from New Holland in such
quantities as to make a veritable Pot-House of Onondaga." To rid him of these afflictions for a time, the
less cruel Cayugas invited Le Moyne to visit their
villages. Here there was established a Huron village
entirely Christian. A month later Father Le Moyne returned to Onondaga, where Garacontié had arrived from

[1] Letter to a friend at Three Rivers. The captive was soon
delivered through the intervention of Garacontié. Jes. Rels. xlvii.
93.
[2] This crucifix, about two feet in height, had been carried off the
year previous by the Mohawks from Argentenay on the Island of
Orleans. Garacontié saw it at Agnié, and obtained it by giving
them a rich present and holding an eloquent eulogy on the Crucifix.
Cf. Relation. 1661-1662. Jes. Rels. xlvii. 215.

his embassy to Montreal.[1]   Under his protection, the missionary continued his apostolic work, while the small pox was raging in the village.   He was able to say mass daily in the rude chapel.   When the wine began to fail, he wrote to the Dutch that he might need some for his health, as he knew that they would not give him any for the sacrifice of the mass.   The Dutch sent him a small bottle, well sealed, by a savage, who was told that he must not drink of this medicine needed by the Father, unless he wished to contract a serious illness.   On his arrival at Onondaga, the Indian asked to taste a little of that medicine to see whether it was as bad as the Dutch had said.   Le Moyne cut up some Barbadoes nuts in a little of this wine, and gave it to the savage. The medicine was "of such purgative effect as to deprive him of all desire to ask for a second dose."[2]

In the spring, the liberation of the French at Onondaga was somewhat delayed.   One of their number, named Liberté, had been treacherously murdered by his Indian masters, because he refused to live in concubinage with an Indian woman, whom they wished to give to him.[3]   However, in the summer the savages fulfilled their pledged word.   "On the last day of August, 1662, Father Le Moyne made his appearance in a canoe below the falls of St. Louis, having around him all those happy rescued ones and a score of Onnontagheronnons who from being his enemies had become their boatmen. . .   They landed amid the cheers and embraces of all the French of Montreal and followed their Pastor

[1] Relation. 1661-1662. Jes. Rels. xlvii. 183-189.
[2] Ibid. 197-199.
[3] Ibid. 201-203.

to render thanks to God in the church."[1]   The war between the Iroquois and the Andastes prevented the renewal of the French missions in that country during the two following years, while the domination of the Dutch in New Netherland still continued.

[1] Relation. 1661-1662. Jes. Rels. xlvii. 191-193.

APPENDIX A

CHRONICLE OF NEW NETHERLAND

1609. Henry Hudson sails along the coast of North America from New Foundland to Chesapeake Bay and explores the Hudson River.
Truce of twelve years signed between Spain and the United Netherlands.

1610. Beginning of occasional fur trading by the Dutch.

1614. New Netherland Co. chartered with a monopoly of the trade for three years.

1620. Petition of the Puritans in Holland for permission to emigrate to New Netherland is refused. Captain Thomas Dermer, an English navigator, while visiting Manhattan Island, asserts English claim to this territory.

1621. The truce with Spain terminates.
Dutch West India Company chartered with the monopoly of the trade to America, etc., for twenty-four years. Colonization is optional to the Company, founded mainly to assist in the war against Spain.

1624. First colony—thirty families—is sent with Cornelis Jacobson May, as Director. Fort Orange on the Hudson, and Fort Nassau on the Delaware erected. A small colony sent to the Connecticut River, where Fort Good Hope is planned. Settlement of Long Island begun.

1625. William Verhulst Director. New settlers arrive with live stock, etc.

1626. Peter Minuit, Director General, buys Manhattan Island, where the erection of Fort Amsterdam and a place of worship is begun.

1627. On the opening of trade between New Netherland and New Plymouth, Bradford warns Minuit to clear the Dutch title to New Netherland, which is within English territory.

1628. Population at Manhattan two hundred and seventy souls. Arrival of first clergyman, Jonas Michaelius.

1629. Charter of Freedoms and Exemptions: grants in the form patroonships and colonies outside of Manhattan Island. First explicit legal recognition of the Dutch Reformed Church, for which the patroons and colonists are bound to provide.

1630. Foundation of patroonships: on the Delaware, Swanendael; on the Hudson at its mouth, Pavonia, and at Fort Orange Rensselaerswyck. The last patroonship was the only permanent foundation of this kind in New Netherland.

1632. Minuit recalled.
Lords Say and Seal, etc., receive from the Earl of Warwick the grant of Connecticut, but neglect colonization till several years later.

1633. Wouter Van Twiller, Director General. Everardus Bogardus, the second Dutch minister. Adam Rolandsen, the first schoolmaster. The "William of London" goes up the Hudson to trade, on the plea that this is English territory. Fort Good Hope on the Connecticut completed. A wooden church erected at Manhattan. Winthrop protests against Dutch occupation of Connecticut, which is claimed to be within the possessions of the English King. A little above Fort Good Hope, Plymouth erects a stockade (Windsor.)

1634. Trouble between the Dutch and the Raritans about New Amsterdam.
Pequods surrender to Massachusetts their rights to the Connecticut River country.

1635. A "Part of New England" and Long Island granted by the Plymouth Council to Lord Stirling. English encroachments un the Connecticut. Eight hundred English in Connecticut Valley. English settlements at Wethersfield and Windsor, and the following year at Springfield.

1638. William Kieft, Director General.
Swedes settle on the Delaware and build Fort Christina. New Sweden founded in spite of the protests of Kieft by the former Director Minuit.

1639. English settlements along Long Island Sound: New Haven, Stratford, Norwalk, Greenwich, encroachments on Dutch territory. Organization of Connecticut, and New Haven commonwealths.

1640. Farret visits Manhattan and in the name of Lord Stirling lays claim to all Long Island. He is arrested, but then dismissed. English attempt to settle there, but are expelled.
New Charter of Freedoms and Exemptions extended to all in friendly relations with the United Provinces, but pro-

1640. hibits the public exercise of any other religion than the Reformed.
Trouble with the Raritan Indians.

1641. The Twelve Select Men representing the commonalty oppose hostilities with the Indians.
Conditions, under which a party of Englishmen with their preacher may come and settle in New Netherland, presented. These modelled on the charter of 1640.

1642. The Twelve Select Men, asembled by Kieft agree to hostilities with the Indians, but demand civic reforms, and are dismissed in consequence with the prohibition to hold any further assembly.
English settle under Dutch jurisdiction: at Mespath Long Island, at Throg's Neck, Westchester, and at Pelham Neck. Friction between English and Dutch continues in Connecticut Valley. English intruded on Delaware are expelled.
Stone church in New Amsterdam begun. John Megapolensis, first minister of Rensselaerswyck. Father Jogues, Jesuit missionary, captured by the Mohawks, his companion Renè Goupil killed.

1643. General rising of Algonquins provoked by the cruel massacre of the Indians by the Dutch. A disastrous Indian war ensues. The "Eight Men" elected by commonalty authorize hostilities. English settlements at Throg's Neck and Mespath destroyed. Lady Moody with others settles at Gravesend.
The "Eight Men" send a "Remonstrance" to Amsterdam and to the Hague anent the ruinous state of affairs in New Netherland with a petition for immediate relief.

Sir Edmund Plowden, "Earl Palatine of New Albion",
claims territory, comprising the present State of New Jersey, under a grant from the King of England.
Father Jogues escapes from the Mohawks.

1644. Hempstead, L. I. settled by Englishmen.
Indian war: one hundred and twenty Indians killed near Hempstead, seven hundred killed near Stamford. Westchester and Long Island Indians sue for peace. River Indians still hostile.
The West India Company bankrupt. First Excise laws enacted. The commonalty discontented. Memorial of the "Eight Men" to the West India Company.
Two exploring expeditions sent to the Delaware River from Boston meet with opposition of the Dutch and the Swedes.
Fort erected on Beeren Island, Rensselaerswyck, attempts to levy toll on all vessels passing it with conflicting jurisdictions as a result.
Father Bressani, S. J. ransomed by the Dutch from the Mohawks and sent to Europe.

1645. General peace with the Indians.
English settlers return to Mespath and reestablish colony in its vicinity under the name of Newtown. Flushing founded by Massachusetts exiles. Gravesend patent issued.
Curaçoa, Aruba and neighboring West India Islands placed under the jurisdiction of the Director of New Netherland.
Quarrel between Director Kieft and Rev. Bogardus.

1646. New Haven encroaches on Dutch territory in the North and the Swedes do the same in the South. Kieft protests against the meeting of the New England commissioners at New Haven, which he claims to be within the limits of New Netherland. Amsterdam Chamber instructs Kieft to oppose all further English encroachments with all means at his disposal short of war. The Swedes pull down the arms of Holland erected on the site of Philadelphia, purchased by the Dutch from the Indians.
Colendonck founded near Spyt den Duyvel. Patent issued for Katskill. Breuckelen incorporated.
Father Jogues, S. J. put to death by the Mohawks.

1647 Peter Stuyvesant, Director. Population of New Netherland estimated at 2000.
Cornelis Melyn and Jochem Pietersen Kuyter, two of the "Eight Men," prosecuted for their criticism of the previous administration, fined and banished.
The board of "Nine Men" appointed to represent the commonalty, and to furnish revenue in support of the colonial government.
Conflicts with the English. Lady Stirling's agent represents himself at Flushing and Hempstead as her governor of Long Island. He is arrested and sent to Holland, but escapes in England. Stuyvesant declares Dutch claim to all territory between the Delaware and the Connecticut and then he extends claim to territory between Cape Henlopen and Cap Cod. A Dutch ship seized at New Haven and brought to Manhattan.

1648. Conflicts with the Swedes on the Delaware. Swedes crowd the Dutch. Dutch trade ruined. New England complains of Dutch trading regulations. Stuyvesant anxious for a settlement of differences and for the establishment of an alliance. Unsettled condition of England prevents a settlement in Europe. Directors of West India Company recommend Stuyvesant "to endeavor to live in the best possible terms," as the English are too strong for the Dutch.
General discontent results in the Dutch Province from the loss of trade. The "Nine Men" propose a mission to Holland to make known the state of the province.

1649. The journal of the "Nine Men", kept by Van der Donck for

1649. the preparation of the Remonstrance to be sent to Holland, seized by Stuyvesant. Van der Donck tried for libel is expelled from the board of "Nine Men." Proceedings against Melyn and Kuyter disapproved. Melyn returns to New Netherland with a safe-conduct and a writ citing the Director to appear at the Hague. Delegates sent to present the Remonstrance of New Netherland to the States General for a redress of abuses. Stuyvesant sends Van Tienhoven, his secretary, to appear for him at The Hague. The magistrates at Gravesend give him a declaration of their confidence in Stuyvesant's "wisdom and justice in the administration of the common weal."

1650. Reforms for New Netherland, reported by a committee of the States General, are opposed by the West India Company. The "Nine Men," continue to complain.

Treaty concluded between English and Dutch at Hartford determines boundary between New Netherland and New England. Dutch complain that Stuyvesant ceded too much land. Massachusetts claims that this settlement does not prejudice its right to territory on the Hudson River.

1651. Stuyvesant stops English from New Haven at Manhattan, as they expressed the intention to settle on the Delaware. They are sent back to New Haven. New England manifests hostile spirit towards New Netherland.

Stuyvesant strengthens Dutch position on the Delaware by the erection of Fort Casimir in spite of the protests of the Swedish governor.

Arbitrary government continues in New Netherland.

1652. Trouble between Stuyvesant and Rensselaerswyck ends in the annexation of Beverwyck by the former.

Settlements begun at Esopus, Newtown, Flatbush and New Utrecht. Population of New Amsterdam estimated at about eight hundred souls. Municipal government given to this city. Naval war between Dutch and English. Stuyvesant advised to engage Indians in the event of hostilities on the part of New England. These advices captured by the English. Stuyvesant directed to be on his guard, but not to give any provocation.

1653. Organization of a Municipal Government for New Amsterdam. Appointment of Burgomasters and Schepens.

Stuyvesant proposes the continuance of peaceful relations between the Dutch and the English in New England and Virginia in spite of the Dutch-English war. New Amsterdam put into the state of defense by a repair of the fort and the erection of a palisade about the town.

The Second Amboyna Tragedy; or a Faithful Account of a Bloody, Treacherous and Cruel Plot of the Dutch in America to murder the English colonists, published in

1653. London. Stuyvesant suggests that New England agents visit New Netherland to examine the evidence of such a plot, which is done.

Connecticut and New Haven urge war with New Netherland, but Massachusetts persistently refuses to engage in such war. Captain Underhill raises the parliament flag on Long Island, and is banished. He seizes Fort Good Hope "with permission from the General Court of Hartford."

Convention of delegates from various towns of the Province assemble at New Amsterdam, and vote a Remonstrance on the State of New Netherland, demanding a representative government, etc. This petition is sent to Holland. Stuyvesant dissolves the convention.

1654. Lutherans at New Amsterdam are denied permission to call a minister of their own persuasion and to worship publicly by themselves.

An English expedition against New Netherland sails from England. Troops raised in New England, but the conclusion of peace prevents the invasion of New Netherland.

The Swedes, under their new governor Rising, capture the Dutch fort Casimir, and call it Fort Trinity. A Swedish ship seized at Manhattan. English settle in Westchester in spite of Stuyvesant's prohibition to do so. Oyster Bay applies to New Haven to be under its jurisdiction. No attention is paid to Stuyvesant's complaints.

Dutch ambassadors try to settle boundary question in England. Cromwell has received no information from New England and refuses to decide the question on the allegations of only one party.

1655. Some English raise the flag of England at Gravesend, L. I., and arrests follow. English settlers in West Chester refuse to recognize Dutch jurisdiction before the settlement of the boundary by England.

Swedes on the Delaware reduced on the order of the West India Company. Lutheran Swedes are allowed the ministry of one Lutheran clergyman. The vice-director instructed by Stuyvesant to "maintain and protect the Reformed Religion." Indians invade New Amsterdam; Hoboken, Pavonia and Staten Island laid waste. General consternation.

French settle at Onondaga. Mission begun by Fathers Chaumonot and Dablon. Jesuit chapel erected.

1656. Stuyvesant orders the formation of compact villages in imitation of "our New England neighbors" for better defense against the Indians.

"Conventicles," or places of worship not in harmony with the established Dutch church are prohibited under heavy fines. Religious persecution ensues.

The English of Westchester forced to acknowledge Dutch

1656. jurisdiction. Hartford treaty ratified by the States
General. Jamaica founded on Long Island.
New Amsterdam surveyed; one hundred and twenty houses,
one thousand souls.
West India Company cedes some territory on the Delaware
to the City of Amsterdam.

1657. The Great and Small Burgher-right established in New
Amsterdam. The City of Amsterdam establishes its
colony of New Amstel on the Delaware.
Cromwell orders the English on Long Island not to betray
the rights of their nation "by subjecting themselves and
lands to a foreign state."
Increased religious intolerance: Lutheran minister banished, Quakers persecuted.

1658 The Flushing protest in favor of religious liberty meets with
measures of repression. Continuation of Quaker persecution. Fines imposed for the refusal to contribute to
the support of the Dutch clergy. Flushing charter
altered. New Harlem and Communipa founded. Bergen
purchased.
French abandon settlement at Onondaga. Trade opened
by sea with Canada at the request of the Dutch.
Trouble with Esopus Indians. Dutch village laid out there.

1659. Massachusetts attempts to encroach on the Hudson River.
New Netherland permitted to trade with France, Spain,
Italy and the Caribbean Islands.
War with the Esopus Indians.
Maryland claims the Delaware. Dutch send embassy to
that Province and demand a commission to define the
boundary between New Netherland and Maryland or a
settlement of the question in Europe.

1660. Controversy on New England and New Netherland claims
continues.
Peace concluded with the Esopus Indians.
Negotiations between Stuyvesant and Virginia. Governor
Berkely does not recognize Dutch title to the Delaware.
Lord Baltimore renews his claim to this territory.

1661. On the Restoration in England, the West India Company,
with the approbation of the States General, gives "to all
Christian people of tender conscience, in England or
elsewhere oppressed, full liberty to erect a colony" in New
Netherland.
Persecution of the Quakers continued.
Some rigid Puritans of New Haven negotiate for settlement
under Dutch jurisdiction at Achter Kol.
Wiltwyck, at Esopus, incorporated. Schenectady purchased. Bushwyck, New Utrecht and Bergen incorporated.

1662   Connecticut receives a royal charter to all territory south
of Massachusetts to the ocean and West to the Pacific
ocean with "the islands thereunto adjoining." Westchester and English towns on Long Island annexed.
City of Amsterdam grants land on the Delaware to a colony
of Mennonites.
New Proclamation against the public exercise of any religion
but that of the Dutch Reformed   Continued persecution
of the Quakers. John Bowne and others banished.

1663.   The whole of the Delaware River surrendered to the City of
Amsterdam.
The authorities in Holland reprove Stuyvesant's severity
in his treatment of dissenters. They would like some
connivance, "at least the consciences of men ought to
remain free and unshackled." The Directors insist on
liberty of conscience, but not on liberty of worship, public
or private.
New Haven Puritans continue to negotiate for a settlement
under Dutch jurisdiction.
Massacre of the Dutch at the Esopus. Vigorous war against
these Indians.
Connecticut foments a revolt of the English on Long Island.
Stuyvesant tries to refer "the matters unsettled to both
superiors." Connecticut knows no New Netherland
without "a patent for it from his majesty, but agrees not
to exercise any jurisdiction "over the English plantations
on the westerly end of Long Island," provided the Dutch
agree to the same.
Convention of Delegates from the Dutch towns in New
Amsterdam. Remonstrance, with an exposition of the
dangers from the English, adopted and dispatched to
Amsterdam.
Revolution on Long Island. Names of the English villages
changed.

1664.   New Netherland granted to the Duke of York. The English
towns of Long Island elect Captain John Scott "to act as
their president until his Royal Highness the Duke of
York or his majesty should establish a government
among them." Stuyvesant agrees to have the English
towns under the King of England for twelve months until
the settlement of the question by his majesty and the
States General, and Scott agrees to have the Dutch towns
remain for the same period under the States General.
General Provincial Assembly of the Dutch at New Amsterdam refuses to vote supplies in defense of the Province
against the Indians and the English.
Peace with the Esopus Indians.
English towns received under the government of Connecticut, which claims Long Island for one of those Islands
expressed in the charter. Scott imprisoned by Connecticut. Winthrop removes Scott's officers and installs

1664.   others. Stuyvesant urges Dutch title and Hartford
          treaty to no effect. New Netherland reduced by the
          English and named New York in honor of its proprietor.
          Population of New Netherland: Province, 10,000; New
          Amsterdam, 1600.

          Population of New England; 50,000.
          Population of Virginia; 35,000.
          Population of Maryland; 15,000.

APPENDIX B

A SELECT BIBLIOGRAPHY

(A) WORKS OF BIBLIOGRAPHY

(i) *Guides to Printed Materials*

GENERAL

Adams, C. K., Manual of Historical Literature, 2d ed. New York, 1889.
Channing, E. and Hart, A. B., Guide to the Study of American History, Boston, 1896.
Larned, J. N., ed., The Literature of American History, Boston, 1902. Supplements for 1901, 1902, 1903, 1904.
Sabin, Joseph, ed. Dictionary of books relating to America, 1868. 19 vols to date.
Richardson, Morse, Anson. Writings on American History 1902. 1904.
McLaughlin, Slade, Lewis. Writings on American History 1903. 1905.
Griffin, Grace Gardner. Writings on American History 1906, 1908.

PERIODICAL

Griffin, A. P. C., Bibliography of American Historical Societies. (The United States and Dominion of Canada). 2d ed., 1907. Annual Report of American Historical Association, vol. ii. 1907.

PROVINCIAL

Asher, G. M., Bibliographical and Historical Essay on the Dutch Books and Pamphlets relating to New Netherland, Amsterdam, 1854-1867.
Fernow, B., Critical Essay on the Sources of Information (for the History of New Netherland or the Dutch in America), in Narrative and Critical History of America, ed. Justin Winsor. vol. iv. 409-438
Flagg, C. A., and Jennings, J. T., Bibliography of New York

Colonial History. New York State Library Bulletin, 56.
Bibliography 24, 1901.
Keen, G. B., Critical Essay on the Sources of Information
(for the History of New Sweden or the Swedes on the Dela-
ware), in Narrative and Critical History of America, ed.
Justin Winsor, vol. iv. 468-502, 1884.
Onderdonck, H., Jr., Bibliography of Long Island, in Furman,
Antiquities of Long Island, ed. by F. Moore, New York, 1875.

New York Public Library Bulletin:
Check List of American County and State Histories in the
New York Public Library, vol. v, 11.
Works Relating to the State of New York in the New York
Public Library, vol. iv. 5-6.
Check List of the Works Relating to the History of Brook-
lyn and other places on Long Island now included in the
City of New York, in the New York Public Library, vol.
vi 3.
List of Works Relating to New York City History in the
New York Public Library, vol. v. 3.

RELIGIOUS

Bowerman. A Selected Bibliography of the Religious Denomi-
nations of the United States, New York, 1896.
Hurst, J F., Literature of Theology (with a bibliography of
American Church History), New York, 1896.
Jackson, S. M. Bibliography of American Church History,
1820-1893, in vol xii. of American Church History Series,
New York, 1908.
New York Public Library Bulletin. List on the Churches and
the Ecclesiastical History of New York in the New York Pub-
lic Library, vol. v. 5.

(ii) Guides to Manuscript Materials

Andrews, C. M. Davenport, Frances. Guide to Manuscript
Materials for the History of the United States to 1783 in the
British Museum, in Minor London Archives and in the librar-
ies of Oxford and Cambridge, Washington, 1908.
Annotated List of the Principal Manuscripts in the New York
State Library. State Library Bulletin. History 3, Albany,
1899.
Brodhead, J. Romeyn. Calendar to the Holland Documents
in the Office of the Secretary of State at Albany, Transcribed
from the originals in the Royal Archives at The Hague and
the Archives of the City of Amsterdam in New York Papers.
Final Report to the Governor, February 12, 1845. Senate
Document 47, Albany, 1845.
Catalogue of Historical Papers and Parchments received from
the Office of the Secretary of State and deposited in the New
York State Library, Albany, 1849.
Check List of the Municipal and other Documents Relating to

New York City in the New York Public Library, in NewYork Public Library Bulletin, vol. v. 1.
Manuscripts Relating to the History of New Netherland and New York in the New York Public Library. New York Public Library Bulletin, vol. v. 7.
O'Callaghan, E B. Calendar of New York Historical Manuscripts, vol. i. (Dutch), 1630-1664, Albany, 1865.
O'Callaghan, E. B. Index to vols. i, ii, iii, of Translations of Dutch Manuscripts in the Office of the Secretary of State of New York, Albany, 1870.
Osgood, H. L. Report on the Public Archives of New York. American Historical Association Report, 1900, vol ii, pp. 67-250, Washington, 1901.
Van Tyne - Leland. Guide to the Archives at Washington, 2d ed. Washington, 1907.

(B) MANUSCRIPT DOCUMENTS

NEW YORK STATE LIBRARY

Transcripts of Documents in the Royal Archives at The Hague and the Archives of the City of Amsterdam, 1603-1678, Sixteen Volumes.
(Procured 1841 by John Romeyn Brohhead; translated and edited by E. B. O'Callaghan, as Documents Relating to the Colonial History of the State of New York, vols. i, ii. Holland Documents, Albany, 1856-58.)

New York Colonial Manuscripts (Dutch), 1638-1664. (Transactions of the Colonial Government).

Vols. i-iii. Register of Provincial Secretary, 1638-1660.
iv-x. Council minutes, 1638-1665.
xi-xv. Correspondence of Director General. 1646-1664.
xvi. Placards, writs and Fort Orange Records, 1647-1663.
xvii. Curaçoa Papers, 1640-1665.
xviii-xxi. Delaware Papers, 1646-1682.

(A defective translation of most of these records by Francis Adriaen Van der Kemp in Twenty-four Manuscript Volumes, known as "Albany Records." A new translation of Vols. i-iii, by E. B. O'Callaghan in one Manuscript Volume, to which the author published an "Index to Vols. i-ii-iii of Translations of Dutch Manuscripts in the Office of the Secretary of State, Albany, 1870.
Translations from vol. iv. in a Second Manuscript Volume by E B. O'Callaghan with a Manuscript Index.
Translation of pp. 1-14 of vol. v. and of p. 33 of vol. xvi. by E B. O'Callaghan in loose sheets.
Many documents from this series printed in vols. xii-xiv. of Documents Relating to the Colonial History of New York, edited by B. Fernow, Albany, 1877-1883.)

Dutch Patents.
 Book GG. 1636-1649.
 Book HH. 1654-1664.

(Manuscript Index: "Index; Account of Dutch Records;
Alphabetical Index of the Two Dutch Books of Provincial
Patents GG and HH."
List of Patents in GG and HH, in O'Callaghan's Cal. Hist.
MSS. vol. i, pp. 36 4-387.
Translations of Book GG, vol. xxvi. 1642-1649, 514 pp. F.
by D. Westbrook, July 23, 1841—"on whole satisfactory
and reliable."
Contents: Patents of July 12, 1630—September 20, 1651, in
GG. Deed of Maryn Andriesen to Jan Jansen Damen,
September 20, 1642 (N. Y. Col. MSS. ii, 53). Commissions
to Martin Crieger and Cornelis van Ruyven, September
22, 23, 1659 (N. Y. Col. MSS. xvii. 68).
Translations of Dutch patents and transports, 1652-1674, 86
pp. F. by James Van Ingen.—"carefully prepared."
Contents: Part 1, of Book HH. Patents of September 5,
1652—October 15, 1653. Translations of Dutch Patents,
1654-1655, 171, pp. F. by James Van Ingen—"Correct and
satisfactory."
Contents: Part 2 of HH. Patents of February 26, 1655—
April 5, 1664. Translation of "Index" of Dutch Patents,
1630-1661. 49 pp. F. Index of Names to the Translations—
"not implicity to be relied upon."

ALBANY COUNTY CLERK'S OFFICE

Court minutes of Fort Orange:
 Vol. i. 1652-1656, 321 pp. F.
 Contents: Minutes of April 15, 1652—December 12, 1656,
MS. Cal. by B. Fernow (Fort Orange Recs of October 4,
1656—December 11, 1657 are in N. Y. Col. MSS. vol. xvi.
Part 2, pp. 1. 124.
 Vol. ii. 1658-1660; Mortgage No. 1, 1652-1660, 447 pp F.
 Contents: Title on front page: "Fort Orange Proceedings,
deeds, Indian treaties, bills of sale, etc., bonds, etc., powers
of attorney, January, 1652—November, 1660." 211 pp. Min-
utes of the Court of Fort Orange, January 8, 1658—Decem-
ber 2, 1659, calendared by O'Callaghan, Cal. Hist. MSS. vol.
i. (Dutch), pp. 317-322.
Mortgages, etc., calendared in MS. Cal. in County Clerk's
Office.
(Fort Orange Recs. of January 13, December 30, 1660 in
N. Y. Col. MSS. vol. xvi. part 3, pp. 133-232.)

Notarial Papers of Beverwyck.
 Vol. i. 616 pp. F. 1660-1676.
 Contents: Contracts, leases, inventories, bonds, indentures of
apprenticeship, powers of attorney, etc., acknowledged
before Dirck Van Schelluyne and Adriaen Van Ylpendam,

notaries public, August 17, 1660—January 6, 1676-1677. Calendared by B. Fernow.

Deed-book, No. 1, A, 1656-1678, 210 pp. F.
Contents: Deeds of October 16, 1656—June 20, 1678. Cal. by B. Fernow

Deed-book, No. 2, B, 1654-1680, 869 pp. F.
Contents: Deeds of August 19, 1654—July ,1679. Cal. by B. Fernow

(Both Deed-books translated and edited by Jonathan Pearson as "Early Records of the City and County of Albany and Colony of Rensselaerswyck, 1656-1657." Albany, 1869; reprinted with a "Key to the Names of Persons," "Contributions for the genealogies of the first settlers of Albany," and "Diagram of the home lots of the village of Beverwyck," in Munsell's Collections on the History of Albany, vol. iii. pp. 1-224, iv. pp. 84-510.)

ULSTER COUNTY CLERK'S OFFICE (KINGSTON)

Court Records of Wiltwyck, 1661-1664, pp. F. vol. i.
Contents: Copy of bond by inhabitants of Wiltwyck to demolish separate dwellings and surround the village with a stockade, May 31, 1658.
Court minutes of July 12, 1661—May, 1664.
(Translation in MS. vol. i. 645 pp. by Mr. D.Versteeg.—"not faultless, but creditable and in general reliable."
Contents: Bond of May 31, 1658 and records of July 12, 1661—February 16, 1672-3.

NEW YORK CITY CLERK'S OFFICE, CITY HALL

Minutes of the Burgomasters and Schepens of New Amsterdam 1653-1674, 6 MS. Volumes F.
(Dutch till 1665 and during Dutch reoccupation, 1673-4.
Vol. i. has the ordinances of the Director General and Council of New Netherland in the first 73 pages. These were edited by O'Callaghan in 1868 as "Laws and Ordinances of New Netherland, and by B. Fernow in his "Records of New Amsterdam." vol. i.
Translation of vol. i., ordinances and minutes to September, 1654, by Mr. Westbrook.—"poor."
Translation of remaining 5 volumes by O'Callaghan in 1848.
Translation printed in 1897 as "Records of New Amsterdam." 7 Vols. ed. B. Fernow: New translation of MS. vol. i., and revision of 5 MS. vols. translated by O'Callaghan.)

Notarial Records:

Vol.	i.	Burgomasters and Schepens, 1653-1675. (This volume with the Court Records.)
	ii.	Burgomasters and Schepens, 1654-1660.
	iii.	Burgomasters and Schepens, 1658-1660.
	iv.	Burgomasters and Schepens, 1661-1663.
	v.	Burgomasters and Schepens, 1663-1665.

vi. Burgomasters and Schepens, 1662-1664.
viii. Burgomasters and Schepens, 1657-1661.
Two Additional Volumes:
   Vol. i. Original records of Burgomasters and Orphanmasters, Surrogates.
   ii. Record of deeds, bonds etc., of New Orange, 1671-74.

   (Translations by O'Callaghan in MS.)
Vol. 1. Mortgages of lots and pieces of land in the City of New Amsterdam, 1654-1660. vol. ii. of original.
   2. Deeds and conveyances of real estate in City of New Amsterdam, 1659-1665, 380 pp. Contents of iii. and parts of v. and vi. of original.
   3. Deeds and conveyances of real estate in City of New Amsterdam, 1654-1638, 311 pp. Contents of iii. and parts of v. and vi. of original.
   4. Register of Salomon Lachair, notary public of New Amsterdam, 1662-1664, 432 pp. vols. iv. and viii. and part of Orphan's Court Records of original.
   5. Register of Waleyn van der Veen, notary public of New Amsterdam, 1662-1664, 115 pp. vol. vi., in part, of original.
   6. Deeds and Mortgages of lots and tracts of land in the City of New York and New Orange, 1664-1675, 233 pp. vol. ii. of Additional Volumes and a part of vol. v. of original.
   7. Powers of attorney, acknowledgments, indentures of apprenticeship, inventories, deeds, etc., 1651-1656. 185 pp.: vol. i. of original, in part.
   8. Minutes of the Orphans' Court of New Amsterdam, 1656-1668, 399 pp. vol. i. of Additional Volumes. Printed by B. Fernow, "Minutes of Orphan Masters' Court of New Amsterdam, 1656-1663; Minutes of the Executive Boards of the Burgomasters of New Amsterdam; and Records of Waleyn Van der Veen, Notary Public, 1662-1664, New York, 1907.

HALL OF RECORDS, KINGS COUNTY, BROOKLYN

Gravesend Records (wholly in English).
   Vol. i. Town Records, 1646-1653.
   i. Town Records, 1653-1669.
   i. Town Records, 1656-1844.
   i. Town Records, 1662-1699.
   i. Town Records, 1645-1701.
      (There is hardly a remark of a religious nature in these books except in the town charter).

New Utrecht Record (wholly Dutch).
   Vol. i. Town Records 1657.
      The Dutch title: Het Bouk Van Het Durp Utrecht. A° 1657. The book is prefaced by two religious poems of Nicasius de Sille: "Het Aerdt-Rijck spreeckt tot sijne opquekers," and

"Ghesang op de wijse van den 116 Psalm." The book also contains a digest of the placards promulgated in the Province. Regulation of the liquor traffic, conventicles, marriage regulations, etc., under title: "Corte aenwijsinghe van enighe placaten over beganene uisusen, etc."
Vol. ii. 1661-1686 (Dutch). Deeds and Miscellaneous instruments.

Court Records of Flatbush (Dutch).
Court minutes, etc., Liber B. 1659-1664.

HALL OF RECORDS, NEW YORK CITY

Newtown Records   (English).
Court Records, 1659-1690.
(Octavo volume bound with a folio volume, beginning in 1695, and giving earlier documents, but all after 1663. The pages of this folio volume are entitled by subjects of a theological treatise in Latin, alphabetically arranged. It was apparently planned as a Dictionary of Moral Theology. The book was then inverted and used for a summary of some parts of the Old Testament: Books of Samuel, Kings, Chronicles, all in English. The Court Records then begin.)

Jamaica Town Records.
1 Vol. 1660-1772. 552 pp.
Contents: deeds, bills of sale, miscellaneous contracts, mostly indentures, etc., with occasional records of town meetings.

HEMPSTEAD, L. I.

Book A. Town Records, 1657-1662.
Book B. Town Records, 1662-1680.
(Book A is prefaced by "An Alphabet to the most Notarial things in this Book, relating to the Publick." The books are printed in the "Records of the Towns of North and South Hempstead." 8 vols. Jamaica, 1896.

LIBRARY OF CONGRESS, WASHINGTON

Dutch West India Company: Extracts of resolutions, minutes of proceedings, etc., 1659-1675, 80 pp. in Dutch.
Miscellaneous papers relating to the Company, Portugal and Brazil, etc. 1649-1655 (?).

LIBRARY OF HISTORICAL SOCIETY OF PENNSYLVANIA, PHILADELPHIA

Dutch West India Company Manuscripts.
Records, 1000 pp. F. 1635-1663.
Minutes: 1655-1663 in a fair state of preservation.

Transcripts of Manuscripts from Swedish Archives: Stockholm, Skokloster, Palmskiöld Collections of Library of University of Upsala, and Lund.
Contents: papers of Usselinx, correspondence of Oxenstierna with Spring, Blommaert, Minuit, papers on Swedish, West

India Company, on expeditions to Delaware; commissions and instructions for officers of the colony; letters and reports of governors; other colonial records, diplomatic intercourse with foreign nations.
(The Correspondence between Oxenstierna and Blommaert has been edited in the original by G. W. Kernkamp, Brieven van Samuel Blommaert aan den Zweedsche Rijkskanselier Axel Oxenstierna, 1635-1641. in Bijdragen en Medeelingen van het Historisch Genootschap (Utecht). 29 dell, Amsterdam, 1908.

LIBRARY OF THE NEW YORK HISTORICAL SOCIETY

New Netherland Papers.   Dutch Manuscripts.

LENOX LIBRARY, NEW YORK

New Netherland Papers: 1636-1660.
Contents: Letters of governors, petitions, extracts from letters and other papers in the colony, accounts kept with the home government, list of houses and various other colonial documents, about thirty items, mostly contemporary or early copies, with some modern transcripts. Unbound. From the Brevoort collection. Cf. Catalogue of the Moore Library. pt. 2. no. 1791.

HOLLAND SOCIETY LIBRARY, NEW YORK

Minutes of the Consistory of Brooklyn, Sept. 5, 1660—July 30, 1664. (MS. Translation by D. Versteeg.)

SAGE LIBRARY, NEW BRUNSWICK, N. J.

Ecclesiastical Records of the Dutch Reformed Church in New Netherland, obtained from Holland Archives: Classis of Amsterdam, Synod of North Holland in Amsterdam, General Synod at The Hague.
1. Original.
2. Transcripts.
(Nearly all of these printed in the Ecclesiastical Records of New York. Vol. i. Cf. Introduction to this work for a classification of this material).

(C) PRINTED DOCUMENTS AND SOURCES

PROVINCIAL

Aitzema, L. van, Saken, van Staet en Oorlogh in ende omtrent de Vereenigde Nederlanden. 15 vols. The Hague, 1657-1671; 7 vols. 1669-72.
(Extracts relating to New Netherland Transl. in New York Historical Society Collections. 2d. Series, vol. ii. 1849.)
Breeden Raedt aende Vereenichte Nederlandsche Provintien

BIBLIOGRAPHY

339

. . . gemaeckt ende gestelt uijt diverse . . . memorien
door I. A. G. W. C. Antwerp. 1649.
(Broad Advice etc. Translation by Henry C. Murphy in New
York Historical Society Collections, 2d. Series, vol. iii. 237
1857; and E. B. O'Callaghan in Documentary History of
New York. vol. iv. 65. 1849.)
Castell, William. A short Discoverie of the Coasts and Conti-
nent of America. London, Printed in the year 1644.
(A chapter of New Netherland on pp. 21-23. An extract
printed in New York Historical Society Collections. 2d.
Series vol. iii. 1857.
De Laet, Johan. Nieuwe Weredlt, ofte Beschrijvinghe van
West Indien. 1625, 1630, 1633, 1640.
(Extracts relating to New Netherland transl. in New York
Historical Society Collections. 2d. Series. i. 282-316. 1841;
ii. 373. 1849.
Revised version in Narratives of New Netherland, ed. J.
Franklin Jameson. pp. 36-60. 1909.)
De Rasières, Isaak, to Samuel Blommaert. 1628?
(Translation by Brodhead: "New Netherland in 1627." in
New York Historical Society Collections. 2d. Series. ii.
339-354. 1849).
Revised version by W. I. Hull in Narratives of New Nether-
land. ed. J. Franklin Jameson. pp. 102-115. 1909.
Documents Relating to the Colonial History of the State of
New York; 1st. Series. 11 vols. ed. E. B. O'Callaghan. 2d.
Series. 3 vols. ed. B. Fernow. Albany. 1856-61.
Donck, Adriaen van der. Nieuw Nederlandt, Beschrijvinghe
van, gelijck het tegenwoordigh in staet is. Amsterdam.
1655, 1656.
(Transl. by J. Johnson, "Description of the New Netherlands,"
in New York Historical Society Collections. 2d. Series. i.
1841).
Hazard, E. Historical Collections consisting of State Papers
and other Authentic Documents Intended as Materials for an
History of the United States of America. 2 vols., Philadel-
phia. 1792-94.
(Extracts relating to New Netherland in N. Y. Hist. Soc.
Collections. 1809.)
Jameson, J. Franklin, ed. Naratives of New Netherland,
1609-1664. New York. 1909.
Meteren, E. van. Historie der Nederlandsche ende haerder
Naburen Oorlogen ende Geschiedenissen tot ded Jare 1612.
Ed. 1st. Delft. 1599; 2d. Delft. 1605; 3d. Utrecht. 1609; 4th.
The Hague. 1614.
(Extracts relating to New Netherland in ed. 1611 and 1614
transl. from ed. 1611 by Henry C. Murphy: "Henry Hud-
son in Holland." The Hague, 1859. pp. 62-65. transl. from
ed. 1614 by G. M. Asher: Henry Hudson the Navigator. (Hak-
luyt Society. 1860. pp. 147-153. Revised version of
Asher's translation in Narratives of New Netherland. ed. J.
Franklin Jameson. pp. 6-9. 1909.)

Murphy, Henry C. Nieuw Nederlandt's Anthologie. Anthology of New Netherland; or Translations from the early Dutch poets of New York, with memoirs of their lives, New York. 1865. Bradford Club.

O'Callaghan, E. B. Laws and Ordinances of New Netherland, 1638-1674. Albany, 1868.

O'Callaghan, E. B. Documentary History of New York; arranged under the Secretary of State. 4 vols. Albany, 1849-51.

Vertoogh van Nieu-Neder-Land, Weghens de Ghelegentheydt, Vruchtbaerheydt, en Soberen Staet desselfs. The Hague, 1650.
(The manuscript, which is a little different from the printed tract, transl. as "Remonstrance of New Netherland," 1856, in New York Colonial Documents. i. 271-316, reprinted in Pennsylvania Archives, 2d. Series. v. 124-170.
The printed tract transl. by Henry C. Murphy in New York Historical Society Collections, 2d. Series. ii. 251-329.   1849; by Mr. James Lenox in a separate pamphlet, also containing the Breeden Raedt; finally a revised version of this by A. Clinton Crowell in Narratives of New Netherland. ed. J. Franklin Jameson. pp. 293-354.)

Vries, David Pieterz de, Korte historiael ende journaels aenteyckeninge van verscheyden voyagiens in de vier deelen des wereldts-ronde als Europa, Africa, Asia ende Amerika gedaen, etc. Alckmaer, 1655.
(Extracts relating to Newfoundland, New Netherland and Virginia, transl. by Henry C. Murphy in New York Historical Society Collections.   2d. Series. iii. 1-129.   Separate print by James Lenox, 1853.
Extracts relating to New Netherland, 1633-1643 in a revised version of Mr. Murphy's translation, in Narratives of New Netherland, ed. J. Franklin Jameson, New York, 1909).

United States Commission on Boundary between Venezuela and British Guiana.   Report of, vol. ii.   Extracts from Dutch Archives.   Also Senate Document No. 91, 55th Congress, 2d Session (1898).

Wassenaer. N. van. Historisch Verhael alder ghedenckweerdichste Geschiedenissen die hier en daer in Europa etc., voorgevallen syn. 21 vols. Amsterdam, 1622-1635.
(Parts relating to New Netherland transl. as "Description and First Settlement of New Netherland," in Documentary History of New York iii. 27-48, in New York Historical Society Proceedings, 1858, and finally a revised translation ed. by J. Franklin Jameson in his Narratives of New Netherland, pp. 61-69, 1909.)

REGIONAL

PATROONSHIP OF RENSSELAERSWYCK

Van Rensselaer Bowier Manuscripts, Being the Letters of

Kiliaen Van Rensselaer, 1630-1643, and other Documents Relating to the Colony of Rensselaerswyck. Albany, 1908.

SWEDISH SETTLEMENTS

Ampliation oder Erweitrung des Privilegii so der Allerdurchläuchtigste Groszmächtigste Fürst and Herr, Herr Gustavus Adolphus,der Schweden, Gothen und Wenden König; Grosz-Fürst in Finnland, Hertzog zu Ehesten and Carelen, Herr zu Ingermanland, etc. Der neuen Australischen oder Süder-Compagnie durch Schweden and nunmehr auch Teutschland, allergnädigst ertheilet und verliehen. Gedruckt zu Heylbrunn, boy Christoph Krausen. Im Jahr 1633. Mense Aprili. Reprint in Marquad's Tractatus. ii. 552-55.

Ampliation oder Erweiterung von dem Octroij und Privilegio der newen Süyder-Handels Compagnia, durch Last and Befehl von die Deputirten der löblichen Confoederirten Herren, Ständen, der vier Ober-Cräysen zu Franckfurth, anzustellen verordnet, den 12 December, Anno 1634. Gedruckt zu Hamburg, durch Heinrich Werner, im Jahr Christi 1635.

Argonautica Gustaviana, das ist: Nothwendige Nach-Richt van der Neuen Seefahrt und Kauffhandlung, so von dem Weilandt Allerdurchleuchtigsten Groszmächtigsten und Siegreichesten Fürsten und Herrn, Herrn Gustavo Adolpho Magno, . . . durch anrichtung einer General Handel-Compagnie . . . vor wenig Jahren zu stifften angefangen: anjetzo aber der Teutschen Evangelischen Nation . . . zu unermesslichen Nutz und Frommen . . . mitgetheilet worden . . . Gedruckt zu Franckfurt am Mayn, bey Caspar Rödteln, im Jahr Christi, 1633. Mense Junio.

Fullmagt för Wellam Usselinx at inrätta et Gen. Handels-Comp. til Asien, Afr., Amer. och Terra Magell. Dat. Stockh. d. 21 Dec., 1624.
(Translation in Col. Doc. N. Y. vol. xii. 1-2.)

Handlingar rörande Skandinaviens historia, tjugondenionde delen. Stockholm, 1848.
(Some letters of the Swedish Government regarding New Sweden.)

Hazard, Samuel, Annals of Pennsylvania from the Discovery of the Delaware, 1609-1682. Philadelphia, 1850.

Hazard, Samuel, Register of Pennsylvania. Vols. iv. v. Philadelphia, 1828-36. (Publication of Manuscripts in the Library of American Philosophical Society, especially of translations from a French version of copies of Swedish documents, procured at Stockholm by Jonathan Russel, Minister of the United States to the Court of Sweden.)

Instruction oder Anleitung: Welcher Gestalt die Einzeichnung zu der neuen Süder-Compagnie, durch Schweden und nunmehr auch Teutschland zu befördern, und an die Hand zu nehmen; derselben auch mit ehestem ein Anfang zu machen. Gedruckt zu Heylbrunn bey Christoph Krausen. 1633, Mens. Aprili.

342 RELIGION IN NEW NETHERLAND

(Reprint in Marquad's Tractatus. ii. 542-52.)

Kernkamp, G. W. Brieven van Samuel Blommaert aan den Zweedischen Rijkskanseleir Axel Oxenstierna, 1635-1641. Bijdragen en Mededeelingen van het Historisc Genootschap. (Utrecht). 29 Deel., Amsterdam, 1908.

Kurtzer Extract der vornemsten Haupt-Puncten, so biszher weitläuffig und gründlich erwiesen, und nochmals, jedermänniglich, unwiedersprechlich für Augen gestellet sollen werden. In Sachend er neuen Süder-Compagnie. Gedruckt zu Heylbrunn bey Christoph Krausen, Anno, 1633. Mens. Aprili.
(Reprint in Marquad's Tractatus. ii. 541-2.)

Manifest und Vertragbrieff, der Australischen Companey im Königreich Scweden auffgerichtet. Im Jahr MDCXXIV. (Reprint in the Auszführlicher Bericht über den Manifest.)

Marquadus, Johannes. Tractatus Politico-Juridicus de Jure Mercatorum et Commerciorum Singulari. 2 vols. Frankfort, 1662.

Navorscher, De. Two letters from Johannes Bogaert, "Schrijver," to Bontemantel, Director of Dutch West India Company. August 28 and October 31, 1655, N. S. in regard to the arrival of the ship De Waag at New Amsterdam with some details on the conquest of New Sweden, not elsewhere noted. Amsterdam, 1858.
(Translation by Henry C. Murphy in Hist. Mag. ii. 257 et seq. New York, 1858.)

Octroy eller Privilegier, som then Stormägtigste Högborne Furste och Herre, Herr Gustaf Adolph, Sweriges, Göthes och Wendes Konung, etc. Det Swenska nysz uprättade Södra Compagniet nädigst hafwer bebrefwat. Dat. Stockholm. d. 14 Junii, 1626. (Cited in Acrelius).

Octroy und Privilegium so der Allerdurchläuchtigste Groszmächtigste Fürst und Herr, Her Gustavus Adolphus, der Schweden, Gothen und Wenden König, Grosz-Fürst in Finnland, Hertzog zu Ehesten und Carelen, Herr zu Ingermanland, etc. Der im Königreich Schweden jüngsthin auffgerichteten Süder-Compagnie allergnädigst gegeben und verliehen. Stockholm, gedruckt bey Ignatio Meurern. Im Jahr, 1626.
(Reprint in Marquad's Tractatus. ii. 545-52. Translation in Col. Doc. N. Y. xii. 7 et seq.)

Octroy ofte Privilegie soo by den alderdoorluchtigsten Grootmachtigen Vorst ende Heer, Heer Gustaef Adolph, der Sweden Gothen ende Wenden Koningh, Grootvorst in Finland, Hertogh tot Ehesten ende Carelen, Heer tot Ingermanland, etc., aen de nieuw opgerichte Zuyder Compagnie in 't Koningrijck Sweden onlangs genadigst gegeben ende verleend is, Mitsgaders een naerder Bericht over 't selve Octroy ende Verdragh-brief door Willem Usselinx. In's Gravenhage, By Aert Meuris, Boeckverkooper in de Papestraat in den Bybel, anno 1627. It also contains Usselinx's Utförligh Förklaring.

Pennsylvania Archives. 2d. Series, vol. v. (Reprint of documents on New Sweden from Col. Docs. N. Y. i. ii. iii.) vol. vii. (Reprints of documents on New Sweden from Col. Docs., N. Y. xii.)

Stiernman, Anders Anton v. Samling utaf Kongl. Bref, Stadgar och Förordningar, etc. angaende Sveriges Rikes Commercie, Politie, och Œconomie uti gemen. Onfran ar 1523 in til närvarande tid. Uppa Hans Konigl. Maj. ts nadigesta befallning gjord. Första del. Stockholm, 1747; andra del. Ibid. 1750; trejda del. Ibid. 1753; fjerde del. Ibid. 1760; femte del. Ibid. 1766; sjette del. ibid. 1775. (Documents relating to Swedish West India Company and New Sweden.)

Stiernman Anders Anton v. Monumenta Politico-Ecclesiastica. Ex-Archivio Palmskiöldiano nunc primum in lucem edita. Praeside Olavo Calsio. Upsaliae. MDCCL. (Documents relating to Swedish West India Company and New Sweden.)

Sw. Rikes Gen. Handels Compagnies Contract, dirigerat til Asiam Africam och Magelliam samt desz Conditiones. Stockh. ar 1625.

Der Reiche Scweden Gera. Compagnies Handlungs Contract, Dirigiret naher Asiam, Africam, vnd Magelanicam Samt dessen Conditionen vnnd Wilköhren. Mit Kön. May. zu Schweden, vnsers Allergnädigsten Könings vnd Herrn gnediger Bewilligung, auch hierauff ertheilten Privilegien, in öffentlichen Druck publiciret. Stockholm, 1625. (Translation in Col. Doc. N. Y. xii. 2 et seq.)

Uthförligh Förklaring öfwer Handels Contractet angaendes thet Södre Compagniet uthi Konungarijket i Swerighe. Stält igenom Wilhelm Usselinx, Och nu aff thet Nederländske Spraket uthsatt pa Swenska, aff Erico Schrodero. Trackt i Stockholm, aff Ignatio Meurer, Ahr, 1626.

Auszführlicher Bericht über den Manifest; oder Vertrag-Brieff der Australischen oder Süder Compagney im Königreich Schweden. Durch Wilhelm Usselinx. Ausz dem Niederländischen in die Hoch-deutsche Sprache übergesetzt. Stockholm, Gedruckt durch Christoffer Reusner. Anno MDCXXVI.

ENGLISH SETTLEMENTS

Adams, C. F. ed. Antinomianism in the Colony of Massachusetts Bay, 1636-38. Prince Society Publication. Boston, 1894.

Lechford, Thomas. Plain dealing; or News from New England. London, 1642. –with an introduction and notes by J. H. Trumbull. Boston, 1867. In Mass. Hist. Soc. Collections. Vol. 23. 1833.

Lechford, Thomas. Note-Book, 1638-1641. ed. Everett Hale Jr.

Underhill, John. Newes from America. London, 1638. Fac-simile publ. by the Underhill Soc. N. Y. 1902. Reprint in Mass. Hist. Soc. Collections. 3d Series. Vol. vi.— ed. by

344   RELIGION IN NEW NETHERLAND

Orr. Charles: History of the Pequot war, etc., Cleveland, 1897.
Winthrop, John. History of New England. In Original Narratives of Early America, ed. by J. Kendall Hosmer as Winthrop's Journal. 2 Vols., 1908.

MUNICIPAL

Fernow, Berthold, ed. Records of New Amsterdam from 1653 to 1674 Minutes of the Court of Burgomasters and Schepens 1653-1674, Administrative Minutes, 1657-1661. 7 Vols. New York, 1897.
(The administrative minutes from February 11, 1661, May 20, 1664, were not printed. These valuable records were discovered among the personal effects of the late Lieutenant B. E. Fernow, and returned by Dr. Burrage, the State historian of Maine, to the librarian of the City of New York.)
Munsell, Joel. Annals of Albany. 10 vols. Albany, 1850-9.
Munsell, Joel. Collections on the history of Albany from its discovery to the present time. 4 vols. Albany, 1865-71.
Pearson, Jonothan. Early Records of the City and County of Albany and Colony of Rensselaerswyck, 1656-1675. Albany, 1869-1872.
(Reprinted with a "Key to the names of persons," "Contributions for the geneologies of the first settlers of Albany," and "Diagram of the home lots of the village of Beverwyck," in Munsell's Collections, etc. vols. iii. 1-224; iv. 84-510.)
Records of the Towns of North Hempstead. 8 vols. 1896.
Valentine, David Thomas, comp. Manual of the corporation of the City of New York, N. Y., 1842-70. Historical index to Manuals, 1841-70. New York, 1900.
(No volume issued for 1867. New series beginning in 1868 is less valuable from a historical point of view, than the preceeding issues to 1850, which contain important historical materials: extracts from early records of the city, Dutch and English, etc.)

RELIGIOUS

Bowne, John. Journal of, partly printed by Onderdonck, H. Jr. in the American Historical Record. i. 4-8, Jan. 1872. "Persecution of an early friend or quaker copied from his journal." Manuscript copy by the same author in Long Island Historical Society Library, Brooklyn, preceded by a copy of Bowne's Account book.
Ecclesiastical Records of the State of New York. 6 Vols. Albany, 1901-1905.
(Vol. i. covers Dutch period. Published by the State under the supervision of Hugh Hastings, State Historian. Documents compiled and edited by E. T. Corwin.)
Fernow, B. ed. Minutes of Orphan Masters' Court of New Amsterdam, 1656-1663; Minutes of the Executive Boards of the Burgomasters of New Amsterdam; and Records of

Walewyn van der Veen, Notary Public, 1662-1664. New York, 1907.

Jesuit Relations, and Allied Documents. ed. R. G. Thwaites. 1610-1791. 73 Vols. Cleveland, 1896-1901.

1642-1643. Vimont, Relation de la Nouvelle France, 1642-1643. Cramoisy. 1644, Jes. Rels. xxiii. xxiv. xxv.

1643. Jogues. Lettre du P. Isaac Jogues du village des Iroquois, 30 juin, 1643.

1643-1644. Vimont. Relation de la Nouvelle-France. 1643-1644.. Paris, Cramoisy, 1645. Jes. Rels. xxv. xxvi. xxvii.

1645-1646. Lalemant et Raguenau. Relation de la Nouvelle-France, 1645-1646. Paris, Cramoisy, 1647. Jes. Rels. xxviii. xxix. xxx.

1645-1649. Breve Relatione d'alcune missioni nella Nuova Francia, 1645-1649. Macerata, 1653, Jes., Rels. xxxviii. xxxix. xl.

1646. Jogues, Isaac. Novum Belgium. Jes. Rels. xxviii. (O'Callaghan, Doc. Hist. N. Y., iv. 15-17; 4to ed. 21-24, 80 ed.; 1851. J. G. Shea, N. Y. Hist. Soc. Collections. 2d Series. iii. 215-219.
Revised version of Shea's translation in Narratives of New Netherland, pp. 259-263, 1909.)

Jogues, Isaac. Notice sur René Goupil, undated. Jes. Rels. xxviii.

1647. Lalemant. Relation de la Nouvell-France sour le Grand Fleuve de St. Laurens. 1647, Paris, Cramoisy, 1648. Jes. Rels. xxx. xxxi. xxxii.

1652-1653. Le Mercier. Relation de la Nouvelle-France, 1652-53. Paris, Cramoisy, 1654. Jes. Rels. xl.

1653. Journal des Jésuites, Janvier à Décembre, 1653. Jes. Rels. xxxviii.

1653-1654. Le Mercier. Relation de la Nouvelle-France, 1653-54. Paris, Cramoisy, 1655. Jes. Rels. xli.

1654. Journal des Jésuites, Janvier à Février, 1654. Jes. Rels. xli.

1655. Copie de deux Lettres envoiées de la Nouvelle-France, 1655. Paris, Cramoisy, 1656. Jes. Rels. xli.

1655-1656. de Quens, Jean. Relation de la Nouvelle-France, 1655-1656. Paris, Cramoisy, 1657. Jes. Rels. xlii. Mort du Frère Liégeois., 1655-1656. Jes. Rels. xlii.

1656. Le Mercier. Journal des Jésuites, Octobre à Décembre 1656. Jes. Rels. xlii.

1656-1657. Le Jeune. Relation de la Nouvelle-France, 1656-57. Paris, Cramoisy, 1658. Jes. Rels. xliii. xliv.

1657. Journal des Jésuites, Janvier à Décembre, 1657. Jes. Rels. xliii.

1657-1658. Ragueneau. Relation de la Nouvelle-France, 1657-58. Paris, Cramoisy, 1659. Jes. Rels. xliv.

1658. Journal des Jésuites, Janvier à Décembre, 1658. Jes. Rels. xliv.

1659. Lalemant. Lettres envoiées de la Nouvelle-France, 1659. Paris, Cramoisy, 1660. Jes. Rels. xlv.
Journal des Jésuites, Janvier à Décembre, 1659. Jes. Rels. xlv.
1659-1660. Relaton de la Nouvelle-France, 1659-1660. Paris, Cramoisy, 1661. Jes. Rels. xlv.
1660. Journal des Jésuites, Janvier à Décembre, 1660. Jes. Rels. xlv.
1660-1661. Le Jeune, Relation de la Nouvelle-France, 1660-1661. Paris, Cramoisy, 1662. Jes. Rels. xlvi. xlvii.
1661. Chaumonot. Lettre du P. J. M. Chaumonot. Québec, 20 Octobre, 1661. Jes. Rels. xlvi.
1661-1662 Lalemant. Relation de la Nouvell-France, 1661-1662. Paris, Cramoisy, 1663. Jes. Rels. xlvii.
1662. Journal des Jésuites, Janvier à Décembre, 1662. Jes. Rels. xlvii.
1663. Journal des Jésuites, Janvier à Décembre, 1663. Jes. Rels. xlvii.
Megapolensis, John. Een kort Ontwerp vande Makvase Indiaenen, haer Landt, Tale, Statuere, Dracht, Godes-Dienst ende Magistrature, aldus beschreven ende nu kortelijck den 26 Augusti, 1644 opgesonden uyt Nieuwe Neder-Landt, door Johannem Megapolensem juniorem, Predikant aldaer. Alkmaer. No date.
(Printed in 1651. Amsterdam by Joost Hartgers in his "Beschrijvinghe van Virginia, Nieuw Nederlandt, etc."
Translation by Ebenezer Hazard in "Historical Collections, i. 517-526. 1792. Revised version by J. R. Brodhead in N. Y. Historical Society Collections. 2d Series. iii. 137-160. A more revised version in Narratives of New Netherland. ed. J. Franklin Jameson. pp. 168-180.)
Megapolensis, Reverend Johannis, Reply of — to a Letter of Father Simon Le Moyne, a French Jesuit Missionary of Canada, 1658. Collegiate Church, New York, 1907.
Versteeg, Dingman. Manhattan in 1628, as described in the recently discovered Autograph Letter of Jonas Michaelius, written from the settlement on the 8th of August of that year and now first published. New York, 1904.
(Letter to Joannes Foreest of Horn and Director of the West India Company. Found in the sale of Manuscripts in Amsterdam, 1902.)

(D) SECONDARY WORKS

General Histories

Hart, A. B. ed. The American Nation. A History from Original Sources by Associated Scholars   New York, 1904.
Doyle, J. A. The English Colonies in America. 5 vols. New York, 1889-1907.

Osgood, H. L. The American Colonies in the 17th Century 3 vols. New York, 1904-1907.
Winsor, J. ed. The Narrative and Critical History of America. 8 vols. Boston, 1886-1889.

(E) SPECIAL WORKS

PROVINCIAL

Brodhead, J. Romeyn. History of the State of New York 1607-1691. 2 vols. New York, 1853-1871.
Fiske, J. Dutch and Quaker Colonies in America. 2 vols. Boston, 1899.
Lambrechtsen, N. C. Korte Beschrijving van de Ontbedekkung en der Verdere Lotgevallen van Nieuw-Nederland. Middelburg, 1881.
(Transl. by F. A. Van der Kemp, as "Short Description of the Discovery and Subsequent History of New Netherland," in New York Historical Society, Collections, 1841.)
O'Callaghan, E. B. History of New Netherland. 2 vols. New York, 1855.
O'Callaghan, E. B. Register of New Netherland. Albany, 1865.

REGIONAL

SWEDISH SETTLEMENTS ON THE SOUTH RIVER (DELAWARE)

Acrelius, Israel. Beschrifning Om De Swenska Församlingars Forna och Närwarande Tilstand Uti Det sa Kallade Nya Sverige. Stockholm, 1759.
(Transl. by W. M. Reynolds, as History of New Sweden in Memoirs of Hist. Soc. of Pennsylvania. vol. ix. Philadelphia, 1874.)
Arfwedson, Carl David. De Colonia Svecia Historiola. Upsala, 1825.
(Several important documents not printed elsewhere "Een Berättelse on Nova Suecia uthi America," "Relation öfwer thet ahnfall thermed the Hollandske under P. Stüvesant, etc.," transl. by Marsh in N. Y. Hist. Soc. Collections. 2d Ser. i. 443 et seq.; "Series Sacerdotum, qui a Svecia missi sunt in Americam," transl. in Du Ponceau: Campanius. p. 109 et seq.
Campanius, Holmiensis, Thomas. Kort Beskrifning om Provincien Nya Swerige uit America. Stockholm, 1702.
(Transl. by P. S. De Ponceau: Short decription of Province of New Sweden. Philadelphia, 1834. Memoirs of the Hist. Soc. of Pennsylvania. vol. iii. An extract in N. Y. Hist. Soc. Collections. 1st Ser. ii. 343 et seq. 1841.)
Carson, Hampton L. The Dutch and Swedish Settlements on the Delaware. Pennsylvania Mag. of Hist. and Biogr. January, 1909.

348   RELIGION IN NEW NETHERLAND

Ferris, Benjamin. A History of the Original Settlements on
the Delaware. Wilmington, 1846.
Keen, Gregory B. The Dutch and Swedish Colonies on the
Delaware. Delaware County Historical Society. vol. i.
Chester, Pa., 1902.
Keen, Gregory B. New Sweden, or the Swedes on the Dela-
ware. In Justin Winsor's Critical and Narrative History of
America. vol. iv. 442-488.
Odhner, Professor Clases Theodor. Sveriges Inre Historia
under Drottning Christinas Förmyndare. Stockholm, 1865.
(Parts transl. by Keen:" C. T. Odhner's account of Willem
Usselinx and the South, Ship, and West India Companies of
Sweden. The report of Governor Johan Printz of New
Sweden for 1647, and the reply of Count Axel Oxenstierna,
Chancellor of Sweden," in Pennsylvania Mag. of Hist. vol.
vii.)
Odhner, C. T. Kolonien. Nya Sveriges Grundlaggung, 1637-
1642, in Historiskt Bibliotek, Ny Följd. i. Stockholm. 1876.
(Translation by Keen. Pennsylvania Mag. of Hist. iii. 269,
etc., 395, etc., 469 etc., Philadelphia, 1879.
Sprinchorn, Carl. K. S. Kolonien Nya Sveriges Historia. in
Historisk Bibliotek, 1879.
(Transl. by Keen. Pennsylvania Mag. of Hist. and Biogr. vii.
viii.)

ENGLISH SETTLEMENTS ON LONG ISLAND

Bergen, Teunis. Early History of Kings County.
Flint, Martha Bockée. Early Long Island. A Colonial Study.
New York, 1896.
Furman, Gabriel. Antiquities of Long Island with a Bib-
liography by Henry Onderdonk, Jr., 1875.
Onderdonk, H. Jr. Queens County in Olden Times, in Ameri-
can Historical Record i. 1872.
Thompson, B. J. History of Long Island, including also a
particular account of the Different Churches and Ministers.
3 Vols. 1843.

MUNICIPAL

Innes, J. H. New Amsterdam and Its People. New York,
1902.
Mandeville, Henry G. Flushing, Past and Present. Flushing,
L. I. 1860.
Moore, Charles B. Early Hempstead. Hempstead. 1870.
Onderdonk, Henry, Jr. Annals of Hempstead. Hempstead,
1878.
Onderdonck, Henry, Jr. Antiquities of Hempstead, 1878.
Ostrander. A History of the City of Brooklyn and Kings
County, 1894.
Riker, James. Annals of Newtown, 1852.
Stiles, Henry R. History of Brooklyn including the Old Town
and Village of Brooklyn, the Town of Bushwyck, etc. 3 Vols.
Brooklyn, 1867.

Strong, Thomas M. The History of the Town of Flatbush.
    1842. Reprint, 1908.
Valentine, David T. History of the City of New York. New
    York, 1853.
Van Rensselaer, Mrs. Schuyler. History of the City of New
    York. 2 vols. New York, 1909.
Waller, Henry D. History of the Town of Flushing, L. I.
    Flushing, 1899.
Wilson, James Grant. ed. Memorial History of the City of
    New York. New York, 1891, 1893. 4 vols.

RELIGIOUS

Beekman, A. J. History of the Reformed Dutch Church of the
    Town of Brooklyn, 1886.
Bennett, W. Harper. Catholic Footsteps in Old New York.
    New York, 1909.
Besse, Joseph. Collection of the sufferings of the people
    called Quakers, 1650-89; from original records and other
    authentic accounts. 2 vols. London, 1753.
Briggs, C. A. American Presbyterianism; its origin and early
    history. New York 1885.
Briggs, C. A. Puritanism in New York. Mag. of Am. Hist.
    vol. xiii. 39-58, 1885.
Bjorck, Tobias E. Dissertatio Gradualis de Plantatione
    Ecclesiæ Svecanae in America. Upsala, 1731.
Campbell, T. J. Pioneer Priests of North America. New
    York, 1908.
Cobb, Sanford H. The Rise of Religious Liberty in America.
    New York, 1902.
Cone, G. Herbert. The Jews in Curaçoa. Pubs. Am. Jew.
    Hist. Soc. No. 10. 1902.
Corwin, E. T. Dutch Reformed. Am. Church Hist. Series.
    vol. viii. New York, 1894.
Corwin, E. T. Manual of the Reformed Church in America.
    4th ed. New York, 1902.
Dunshee, Henry Webb. History of the School of the Re-
    formed Protestant Dutch Church in New York, 1853.
Dyer, A. M. Points in the First Chapter in New York Jewish
    History. Am. Jew. Hist. Soc. Publs. No. 3. 1895.
Jacobs, Henry Eyster. Lutherans, Am. Church Hist. Ser. vol.
    iv. New York, 1907.
Kohler, Max J. Beginnings of Jewish History in New York.
    Am. Jew. Hist. Soc. Publs. Nos. 1, 2. 1893-4.
Kohler, Max J. Phases of Jewish Life in New York before
    1800. Am. Jew. Hist. Soc. Publs. No. 3. 1895.
MacDonald, James M. Two Centuries in the History of the
    Presbyterian Church, Jamaica, L. I., 1862.
Newman, A. H. Baptists. Am. Church Hist. Ser. vol. ii.
    New York, 1902.
Onderdonck, H. Jr. The Rise and Growth of the Society of
    Friends On Long Island and In New York, 1657-1826 in
    The Annals of Hempstead, 1643 to 1832. 1878.

Onderdonck. H., Jr.   Antiquities of the Church of Jamaica. 1880.
Onderdonk, Henry, Jr.   Antiquites of the Parish Church of Hempstead, including Oysterbay and the Churches in Suffolk County.   Illustrated from Letters of the Missionaries and other Authentic Documents, 1880.
Oppenheim, Samuel.   The Early History of the Jews in New York, 1654-1664.   New York, 1909.   Also in Am. Jew. Hist. Soc. Publs. No. 18. 1909.
Thomas, Allen C., and Richard H.   The Society of Friends. Am. Church Hist. Ser. vol. xii. 1908.
Thompson, Robert Ellis.   Presbyterians, Am. Church. Hist. Ser. vol. vi. New York, 1902.
Walker, Williston.   Congregationalists, Am. Church Hist. Ser. vol. ii. New York, 1903.
Whittemore, Henry.   History of the First Reformed Protestant Dutch Church of Breuckelen, 1896.

(F) BIOGRAPHY

Kapp, Friedrich.   Peter Minuit aus Wesel.   In Von Sybel's Hist. Zeitschrift. xv. 225 et seq.
Jameson, J. F. Willem Usselinx.   In Am. Hist. Assoc. Reports. vol. ii.   Separate Ed. New York, 1887.
Mickley, Jos. J.   Some Account of William Usselinx and Peter Minuit. Wilmington, 1881.
Tuckerman, Bayard.   Life of Peter Stuyvesant.   New York, 1905.

(G) AUXILIARY INFORMATION

Brakel, Dr. S. van.   De Hollandsche Handelscompagnieën der Zeventiende Eeuw.   Hun Onstaan—Hunne Inrichting.
Blok, Petrus J.   A History of the People of the Netherlands. 4 vols. New York, 1907.
Cambridge Modern History., vol. iii.   The Wars of Religion. New York, 1905.
De Schrevel, H. C.   Remi Drieux, évêque de Bruges et les troubles des Pays Bas.   Revue d'Histoire Ecclésiastique. ii. 828-839; iii. 36-65, 349-369, 644-688; iv. 645-678.
Hubert, Eugène.   Les Pays-Bas Espagnols et La République des Provinces Unis Depuis La Paix de Munster Jusqu'au Traicté D'Utrecht, 1648-1713   La Question Religeuse et Les Relations Diplomatiques.   Bruxelles, 1907.
Knuttel, W. P. C. De toestand der Nederl.   Katholieken ten tijde der Republiek.   2 vols.   The Hague.   1892-4.
Laspeyres.   Geschichte d. volkswirthschaftlichen Anschauungen d. Niederländer z. Zeit d. Republik.   No. xi.   Preischriften d. Fürstlich Jablonowski Gesellschaft v. Leipzig.
Mather, Cotton.   Magnalia Christi Americana; or The ecclesiastical History of New England, 1620-98.   London, 1702.

With introd. and notes by Thomas Robbins, Hartford, 1853. 2 vols.

Netscher, P. N. Les Hollandais au Brésil. La Haye, 1853.

Netscher, P. N. Geschiedenis van de Koloniën Essequebo, Demerary en Berbice s'Gravenhage, 1888.

Oppenheim, Samuel. An Early Jewish Colony in Western Guiana, 1658-1666. And its Relation to the Jews in Surinam, Cayenne and Tobago. Am. Jew. Hist. Soc. publs. No. 16. 1907.

Oppenheim, Samuel. An Early Jewish Colony In Western Guiana. Supplemental Data. Am. Jew. Hist. Soc. Publs. No. 17. 1908.

Rees, O. van. Geschiedenis der Kolonial Politiek van de Republiek der Vereenigde Nederlanden.

Rees, O. van. Geschiedenis der Staathuishondkunde in Nederland tot het Einde de achtiende Eeuw. 2 vols. 1868.